T. J. Hovell-Thurlow

Amsterdam exhibition of demostic economy

T. J. Hovell-Thurlow

Amsterdam exhibition of demostic economy

ISBN/EAN: 9783742838827

Manufactured in Europe, USA, Canada, Australia, Japa

Cover: Foto ©knipser5 / pixelio.de

Manufactured and distributed by brebook publishing software
(www.brebook.com)

T. J. Hovell-Thurlow

Amsterdam exhibition of demostic economy

TRADE UNIONS ABROAD

HINTS FOR HOME LEGISLATION:

REPRINTED FROM A REPORT

ON THE

AMSTERDAM EXHIBITION OF DOMESTIC ECONOMY.

BY

THE HON. T. J. HOVELL-THURLOW.

HARRISON, 59, PALL MALL,

BOOKSELLER TO HER MAJESTY AND H.R.H. THE PRINCE OF WALES.

1870.

HARRISON AND SONS,
PRINTERS IN ORDINARY TO HER MAJESTY,
ST. MARTIN'S LANE.

nently successful; and it was late in the day when Lord Wharncliffe, on his personal responsibility, put an end to the horrors of the scene by bringing over fifty men of Her Majesty's 22nd Regiment from Sheffield. Now, mark the French counterpart of this. At Creuzot the telegraph is put in action, and 3,500 men arrived from Paris in order to, and, what is of more importance, in time to, protect the lives and property of the non-unionists.

Under these circumstances, I maintain that we have much to learn from the Continent in the management of Strikes; and in legislating on this subject, Parliament must be careful not to drown the liberty of the individual in the liberty of association.

The primary duty of a Government is to protect the weak, the industrious, and the orderly, against the strong, the idle, and the violent; and a Statute-book that does not recognize this fact may, with great advantage, take a few pages out of the *Code Napoléon* as modified by the French law of May 27, 1864, and by the Belgian legislation of June 11, 1866.

There is just now much talk of free trade in land; but let us first secure free trade in labour; the one without the other would be of little value as a cure for the social diseases under which the body corporate of society is now suffering in Great Britain.

The Report, of which this volume contains a

PREFACE.

LEGISLATION on Trade Unions having been postponed till next Session, and the demand for copies of this Report being greater than can be met from the limited number printed for presentation to Parliament, I have been induced to publish the present edition, in the hope that a wide diffusion of the information it contains relative to the scope and character of Working-men's Associations on the Continent, may not prove altogether unproductive of beneficial effect on the public opinion of this country, by which, in the first instance, the drafts of our Acts of Parliament are prepared.

At the commencement of this year, we had, at Thorncliffe and at Creuzot, apt illustrations of the different ways of dealing, in England and in France, with Strikes and their consequences. At Thorncliffe the unionists divided their forces into two bodies; the one to attack and hold the pit mouth, and deprive non-unionists of the power to give alarm; the other body being told off to wreck the houses of the men working in the pit. In the execution of these brilliant tactics the unionists were emi-

reprint, is to be found in No. 2 of the Reports of Her Majesty's Secretaries of Embassy and Legation for 1870, presented by command to both Houses of Parliament, and published by Messrs. Harrison of Pall Mall.

T. J. HOVELL-THURLOW.

DUNPHAIL, FORRES, N.B.

CONTENTS.

INTRODUCTION.

THE Exhibition which forms the subject of the present Report was promoted by, and held under the superintendence of, the Society for the Encouragement of Manufactures and Mechanical Industry in the Netherlands. The avowed object of its promoters was to bring to the knowledge of the working classes such articles of household use, furniture, clothing, food, tools, implements, and objects of information or instruction, as combine usefulness with durability, so that the working classes of all countries might be enabled to improve their condition by judicious investment of their wages. A further object which the promoters of this undertaking had at heart was—by arriving at a full knowledge of the utmost purchasing power of the daily, weekly, monthly, or yearly earnings of every class of labourer or artisan —to discover, 1st, how such earnings are commensurate with the wants it is their duty to supply, and, 2ndly, how far such earnings, if not commensurate, can, and consequently should, be raised, without interfering with the natural laws which govern capital and labour, supply and demand, and over-taxing the rich producer for the benefit of the poor

Objects of the Exhibition.

B

consumer. "The labourer is worthy of his hire" is
the motto that the Netherlands International Exhibition of 1869 sought to uphold; and it further
undertook to lay down, by tabling facts and prices,
and to place it in the power of all to ascertain, the hire
that labour of all kinds should be entitled to command, so as to combine the possibility of health,
contentment, and the attainment of intellectual en-
joyments among the working classes of society, with
a reasonable profit-margin to the employer. The
limits of what may be termed legitimate or judicious
strikes would thus, it was hoped, be more clearly
defined, and the world at large might, perchance,
be saved the pain, the evil, the waste, the crime,
entailed by the future repetition of hopeless injudicious strikes, in cases where the employer of labour
is unable to offer better terms, and the hands have
taxed themselves by deductions from their scanty
wages to do what?—to enable them to remain idle
for certain weeks or months, and after being compelled to sell furniture, incur debt, and render their
position more intolerable than before, to return one
morning, with emaciated bodies, and heavy, discontented hearts, to the factory or mill.

Surely such an object, even if somewhat Utopian
in character, must be admitted on all sides to be
entitled to respect; and any contribution to human
knowledge on these matters which the Exhibition
may have called forth, must be deemed cheap at the
price, and well deserving of being scrupulously gar-
nered as valuable material for future legislation.

Interest of
Holland
in these
questions.

That this idea should have been seized and carried out in Holland is singularly characteristic of the
practical nature of her people. The neighbouring
kingdom of Belgium had become the scene of strikes
on a large scale, and the Netherlanders had thus witnessed from afar the good and the evil that co-opera-

tive societies have it in their power to bestow. As through a glass darkly, they had observed "the two-edged purpose" to which the funds of a Trade Union may be applied: how, raised for purposes of peace, they are equally applicable for purposes of war. Other countries than Belgium had suffered from misdirection of the people's savings. In England, in France, and in Germany, abundant instances had illustrated the danger of permitting trade associations to dispose at will of the labour of a population and of its hard-earned savings; and though the spirit of combination among workmen in the Netherlands remained, until 1867, so little developed as to enable Her Majesty's Chargé d'Affaires at the Hague to report, in reply to an official circular despatch, that there was little or no information to be gained on the subject in that country; yet since that date sufficiently rapid strides have been made by the Dutch as to afford already two examples of an imitation, on a small scale it is true, of the practice of their fellow-workmen in other countries in this regard.

These examples were the strikes, in the early spring in last year, of two bodies of men connected in no way with one another; and they were for this reason important as evidences of the extent to which this dangerous remedy—a remedy almost always worse than the disease—was threatening to become one of ready resort in the Netherlands. The bodies of men referred to were the peat-cutters on the Belgian frontier, a rural population, and the skilled artisans in the Amsterdam ship-building yards—a class the exact reverse of rustic in ideas, habits, food, clothing, and all that constitutes the individuality of society. Between these country boors and town handicraftsmen no bond of sympathy could have existed. The disease with which they were infected had evidently crossed the Belgian frontier, even as

the cattle-plague, or some other insidious enemy ; and
when once it had obtained a footing in the country,
had, like the cattle-plague, spread rapidly from one
province to another, until the taint extended through
the kingdom, and was only checked from further
progress by the limit of the ocean.

No time was therefore to be lost in endeavouring
to trace the action of the combination wave in Holland, so as, if possible, to build up social dykes to
check its force for evil. Acting on this sudden impulse the Exhibition has been held, and it has now
become a duty to study its results.

Self-govern-
ment in
Holland.

In no country in the world do the local adminis-
trations and provincial legislatures watch so jealously
over the prosperity of the population as in Holland ;
and in no country does the Government so completely realize the meaning of the phrase " paternal."
This indisputable fact may probably be attributed to
two causes—first, to the desire of the peace-loving,
law-abiding population to be paternally governed ;
and secondly, to the absence of centralization, and
the power consequently intrusted to the Parliament of each country, borough, town, or village :
through which system of self-government the real
rulers of the people are the rulers whom they all
know personally, and whom they have themselves
elected, the Dykegraves, the Burgomasters, and the
Syndics of each district. The great interest, indeed,
that England has ever taken in the Netherlands—an
interest easily comprehensible in former days when
Admirals de Ruyter and Van Tromp swept the
mouth of the Thames with brooms at the masthead,
and fully justified to-day by the fact that we annually
import and export goods to and from the Netherlands
to the value £27,500,000 (or nearly one-fifteenth part
of our whole foreign commerce)—is one that does not
flag when opportunity occurs for penetrating below

the surface presented to the eye of every tourist. By the bulk, however, even of our well-informed and travelled countrymen Holland is simply known and judged from the brilliant writings of the American historian, Mr. Motley, or from a hurried transit, viâ Rotterdam, to the picture galleries and diamond-cutters of the Hague and Amsterdam. Views formed from such aspects, and opinions collected under such conditions, are not only likely to be partial and imperfect, but certain to be erroneous and misleading. The real interest of the Holland of to-day is to be found—not so much in her museums, rich as they are in works of art; not so much in the eloquent bygones of her history, as in the inner homely life of the Dutch husbandman, in the self-government of the Kingdom as exemplified in its provincial legislatures, its communal councils, and village parliaments—in the exemplary precision, the sober and mechanical spirit, with which the Dutch regulate, as Mr. Matthew Arnold has justly observed, all the positive affairs of life; and lastly, in the provinces least known to travellers of Drenthe and Groningen, of Friesland, or of Overyssel, where the national characteristics of the people remain unchanged, and each hour's walk may place before the eye real representations of the life immortalized by Teniers and Ostade—where generations continue to succeed each other, to be born and bred and buried, inheriting and bequeathing their paternal acres under laws and usages as old as Charlemagne and as immutable as the statutes of the Medes and Persians. In these four remote provinces self-government is at home, and reigns supreme, and in the remaining seven provinces of the Netherlands, though not equally supreme in character, it still rules the people with an orderly iron sway, rendered dear to the mind of every Dutchman by the fact that any industrious village lad may look forward to the personal exercise of it in manhood or old age. In Holland, alone perhaps in all the world, we find a perfect realization of that beau-ideal of the masses, a government " by the people, of the people, for the people." This Government has been handed down carefully from generation to generation of liberty-loving Dutch burghers ; well-to-do burghers, with more to lose than to gain from any change, and rightly jealous of infringement of their heritable privileges : the Government and population of each district forming a perfect sample of organized self-rule for the good of all. Robbery and violence unknown—the rich secure, the poor content—one law for rich and poor alike—innumerable charitable institutions, amply endowed, for the maintenance of the sick, the aged, and the destitute —making an aggregate of peace and good-will upon earth that no other land can show such a percentage of upon its total population.

In contemplating so smiling a social and political landscape as the Netherlands thus offer, it is well, however, to bear in mind the common-place though sage reflection, how much easier it is to rule a population of 3,000,000 than of 30,000,000 ; how much easier it is to have a model village than a model town ; and when to this is added some allowance on account of the national *vis inertia* which no doubt contributes to the easy and contented manner in which the untravelled Dutchman goes through all the incidents of life, sufficient reason has been shown for the belief that the tranquillity and prosperity we admire in Holland are not attainable to the same degree at home.

Constitution of the Kingdom of Holland.

The Kingdom of the Netherlands is, as is known, a limited monarchy, devoted to the House of Orange and to the Constitution of 1848. Under it the States-General of the Netherlands consist of two

Chambers, an Upper and a Lower. Both are elective for a term of years; of two or four, to be determined by lot, in the case of the Commons, of nine in the case of the Upper House. There is no ecclesiastical element in either Chamber. The franchise for the Second Chamber varies under the law in rich and poor localities from 20 to 120 florins paid in direct taxation. The existing table of such rating was settled by law in July, 1850, and puts the franchise at 50 florins (4*l.* 3*s.* 4*d.*) for large and wealthy constituencies, such as Rotterdam, or the Hague, and at smaller sums for others, such as Utrecht, Delft, or rural districts such as Tiel. The thirty-nine members of the First Chamber are elected by the Provincial States from among those who, in taxes, contribute most largely towards the financial resources of the State; and this element is by no means confined to the nobility. There are now eighty members of the Second Chamber; the number varying, under the Constitution, according to the population, one member for every 45,000 souls. To provide for the maintenance of this ratio, the Table of Constituencies is revised every five years, and the last quinquennial revision took place in April, 1869. Each member receives 2,000 florins, or £166 13*s.* 4*d.* per annum, as remuneration for his services. Travelling allowances, on a moderate scale, are awarded to the members of both Chambers. Finally, no man can sit, in either House, until he has attained the ripe age of thirty.

In this last provision we find another safeguard against the outbreak of national energy in its youth. Men do not enter the Netherlands Parliament to make a position or reputation, but rather as a consequence of having obtained some previous distinction. And when it is further known that the organization of the Dutch Government does not include Parliamentary

Under-Secretaries for the several Departments of
State, nor Junior Lords of the Treasury or Admiralty,
the sufficiency of the causes will be more readily
appreciated which combine to render the discussions
in the Second Chamber of the States-General, which
holds daily meetings from 11 A.M. to 4 P.M., during
eight or nine months in the year, but a somnolent
representation of the more agitated sittings of the
British House of Commons.

Yet however satisfactory in its working in the
Netherlands this exclusion of the very young from a
voice in the deliberations of the country may be, and
however little, owing to the habits of local self-
government which prevail, the want of trained
Statesmen in the Chambers may be felt, there can be
but little doubt that the causes above-mentioned have
tended powerfully to the formation of a class of
thought which finds expression in the dictum,
" Holland is a *nation éteinte*," or, no longer in the
heyday of its national existence ; and it must be con-
ceded that any cause which contributes, however
remotely, to the formation of such an impression,
whether true or false, can hardly be accepted in an
age of progress as favourable to the growth of the
conditions which secure national strength, wealth,
and independence.

Another and more substantial source of national
danger springing from this exclusion of the young
from parliamentary life is the utter absence of political ambition which it has bred among the *jeunesse
dorée* of the Netherlands. They mostly pass the
time from leaving college to their thirtieth year in
the pursuit of town and country pleasures, and in the
performance of the slender duties attaching to small
sinecures at Court ; to such offices as *Chambellan* or
Ecuyer. Some exceptions exist, indeed, to prevent
the general application of this truth ; some few dis-

tinguish themselves, from time to time, endeavouring
to fit themselves, by travel or by study, for the more
serious duties of their after-lives, on the attainment
of their political majority ; some few among the
youth of the Netherlands upper ten thousand buckle
on the sword, or take to legal or commercial business,
and give evidence of their non-deterioration from the
stock whence they sprung ; but unhappily these are
found in sufficient numbers only to form the exception
rather than the rule.

The part, however, that is played in the Government of the country by the Dutch States-General is,
as has been said, but limited. They pass enactments
regulating the imperial taxation of the country, to
pay the Army and the Navy, or to make main canals
and railways ; they ratify Conventions negotiated
with foreign Powers ; they determine on the policy to
be pursued towards their numerous Colonies ; but in
no sense can it be said that they govern the Dutch
people. The real seat of power at home is in the
eleven local Chambers or Provincial States, which
form small parliaments for the discussion of internal
questions of administration, and in the eleven King's
Commissairies who preside over them, and are assisted
in their executive functions by permanent councils or
committees, elected *inter se*, and styled Provincial
States-Deputies. These regulate the communal taxation to which localities are subject for the requirements of education, drainage, roads, and sanitary
objects. Their decrees are carried out by the Burgomasters of the towns and villages ; and any popular
display of feeling, or opposition to a cess or regulation, is handed up to the Provincial States or King's
Commissary, and speedily disposed of on the merits
of the thing itself, without reference to abstract principles, uniformity of legislation, or other considerations
that tend to hamper justice and entail reference to

higher branches of the State, with consequent agitation to enlist the sympathy or fears of other provinces
or communes.

In this wise is self-government carried out in
Holland; and while in the most august of free
assemblies, the British House of Commons, the discussion of important national questions is constantly
delayed by foolish observations upon small local
matters—for instance, bicycle-practice in High Park
—the Netherlands States-General are enabled to
pursue, unruffled and undisturbed by petty cares,
their deliberations on colonial affairs and other vital
issues of Imperial magnitude.

Site of the
Exhibition.

The commercial capital of this happy land, and
the scene ultimately chosen for the exhibition of
objects produced by every country to meet the wants
of the labouring portion of their respective popu-
lations, bears the time-honoured name of Amsterdam.
When the scheme for an exhibition of domestic economy was first broached in Holland, Utrecht was
selected as the place best fitted for the purpose, as
combining most of the desired conditions.   Geographically, it had great advantages.   The central
city of Holland, it also formed, roughly speaking,
the centre of a circle drawn through London, Paris,
Frankfort, and Berlin—from all of which places it
was nearly equi-distant, and with all of which it was
in the most direct and connected communication.   By
reason of its manufactures, and the European reputation of its looms, it had become the most industrial
of Netherland cities long before the Dutch-Rhenish
Railway had given it exceptional facilities for disposing of its treasures.   As the plans, however, of
the projected exhibition were more matured, and it
became evident from the interest awakened in Great
Britain, in France, and in the neighbouring kingdoms
of Belgium and Prussia, that the European countries

most advanced in civilization were sincerely anxious to co-operate in its labours and to participate in its results, it became also evident that the resources of a provincial town, however well situated and distinguished in itself, would prove unequal to the dignity and necessities of the occasion. On the other hand there existed, at but one hour's additional railway-travelling distance from the European capitals above-mentioned, the great commercial mart of Amsterdam, abounding in palatial buildings, hotel accommodation, docks and shipping, and lastly, though not least, possessed of a building capable of storing the industrial inventions of the nineteenth century, and worthy of being chosen for their display. At Utrecht model cottages must have sought a temporary canvas shelter from the inclemency of autumnal weather, while but a few leagues off there was a crystal palace on the Amstel river, with acres of accommodation under permanent glass and iron.

Furthermore, it seemed to the projectors of the Exhibition that the international character of their work would be more readily appreciated in foreign countries by the selection of a port like Amsterdam, whose harbour, nay, whose very streets, are daily decked with the flags and emblems of foreign merchandize ; whose brokers' bills circulate at par throughout the world ; and whose trade in useful and ornamental wares—in diamonds and in coffee—still entitles its commercial men to take high place among the merchant princes of our age.

The body to whom belongs the credit of promoting the idea of holding in Holland an International Exhibition of articles of daily household use among the working classes, is the Society for the Encouragement of Manufacturers and Mechanical Industry in the Netherlands. This useful association, established under the enlightened patronage of the King in 1851, *Society for the Encouragement of Manufactures and Industry.*

has already had it in its power to render great services to its country, among masters and their workmen, as a judicious go-between. These opportunities have not been neglected, and its growth and practical utility cannot now be measured even by the fact that it counts many of the best names, and many of the leading men in Holland among its ranks, which number 700 strong. These 700 names do not merely represent the payment by their bearers of a small annual contribution towards defraying the expenses of the association. They represent men who, all engaged in active life, some servants of the State, others following mercantile pursuits, devote their leisure and their surplus power to the improvement of their fellow-beings.

The President of the Society, to whose untiring zeal the success of the Exhibition was entirely due, was Baron Donald Mackay, only son of Baron Mackay, who has long occupied the second place in the Kingdom of Holland as permanent Vice-President of the Council of State. The King is President of this body, but never attends its deliberations. The Prince of Orange is a simple member with one vote. The Cabinet are not *ex officio* members, but a number of permanent paid members are appointed for distinguished services in all branches of the administration. As practical President of this august body, to whose decisions the nation bows its head, Baron Mackay has wielded unseen power for good, and contributed not a little to the welfare of his country. His son, carefully trained in the duties of a loyal citizen, and educated at the University of Leyden, embraced, on entering life some ten years ago, diplomacy as a career. As Secretary to the Dutch Legation in London during the time when Baron Bentinck was so justly popular a representative of Holland, Baron Mackay enjoyed exceptional advantages for studying our institutions, both social and political. His Scotch descent, moreover, stood him in good stead in gaining access to much of London, and of British country life usually hermetically sealed to foreigners even of distinction. Directly descended from the Reay family, the chief of the Mackays, he met in Scotland with a hospitable reception from his fellow-clansmen in the north of Sutherland that must have contrasted somewhat strangely with the preconceived notions of his home, as formed among the dykes and polders of Guelderland and South Holland. To experience so varied in the Old World, he next added experience still more varied in the New, by travel on the continent of North America. In this manner his natural gifts of observation, application, and reflexion, became heightened and improved, and gradually he acquired, to an extent but rarely equalled, the character of the international man, in which we have to do with him on the present occasion, as the prime originator and President of the movement represented by the Working Men's Exhibition of 1869.

The difficulties he encountered at the outset of his labours in reconciling the Government and the public to the scheme he had at heart, would probably have proved insurmountable to any other man in Holland, and proved, indeed, all but insurmountable to him. Not only the Conservatives looked with dread on such an innovation as taking so practical an interest in the working-man, but even the Liberals urged that his condition in Holland was so little capable of improvement as compared with that of his class in other industrial countries, as to clothe the venture with the double danger of giving rise to discontent among as yet contented men, and opening the sluice-gates of society to dread infection from the mental poison disseminated by co-operative associations of alleged benefit to mankind, but of whose

Difficulties to be surmounted.

power for evil as well as good the annals of late
years have afforded more than ample proof.

Ultimately, however, the scheme triumphed over
the multitude of opposition with which it had been
attempted to suppress it. In last resort its enemies
had not neglected to make use of a weapon which
often carries more conviction than the closest forms
of reasoning. Failing alike to intimidate or convince,
they had endeavoured to turn the enemy's flank by
holding up the idea to public ridicule. Those, in
short, who do not know how the so-called liberals of
Holland are but little more than liberal in name, and
are practically more conservative than our best conservatives at home, would find it hard to follow or
believe the course of difficulties and stumbling-blocks
which public opinion and private jealousy combined
to interpose between the first conception and the fair
accomplishment of the work into which Baron
Mackay had entered with the energy of a Scot and
the perseverance of a Dutchman.

Co-operation of Great Britain. To make amends, however, for the unpopularity
he incurred at home, Baron Mackay found ample
favour for his scheme abroad. In Belgium, Germany,
France and England, sympathy soon kindled, and in
London he shortly had the satisfaction of finding
the Lord Mayor, Sir James Lawrence, calling public
meetings at the Mansion House, obtaining corporation
votes of money, and presiding over a numerous and
influential committee appointed to consider means for
forwarding the objects of the Exhibition. A glance
at the composition of this Committee will suffice to
show its working character, and the guarantee that
it afforded of Great Britain taking a proper place on
this occasion.

Lord Mayor's Committee. Its members were :—

H. E. Adair, Esq., M.P.

Somerset A. Beaumont, Esq., M.P.

Michael Biddulph, Esq., M.P.
Hon. William Brodrick, M.P.
Edwin Chadwick, Esq., C.B.
Hyde Clarke, Esq., D.C.L.
Charles Critchett, Esq., B.A.
G. F. Coster, Esq.
Ellis A. Davidson, Esq.
J. Van Drunen, Esq. (Vice-Consul for the Netherlands).
M. E. Grant Duff, Esq., M.P.
D. Everwyn, Esq. (Netherlands Legation).
Major-General Sir Vincent Eyre, C.S.I., C.B.
P. Le Neve Foster, Esq., M.A.
J. P. Gassiot, Esq., F.R.S.
Right Hon. Russell Gurney, M.P., P.C.
Hon. Auberon Herbert, M.P.
Robert Hudson, Esq., F.R.S.
Thomas Hughes, Esq., M.P.
Edmund Johnson, Esq.
George J. Shaw Lefevre, Esq., M.P.
Sir John Lubbock, Bart., F.R.S.
J. W. May, Esq., Consul-General for the Netherlands.
Samuel Morley, Esq., M.P.
H. W. Peek, Esq., M.P.
Hodgson Pratt, Esq.
Samuel Redgrave, Esq.
Charles Reed, Esq., M.P.
Rev. W. Rogers, M.A.
Gilbert Sanders, Esq.
Seymour Teulon, Esq.
Thomas Twining, Esq.
George O. Trevelyan, Esq., M.P.

Mr. P. L. Simmonds, who has been connected, more or less, with almost every International Exhibition since the first execution of the Prince Consort's great idea in 1851, was appointed Secretary and Manager to this Committee, and the enterprising establishment of Messrs. J. M. Johnson and Sons of 3, Castle Street, Holborn, who published, at a large money loss, the English edition of the complete Official Catalogue of the Paris Exhibition of 1867, and who have played no insignificant *rôle* in both previous and subsequent undertakings of the kind, placed offices at the disposal of the Exhibition, for the conduct of all business and correspondence. From these offices speedily issued the following circular to the leading exhibiting houses of Great Britain ; and the manner in which many public-spirited firms responded to the invitation was such as to leave no room for doubt of the success of the venture, so far as Great Britain was concerned.

Circular to exhibiting houses.

Circular to Exhibitors.

" Sir,

" As we believe your manufactures to be specially calculated to attract attention at the Netherlands Exhibition, we have pleasure in inclosing a detailed prospectus.

"The Exhibition is to be held at Amsterdam, from July to October next.

" Exhibiting will be attended with scarcely any trouble or expense. Medals and other awards will be liberally distributed.

" The import duties are low (scarcely any exceeding 5 per cent.), and there exists in Holland a strong disposition for increased commerce with Great Britain, so that beneficial results may be anticipated from the Exhibition.

" The space reserved for the United Kingdom being limited, and the allotments having to be made at an early date, it is important that all applications should be forwarded without delay.

" Yours, &c.,

(Signed) " J. M. JOHNSON AND SONS."

The interest that many of the thirteen Members of Parliament on the Lord Mayor's Committee took in the project, now fairly launched, was not confined to the lending of their names. More than one among them consulted his constituents, different Chambers of Commerce, and other associations of all kinds, consulted everything, in short, except his own convenience, on the measures to be taken to procure the co-operation of the manufacturing and industrial centres of the country. For this purpose, local and subordinate Committees were formed at Edinburgh and Leith, Glasgow, Manchester, and Newcastle-on-Tyne ; and the extent to which they ultimately succeeded in their endeavours will be best seen hereafter. These local Committees were composed as follows :—

Edinburgh and Leith.   Local Committees.

The Right Hon. the Lord Provost of Edinburgh.

The Hon. the Provost of Leith.

Josiah Livingston, Esq., Chairman of the Chamber of Commerce.

Professor Archer, Edinburgh Museum of Science and Art.

Donald R. Macgregor, Esq., Edinburgh.

George Harrison, Esq., Edinburgh.

Walter Berry, Esq.

J. J. Mackay, Esq., Edinburgh.

R. W. Thomson, Esq., Edinburgh.

Mungo C. Gibson, Esq., Leith.

David Maclaren, Esq., Edinburgh.

George V. Turnbull, Esq., Consul for the Netherlands, Leith.

C

Glasgow Committee.

Hon. Sir James Lumsden, Lord Provost, President.

William McEwen, Esq., Lord Dean of Guild.

John Ramsay, Esq., President of Chamber of Commerce.

Edward Caird, Esq., M.A.

Jacques von Raalte, Esq., Vice-Consul for the Netherlands.

Manchester Committee.

The Mayor of Manchester, President.

H. S. Shaw, Esq., Vice-President.

J. W. Mouliere, Esq.

S. A. Steinthal, Esq.

John Watts, Esq.

Dr. Isaac Watts, Secretary.

Newcastle-on-Tyne Committee.

William J. M. Lange, Esq.

Anthony M. M. de Charente, Esq.

John Sowerby, Esq.

John T. Dobson, Esq.

D. D. Main, Esq.

Joseph Cowen, Esq., jun.

General arrangements.

Similar committees gradually formed in other countries, and by them a general knowledge of the special objects of the Exhibition, and of the manner in which it was intended to promote them, became disseminated throughout the greater part of Europe. The 15th of May was fixed as the latest date on which applications for space to exhibit could be made to the London Secretary, and the 1st of July as the latest date on which goods intended for exhibition would be received in the building. The opening was fixed for the 15th of the last-named month. The two first of these three dates were departed from, in accordance with the precedents established in previous Exhibitions; it proving practically impossible to procure a complete collection of exhibitors from all the corners of the earth by the day originally determined. The third date, however, underwent no subsequent change from the moment of its being published.

The Central Committee at the Hague, charged with the general arrangements and the task of corresponding with the various foreign and local Committees, was composed as follows :— Central Committees.

Baron D. J. Mackay, President.
Mr. M. L. Hermans, Vice-President.
Dr. J. Th. Mouton, Secretary.
Mr. H. L. Enthoven, Treasurer.
Mr. F. W. Van der Putten.
Mr. W. J. Van Zeggelen.
Mr. J. Wijdoogen.
Mr. H. W. Veth.
Mr. J. Van der Wall Bake.
M. A. Van Naamen Van Eemnes.

And the organizing machinery was ultimately completed by the appointment of the following gentlemen to form a Board of Installation at Amsterdam itself :—

Mr. W. Van der Vliet, President.
Mr. J. Gosschalk, Secretary.
M. G. A. Heineken, Treasurer.
Mr. Charles Boissevain.
Mr. R. W. J. C. Van der Wall Bake.
Mr. J. J. F. Verdonck.

Thus encouraged from without, the Exhibition ultimately began to find favour in the eyes of the Dutch themselves; and many who had been loudest in their denunciations became numbered among its zealous advocates. Some pretended its character had undergone a change; that a certain revolutionary element had been eliminated, or absorbed and rendered harmless, by contact with conservative corporations, such as that of the City of London; others, finding the scheme growing daily in popularity, suddenly became anxious not to appear to their fellow-burghers behind the spirit of the age; while not a few of the courtier class, a class numerous at home, but still more numerous abroad, were easily converted to the merits of an undertaking which had found means to recommend itself to the favour of the kingly, historical, and enlightened House of Orange.

Prompted in part by one or other of the foregoing motives, and also in part no doubt by a generous desire to lend a helping hand to an experiment admitted on all sides to be disinterested, and therefore noble, the Government of the Netherlands had come forward with suggestions and liberal offers of assistance. A Ministerial resolution had appeared in the official "Gazette" of the 10th November, 1868, making known that no import duties would be levied on articles destined for exhibition; and a convincing proof of the well-wishing of the Court and Cabinet was afforded by the fact of the promoters being authorized to announce the Exhibition as held under the patronage of His Majesty the King, of the Government, and of the municipal authorities of Amsterdam.

At the outset of the undertaking, when the limited resources and accommodation of Utrecht were in the thoughts of its chief promoters, it had been notified that articles of luxury and the fine arts, with those of elegance and ornament strictly so-called would not be admitted. From this resolution, however, it became, and perhaps happily, possible to depart in practice (without virtually rescinding the rule), for when Amsterdam was selected as the site, a building unnecessarily large for the immediate objects in view had to be filled ; it became then desirable to accept rather than reject articles of a doubtful character as judged from a purely utilitarian point of view ; and this circumstance proved a golden bridge for the Committee of Installation, in relieving them from the arduous, thankless, and well-nigh impossible task of drawing a hard and fast line between the ornamental and the useful—between articles of luxury and necessity.

Thus things settled into shape, and many matters of detail which might have proved difficult of decision ultimately solved themselves by mutual concession. Still some problems not unnaturally, however unfortunately, withstood the adjusting influences of time and circumstance. Foremost among these ranked the earnest request to exhibitors to attach the wholesale as well as the retail prices to their goods. If this system could have been universally followed out, the beginning of the end might have been foreseen to the robbery now practised on the poorest classes of society, who are of necessity compelled to deal with very small retailers for articles of daily use. A person who buys a ton of coal or a chest of tea at a fashionable establishment gets, in reality, a nearer approach to the value of his money than the poor man's wife, who, unable to leave her home and children, is compelled to purchase her household stores by the ounce from the squalid and too often dishonest vendor of inferior goods at short weight who lives just round the corner. Ignorance

Wholesale and retail question.

of wholesale prices, and the absence of all possible
check upon the profits made by small retailers, are
at once the deadliest enemies of the poor, and those
most difficult to cope with. How far the great point
of making these things known, and seeking a remedy
by publicity, was ultimately carried, will be shown at
a later place in this report.

Final
regulations. To insure the *bona fide* nature of exhibits, the
Central Committee deemed it their duty to reserve
the right of purchasing all goods exhibited at the
prices affixed, and of ordering like goods at the same
price. Exhibitors refusing to comply with this regulation were very properly not to be held entitled to
compete for awards.

The above brief and practical regulations, with
the exclusion of live animals and articles of a very
perishable nature, or liable to spontaneous combus-
tion, were the only restrictions placed on the exhibition of all the animal, vegetable, or mineral
productions, and all the wares and manufactures
of every competing country; and it was duly notified
to the public, by Royal Decree promulgated in the
Government Gazette, that medals and certificates of
honourable mention would be awarded, for cheapness
and general excellence, to the most deserving exhibitors, by an International Jury, nominated by the
King of the Netherlands.

Under this short and simply-worded document
the Exhibition changed its character. From a merely
private undertaking, ostensibly promoted by the
Society for the Encouragement of Manufactures and
Mechanical Industry in the Netherlands, it became
one to the success of which the King and Cabinet
stood pledged. The sole responsibility was lifted
from the shoulders of one man, and that man himself
was transformed from a volunteer, and self-appointed
custodian of the interests of the masses, into an agent

responsible to the King and to his Minister in the Home Department for the performance of duties originally self-imposed. From this point of view the decree above-mentioned forms an important archive in the records of the Exhibition ; and as it will, moreover, be necessary to refer to it hereafter, no apology is needed for inserting the translation which now follows :—

" We, William III, by the Grace of God, King of the Netherlands, Prince of Orange-Nassau, Grand Duke of Luxemburg, &c., &c., &c. ^{Royal Decree} Royal Decree appointing the Jury.

" On the recommendation of our Minister for the Home Department, dated the 6th July, 1869 ;

" Have approved and do decree :

" 1. To name as members of the Jury for deciding awards at the International Exhibition of objects for the household and domestic use of the working classes, to be held at Amsterdam :

" As Honorary President, Mr. C. J. A. den Tex, Burgomaster of Amsterdam ;

" As Member and President, Baron D. J. Mackay, President of the Society for the Encouragement of Manufactures and Mechanical Industry at the Hague.

" As Members :—

" M. d'Andrimont, Liege.
" M. G. Berger, Paris.
" M. Van Camp, Antwerp.
" M. Carcenac, Paris.
" M. J. Clerfeyt, Brussels.
" M. C. N. David, Copenhagen.
" M. A. Deiglmayer, Vienna.
" M. L. Donnat, Paris.
" M. A. H. Eigeman, Leyden.
" M. Gilka, Berlin.
" M. A. Givard, Paris.

" M. L. J. Gron, Copenhagen.
" M. D. Grothe, Delft.
" M. H. Grothe, Berlin.
" Dr. J. W. Gunning, Amsterdam; also 1st
    Secretary.
" M. M. L. Herman, The Hague.
" M. B. Jensen, Copenhagen.
" E. Johnson, Esq., London.
" M. J. J. Kreeneu, Zwolle.
" M. J. P. Krusemen, Amsterdam.
" M. F. Von Liebig, Reichenberg, Bohemia.
" M. J. Martelet, Paris.
" M. Moudron, Lodelinsart, Belgium.
" Dr. J. Th. Mouton, the Hague.
" M. P. N. Muller, Amsterdam.
" P. Le Neve Foster, Esq., London.
" Dr. A. Van Oven, Dort, also 2nd Secretary.
" M. Poncelet, Brussels.
" Hodgson Pratt, Esq., London.
" M. Raeymackers, Antwerp.
" M. Renier, Brussels.
" M. C. V. Rimestadt, Copenhagen.
" Dr. W. Reve, Amsterdam.
" M. Ch. Robert, Paris.
" Dr. Rosenthal, Berlin.
" G. Sanders, Esq., London.
" P. L. Simmonds, Esq., London.
" M. J. Stakrosch, Brunn, Moravia.
" M. Stobwasser, Berlin.
" M. P. Fétar van Elven, Delft.
" M. N. Tetterode, Amsterdam.
" Hon. T. J. Hovell-Thurlow, the Hague.
" M. H. W. Veth, Dort.
" Dr. H. Vogelsang, Delft.
" M. J. Van der Wall Bake, Utrecht.
" Baron de Watteville, Paris.
" M. von Wertheim, Vienna.

" M. Wolff, Berlin.

" As *Jurés Suppléants* (or substitutes) :—

" M. J. Braet Van Neberfeldt, of Amsterdam.
" M. J. J. Buddingh, Arnhem.
" M. A. Chapon, Paris.
" M. F. Cheysson, Paris.
" Er. S. S. Coronel, Leeuwarden.
" M. Corr Van der Maeren, Brussels.
" M. Danbresse, La Louvière, Belgium.
" M. A. Dumaresq, Paris.
" M. Duvelleroy, Paris.
" M. Gillon, Brussels.
" M. W. T. Grasveld, Utrecht.
" M. G. Halphen, Paris.
" M. O. Van Kerckhove, Antwerp.
" M. Kindt, Brussels.
" M. A. Michiels, Antwerp.
" M. Moullott, Paris.
" M. Offermann, Brussels.
" M. A. Schilte, Ysselstein.
" M. P. Smit Van Gelder, Amsterdam.
" M. A. P. Van Stolk, Rotterdam.
" M. Feston, Paris.

" 2. To empower the Central Direction of the Society for the Encouragement of Manufactures and Mechanical Industry—

" (*a.*) To appoint *Jurés Suppléants* on the application of the members of the Jury from Great Britain, North Germany, Austria, Hungary, and Denmark.

" (*b.*) Whenever the number of exhibitors from any one country exceeds thirty, to appoint, on the application of the Commissioners of such country, not more then seven members of the Jury, and an equal number of *Jurés Suppléants*.

" Our Minister of the Home Department is charged with the execution of this Decree.

" *The Loo, July* 8, 1869.

"(Signed) " WILLIAM.

" The Minister of the Home Department:

" (Signed) " FOCK."

Classification of exhibits.

The next point which calls for some remark is the method of classifying exhibits ultimately adopted. Simplicity was the object which the Central Committee sought especially to attain, and bearing in mind the utilitarian aims of the Exhibition, the seven classes under which articles were eventually ranged formed a marked contrast to the more complex classification of previous occasions, and perfectly sufficed to answer all the requirements of reference and order. They were as follows :—

Class I.-—*Houses, &c.*

Dwellings, &c. ; institutions for the use of working men ; plans of dwellings for married and unmarried working men and agricultural labourers ; plans of bedrooms, kitchens, boarding houses, washing and reading-rooms, and places of amusement; portions of these buildings ; model dwellings ; materials for buildings ; experiments with cheap materials, mortar, iron, concrete, &c. ; felt and other coverings for roofs ; foundations ; means to prevent damp, &c.

Class II.—*Furniture and Household Necessaries.*

Chairs, tables, cupboards, lamps, safety-lamps, stoves, ovens, washing and drying machines, table utensils (spoons, forks, knives), carpets, floor-cloths, paperhangings, oil paints, lacquer-work, framed engravings, &c. ; clocks, looking-glasses, mats, iron

bedsteads, cradles, clothes-horses (for linen), pails,
tubs, and barrels, bedding, and table-linen, feathers,
mattrasses filled with various seaweeds and fibres,
hammocks, and cheap curtains; plates and dishes,
glass and earthenware for use as well as ornament,
ornamental plaster figures, cans, basins, pots, and
pans; materials for warming: turf, charcoal, com-
pressed turf, coal, coke, comparisons of heating
powers; materials for lighting: oil, petroleum
(samples of not more than 1 litre $= 1\frac{3}{4}$ pints
English), gas, comparisons of methods of lighting;
materials for promoting cleanliness of persons and
houses: cheap soaps, bleaching methods (with popular directions for use), such as bleaching-water, soda,
chloride of lime, scouring utensils, powders and
polishes, whiting, disinfectants, traps, and means of
destroying vermin; pedlars' wares: small basket-work,
tin-work, coombs, brushes and brooms, mops, service-
pipes, glazed iron-work, copper-work, &c.

Class III.—*Clothing.*

Cotton stuffs (including cambrics), linen, woollen,
and mixed stuffs, all in the piece; ready-made clothing: knitted, netted, and crochet goods, including
over and under garments, waterproof clothing, working dresses for dyke-makers, pilots, fishermen, &c.,
leather aprons, gloves, thumbstalls; coverings for the
head: caps, hats (sou'-westers), women's caps and
bonnets, straw and glazed hats, paper caps; boots and
shoes of wood, leather, felt, straw, gutta-percha,
wool; smaller objects connected with clothing: ornaments, buttons, threads, ribbons, needles, pins,
tobacco-boxes, pocket-books, purses, scissors, rings,
earrings, bracelets, and other cheap trinkets, national
costumes, also those of the Colonies, &c.

Class IV.—*Food.*

Agricultural and industrial productions for food and similar uses ; various sorts of flour, oatmeal, peas, beans, rice, potatoes, chestnuts, maize-flour, potato-flour, spices, sugar, treacle, sweet oils, vinegar, and other condiments, coffee, tea, chicory, and all sorts of sweets and confectionery, if pure and harmless; tobacco for smoking and chewing, snuff; dried food, or food preserved in any way, dried and salted meat and fish, extract of meat, milk powder, preserved vegetables, jams, and fruits, &c.; drinks: beer, spirits, wines, &c.

Class V.—*Mechanics', Farm Labourers,' Gardeners', and other Tools and Implements.*

Tools for working-men, by which is principally meant tools which economize time and labour in any trade, or in domestic arrangements. Tools for gardeners, farm-labourers, dyke-workers, market-gardeners, nets and tackle for fishermen, sowing-machines, ploughs, &c. (with the exception of large, and therefore expensive, agricultural implements), wheelbarrows, implements used in draining, sewing-machines, &c.

Class VI.—*Means for Moral, Intellectual, and Physical Development.*

Education and recreation. Books for the technical education of the working-classes ; works of imagination (popular romances), works for education, popular science, history and biography; prints and engravings coming under the above heads. Gymnastic exercises, methods of defence ; music and musical instruments, national airs, singing methods. Games, popular amusements, children's toys. Papers on the above. Secondary trades ; things to be done in spare time —employments suited for women and girls at home, &c.

Class VII.—*Reports, Statutes, Rules, and Regulations of Associations for Promoting the Well-being of the Working Classes.*

Papers on institutions and associations for promoting the well-being of the working-man :—(*a*), to his advantage ; (*b*), concerning provident funds and societies, savings' banks, co-operative stores, co-operative labour, sick funds, pension funds, &c.

Articles exhibited under this class became the property of the Society for the Encouragement of Manufactures and Mechanical Industry in the Netherlands.

The building in which all these articles were to be displayed, partakes largely of the Crystal Palace style of architecture, but is stronger in its construction, and more permanent in its character than most of the buildings designed for exhibitions. Though late in maturing their International Exhibition, the Dutch were first in the field in planning an imitation of the Prince Consort's building of 1851. In the succeeding year, Dr. Sarphati commenced an agitation to collect subscriptions for this purpose, and in 1856 the foundations were laid of the *Volksvlijt Paleis*, which was opened by the King in 1864. Though constructed of the usual exhibition materials,—wood, iron, and glass,—it has a substantial, Dutch appearance, combined with much grace and symmetry. M. Cornelius Outhoorn, the architect, has reaped great credit in Holland from the design, and good foreign judges have not hesitated to award to it the palm in archi- *[Exhibition building.]*

tectural beauty over the similar structures erected at
Paris, Dublin, or Sydenham. It consists of one
principal nave, supported by very slender cast-iron
columns, which give it appearance of lightness; but
its moderate height, and the side halls, which, though
joined to and opening out of it, are partitioned off
by solid walls, take off the look of scaffolding that
has marred the perfection of other exhibition buildings. In the centre of the nave a dome rises to the
height of 250 feet, crowned by a winged figure, of
fine dimensions, which, from a little distance, stands
out in bold relief against the sky. The position is
well chosen, on the banks of the Amstel River, in the
new part of the town, near the Utrecht Railway
Station, and a small surrounding park contains Café
Restaurants, and other places of out-door amusement
or repose. Hitherto it has been mainly used for
holding flower-shows, concerts, and popular gatherings of all kinds, and has not proved by any means
as profitable an investment as had been hoped by its
projectors.

Arrange-
ment of
exhibits. Being intended, as has been said, to remain an
ornamental and useful public edifice, no special
internal arrangements mark its aptitude for sub-divi-
sion into nations, sections, or compartments. This,
however, did not prove by any means an unmixed
evil. In the International Exhibition held at Paris
in 1867, a theory of arrangement was designed,
perfect at first sight, but generally admitted to have
proved highly inconvenient in practice. The fallacy
of the arrangement of exhibits in zones lies, as Mr.
Cole has clearly put it, in the assumption that every
country will supply an equal proportion of objects in
each group; whereas, when the stern facts are dealt
with, in the actual arrangement of the interior, discordant violations of principle become necessary on
all sides. In all exhibitions preceding that held at

Paris in 1867, there was a tolerable certainty that objects of the same class would be found in one spot. At Paris it was otherwise; for in many cases the section of the zone, where objects belonging to the same group were theoretically supposed to be collected, did not afford sufficient space for them. According to Mr. Cole, this generally proved the case in the small section of zones set apart for the exhibits of small countries. Once out of their appointed zones, no clue existed for discovering their arbitrary position. The object sought might be found in any of the other zones, or outside the main building altogether.

In the Amsterdam Exhibition, difficulties having their origin in too studied an adaptation of the building to the end in view did not arise. The simple plan was therefore adopted of cutting off for each country as much space as was required, the partitions between the several countries being generally constructed by the cases of their respective exhibits being placed back to back, and the internal arrangement in classes by each country within its own prescribed limits being entirely left to the discretion of its own officials. Thus the British section was laid out and arranged by Mr. P. L. Simmonds, the Secretary and Manager of the Lord Mayor's Committee, whose ripe experience in exhibition management enabled him to render the utmost justice to the merits of the articles displayed.

The relative proportion of exhibits from each country represented may be seen by a glance at the following Table, showing the number of exhibitors by classes and by countries :— *Numerical roll of exhibits.*

Country.	Class I.	Class II.	Class III.	Class IV.	Class V.	Class VI.	Class VII.	Total.
Austria	15	24	59	25	13	6	4	146
Baden	..	3	..	..	1	..	..	4
Bavaria	1	5	4	..	3	1	..	14
Belgium	74	93	98	44	35	46	32	422
Denmark	14	13	12	11	5	6	2	63
France	28	100	89	50	56	60	33	415
Great Britain	18	74	43	27	28	10	13	218
Hesse-Darmstadt	..	1	..	..	..	1	..	1
Italy	..	..	..	2	..	..	..	3
Netherlands	84	241	100	115	157	113	36	846
North Germany	28	22	32	15	19	6	12	134
Norway	..	..	1	..	..	1	..	2
Sweden	1	7	3	1	..	1	1	14
Switzerland	1	..	2	1	..	2	..	6
Wurtemberg	..	2	2	1	2	3	170	180
Total of Exhibitors	264	585	449	292	319	256	303	2,468

From this Table it is seen that Great Britain ranked fourth in numerical importance of exhibitors, and it may be added that the articles in this section certainly equalled, if not exceeded, in practical utility and in money value, those of any other country. The three countries that ultimately surpassed Great Britain in number of exhibitors were the Netherlands, who were at home, the limitrophe Kingdom of Belgium, and Imperial France. Yet on the opening day, the 15th July, Great Britain stood first amid foreign nations in the completeness of her arrangements. The French department, at noon on the 14th July, was represented by a large empty space of the floor of the building, roped off and labelled " France." At sundown, however, the French *personnel* and *matériel* arrived in force, speedily took possession of their appointed space, and worked with so great energy throughout the night, that when the opening hour arrived on the morning of the 15th, France, no longer conspicuous by her absence, was represented by lanes of handsome, though as yet empty, cases, and by a voluble and intelligent Frank, who was busily engaged in entering *abonnements* to a *Moniteur de l'Exposition*, to be published weekly in the French department.

It had been hoped, and at one time there had appeared reasonable grounds for hoping, that the King of the Netherlands would open the Exhibition in person, or commission the heir apparent, the Prince of Orange, to open it in His Majesty's name. To the grievous disappointment of those concerned in its success, circumstances prevented the full accomplishment of this desire. Yet, though the King was unable to attend in person, and though illness prevented the Prince of Orange from performing the duties that devolved upon him, sufficient proof was afforded of the interest taken by the House of Orange Nassau

Opening of the Exhibition.

D

in the undertaking, by the appointment of Prince
Henry of the Netherlands to open the Exhibition in
the name of his Royal brother.   This ceremony took
place at noon of the 15th July, 1869, amidst all the
honours that the civic authorities of Amsterdam had
in their power to heap on the occasion.   Punctually
at the hour appointed, the Prince arrived in the
uniform of a Dutch Admiral, and after his formal reception by the burgomaster of Amsterdam, by the
King's Cabinet, and by the members of the Diplomatic Body who had come from the Hague to be
present at the opening, Baron Mackay delivered an
address in the Dutch language, of which the following is a faithful translation :—

Address to
Prince
Henry.

" Your Royal Highness,
        " In the Netherlands every great thing is brought
about under the influence and protection of a Prince
of the House of Orange.
        " His Majesty the King, the Patron of the Society
for the Encouragement of Manufactures and Mechanical Industry, has, during His Majesty's reign,
given many evidences of his devotion to the Industry
of the Netherlands.   We know that His Majesty
looks down with satisfaction on each attempt to
develop industry, and place it in a position to accomplish its difficult mission.   In the name of the
Society, I have the honour here openly to express to
our honoured King my thanks for this new proof of
favour, and for many previous ones conferred upon
this Exhibition, by inviting your Royal Highness to
open it in His Majesty's name.   Your Royal Highness, whose high calling unites the maintenance of
the ancient glory of the Netherlands on the high seas
with the guardianship of our flag, wherever it waves
in the four quarters of the earth, has, by your
presence here this day, placed a seal on this work of

peace, in the successful accomplishment of which our national honour is concerned. Your Royal Highness has been willing to bestow an approving glance upon a Dutch enterprise, conceived and executed in a genuine Dutch spirit; and your Royal Highness must graciously accept the humble expression of our warm gratitude. On our soil it has ever been customary to say little and to do much. This Exhibition is the fruit of calm and ripe deliberation, joined to the restless exertion of many various forces. We desire no vain show, but solid and permanent results, such as accord with the character of our people. The idea of the Exhibition was conceived by a prominent Dutch manufacturer, the President of the blooming Utrecht branch of our Society, Mr. John Van der Wall Bake. With a practical eye he recognised that this Exhibition would supply a want of the present day. How just was his view at once appeared from the manner in which his idea was received. Our Society unanimously resolved in one of its general meetings to proceed to its immediate execution, and our Central Committee commenced, not without fear, its difficult task.

" Abroad and at home, men of all shades of opinion vied with one another in preparing what is this day completed. Manufacturers, the learned, Statesmen, bound themselves to the work with great sacrifice of time and money. With what success their efforts have been crowned can only appear when the judges commissioned by His Majesty to deliver sentence shall have fulfilled their arduous duties. One feeling alone shall govern me on entering the Exhibition ; a feeling of gratitude towards so many who have given their support to it. The number of those to whom we are indebted is indeed too great to enable me to mention them here individually ; and even were I so to do, I might, perhaps, unwillingly be guilty of omissions. I cannot, however, pass over in silence the proofs of interest in the undertaking given by several Foreign Governments in the appointment of Commissioners, by His Majesty's Government, whose co-operation was never refused to us from the commencement, by Provincial and Local Authorities, by Foreign Commissioners, and by the Netherlands Provincial and Local Commissioners who, by their exertions, knew how to spur on so large a number of Exhibitors to take part in our endeavours.

" The Local Committee of Management in the capital, composed of members of the Amsterdam branch of our society, has, under the excellent presidency of Mr. W. Van der Vleit, and of its clever technical secretary, the architect, Mr. J. Gosschalk, proved, by its restless zeal and disinterested devotion, that nothing was too much for it.

" I spoke above of the end in view, and that gives me occasion for saying a few words. Although it was a delicate task that we had undertaken, the organizing Committee was of opinion that it should be looked straight in the face, in a national manner. This has ever been the praiseworthy habit of all well-meaning Netherlanders, and we desired not to depart from it. Our end is material and moral.

" The material side of the Exhibition is evident to the eye ; it gives to our manufacturers the opportunity of acquainting themselves with what is taking place in other countries in the realms of industry ; it also affords to foreign industry opportunities of acquiring a more exact knowledge of our wants ; it thus creates new sources for our trade ; it increases our prosperity ; it causes justice to be rendered to our excellent system of free trade ; it promotes cheapness, and is in this respect entirely different from other Exhibitions.

" But the material side is not the principal end, which is the moral one; the power of the Netherlands nation has at all times consisted mainly in the fact that all inhabitants, to whatever class they may belong, meet one another with kindly confidence. This tie we wish to strengthen, in the conviction that nothing can be more fatal to the prosperity of the Netherlands than the absence of this first condition of welfare. As the result of pernicious influences, the workman had gathered an impression that his interests were separate from those of the work-giver. Yes, that they even were in conflict with them. No sensible workman will allow himself to be thus deluded; no sensible work-giver will make himself uneasy about it. Sad facts are there to prove that nobody experiences more the evils of this strife between unequal powers than the workman himself. The question is whether he shall profit from the experience gained by others, or whether he shall plunge himself into ruin by resort to fallacious principles.

" This Exhibition, projected by the workman's real friends, is a protest against the misleading of those who display before his eyes glittering illusions, the unattainability of which can only produce the bitterest disappointment.

" If this Exhibition closes the way to unlawful expectations of impossible raising of wages by means of fatal strikes, it also justifies reasonable hopes of bettering the condition of the workman without injuring his interests; its aim is to give him the means of turning to the best account the money he earns by intelligent and orderly labour, and to enable him to supply in the best manner all his material as well as moral wants.

" The Exhibition that your Royal Highness is about to open is thus a work of equity and mercy;

of equity, because it strives to establish our social
condition on firm foundations, and to render vain the
designs of those who threaten it; of mercy, because
it occupies itself with the condition of those whose
inferior development often renders them a prey to
specious but really erroneous and dangerous teach-
ings, and hinders them from making the most
judicious use of their earnings and savings.

"What I have had the honour of stating is not a
rash conviction, it is the experience of the lives of
men who are friends of both Dutch and foreign
industry, and who know that even as in a household
or family the prosperity of one member conduces to
the prosperity of the others, so also in the workshop
the prosperity of the workman and that of the work-
giver are inseparable. This Exhibition marches on
the smooth path of right and justice; it does more;
its international character brings with it the presence
of foreigners. The intelligent foreigner will avail
himself of this opportunity to make himself master of
the secret of our prosperity. The sight of a proud
and free nation will make him follow up the causes of
this enviable condition. Let our nation not shun
this examination; let our nation, indeed, invite it,
provided it be not superficial. Netherlands society
is composed of so many varied elements, that a superficial examination can only produce erroneous im-
pressions. The foreigner will be able to reap
advantage from a minute and careful study of our
manners, of our laws, and of our privileges, even as
we propose to derive from his visit the benefit of his
experience.

"One great fact governs our whole history, which
must above all attract the attention of foreigners; it
is that a nation which has remained faithful to the
principles that obtained for it its independence—a
nation which will never forget that the dying cry of

your Royal Highness's great ancestor, 'My God, have pity on me and my poor people!' was the prayer whereby a brilliant future was opened to us—a nation which, so long as Dutch blood flows in Dutch veins, is bound by an indissoluble link of attachment and faith to the House of Orange, mindful of the responsibility that a previous generation has laid upon it, will, whenever it is a question of its rights and privileges, fight by the side of its King under the motto *Je maintiendrai.*"

To this eloquent address, delivered with a fire and spirit of which we Englishmen erroneously deem the phlegmatic Netherlander incapable, but with which the impassioned utterances that have been happily preserved to adorn the pages of European history show the Dutch of all ages have on occasion proved themselves imbued, Prince Henry replied as follows:

"Mr. President of the Central Society for the Encouragement of Manufactures and Mechanical Industry in the Netherlands, and Gentlemen, Members of that Committee, highly Esteemed Representatives of Foreign Powers, Commissioners, Ministers of the King, noble and honoured Burgomasters of Amsterdam, &c., and all of you who manifest by your presence the interest that you take in the proceedings of this day, it is a real pleasure to me to find myself on this spot, in the faithful capital of the Kingdom, to perform the honourable task of opening in the name of the King this International Exhibition of objects for the use of the working classes. Prince Henry's reply.

"Receive, Mr. President, my sincere thanks for the hearty patriotic speech with which you have welcomed me.

"With much satisfaction I have learnt the co-operation your Society has met with at home and abroad in its labours to attain the lofty aims that we find represented in this Exhibition, namely, to raise the social, moral, and material condition of the working man, by manifesting an upright kindly interest in him, and by placing within his grasp means of development.

"May this honourable, but difficult, task that you have undertaken bear the most salutary fruit, both in the Netherlands and in all those countries which prove by their presence at this Exhibition the interest they take in the attainment of similar ends.

"May your manly efforts in all herein concerned meet with the sincere and powerful support that they require, in order to give new strength to the links of mutual confidence, love, and affection, which, for their own quiet and orderly development, it is necessary should exist in every land between the different classes of society.

"The co-operation and support which your Society, Mr. President, has already received from so many quarters and in so many shapes, may, let us hope, prove an earnest of the success of this Exhibition, through which new sources of well-being and development may be discovered in the Netherlands, and in the other countries which have taken part or interest in the objects of this International Exhibition.

"In the name of the King, patron of your Society, I beg, Mr. President, warmly to thank all, Netherlanders and others, for their co-operation in your Exhibition, and especially the Foreign and Native Commissions here present, with the assurance that they are heartily welcome in the Netherlands and in this capital.

"In the name of the King I declare the Interna-

tional Exhibition of objects for the household and
use of the working-man to be now opened."

Immediately upon the conclusion of this reply,
the folding-doors into the nave of the building were
thrown open; and as Prince Henry and his at-
tendants passed through, a thousand voices burst
into the Choral Workman's song, for the following
spirited and accurate translation of which I am
indebted to a poetical friend :—

" No monster of iron on gunpowder fed,
  No clangor of steel, no whizzing of lead,
    Makes the blood in our arteries tingle:
  But the whirl of the wheel, and the whistle of steam,
  And the bubbling hiss of the seething stream,
    Is the sound where our sympathies mingle.

" No laurel that drips with the blood of the brave,
  No crown that hangs over the conqueror's grave,
    No wreath that is woven in weeping;
  The olive that circles the forehead of toil,
  The mood of the master of metal and soil,
    Is the fruit that we glory in reaping.

" Oh! the roar and the foam of the fiery stream!
  Oh! the rush and the shriek of the bursting steam!
    No warrior's clarion is louder;
  We, too, have our iron, our steel, and our lead,
  But ours is living and theirs is dead,
    And the music of Peace is the prouder.

" Then a song shall arise in melodious might,
  To God who has severed the dark from the light,
    And the work and the workmen created;
  By the play of the muscles He holds us in health,
  By the sweat of the brow can endow us with wealth,
    In the love of our labour elated.

" We sow for the weal of the loved ones at home,
  We know in good time that the harvest will come,
    He wins who has honestly striven;
  Our toil is the salt of the bread of to-day,
  And the food of our hearts is the faith that can say,
    ' We, too, have our rest and our heaven.' "

Workman's choral song.

Prince
Henry's
progress
through the
building.

On entering the Exhibition, His Royal Highness found himself in the Netherlands Department; and after a hurried glance at the objects it contained, commenced his progress through the different courts or countries, by a detailed examination of the cutlery and other practical articles of the first necessity, which were displayed in rich profusion among the exhibits from Great Britain.

Some idea may be formed of the relative space occupied by each country, from the accompanying rough-ground plan of the Exhibition building :—

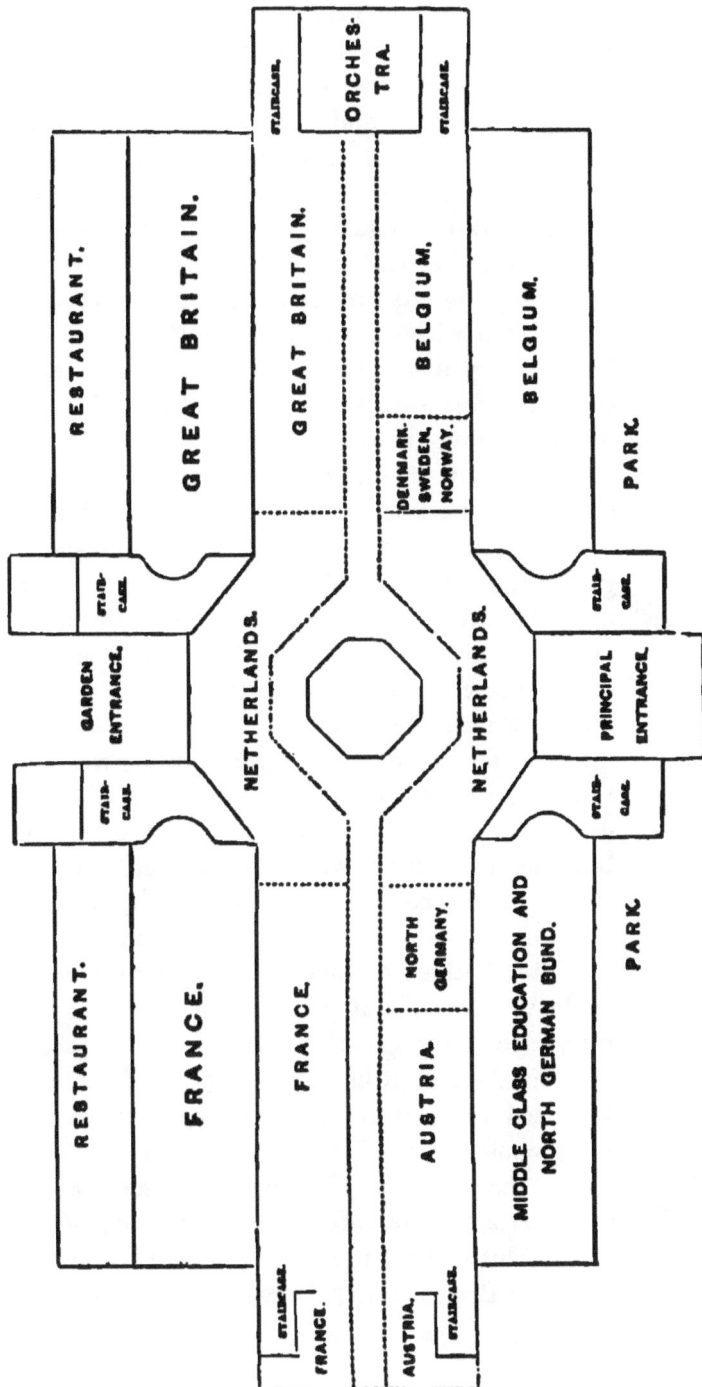

ORCHESTRA.

STAIRCASE.

STAIRCASE.

RESTAURANT.

GREAT BRITAIN.

GREAT BRITAIN.

BELGIUM.

BELGIUM.

DENMARK. SWEDEN. NORWAY.

PARK

STAIRCASE.

STAIRCASE.

GARDEN ENTRANCE.

PRINCIPAL ENTRANCE.

NETHERLANDS.

NETHERLANDS.

STAIRCASE.

STAIRCASE.

RESTAURANT.

FRANCE.

FRANCE.

AUSTRIA.

NORTH GERMANY.

MIDDLE CLASS EDUCATION AND NORTH GERMAN BUND.

PARK

STAIRCASE.

FRANCE.

AUSTRIA.

STAIRCASE.

From England Prince Henry passed into Belgium, and thence made the round of the remaining countries, being received at the entrance of each by its Commissioners and Jurors. Passing out of the building, His Royal Highness examined with great interest and minuteness the accommodation provided for the working classes of all countries visiting the Exhibition. For this purpose three buildings, capable of housing 200 visitors at a time, had been specially erected just without the precincts of the Exhibition, by the organizing Committee, under the efficient superintendence of Mr. Van der Vliet. The accommodation was divided into two classes, for which 60 cents and 40 cents (1s. and 8d.) *per diem* were charged respectively. This included a clean bed, with ample bedding (each room being double-bedded), gaslight, any quantity of water for washing or drinking purposes, and the use of a hand-basin, towel, looking-glass, chair, table, &c. Everything was brand new in these model caravanseries, and a pattern of neatness, cleanliness, and simplicity. The restaurants intended for the working classes visiting the Exhibition were within its precincts, and provided excellent dinners at 9d. a-head, and other refreshment of the best quality at the lowest possible price. The statistics of the use made of these buildings by visitors will be given at a later period of this Report.

Into all these details Prince Henry entered with evident interest and appreciation; and he finally completed the range of his experience by partaking of a luncheon that had been prepared for him in a full-sized model workman's cottage, erected within the grounds.

In the evening His Royal Highness was entertained at a banquet, after, or rather during which, as is the Dutch fashion, some admirable speeches were made by Prince Henry, Baron Mackay, the Belgian

Accommodation for working-class visitors.

Evening entertainments.

Envoy, and the President of the Austrian Commission, who respectively returned thanks for the King, proposed the health of the working-classes, the Diplomatic Body, the Foreign Commissioners, &c. Unfortunately, no provision was made for reporting these speeches, more than one of which was distinguished by a rare combination of courage and skill in dealing with many of the social problems of the age in the presence of the representatives of every kind of autocratic and popular machinery yet invented for the rule and governance of mankind. As was stated at the time in the columns of the *Times*, it is . greatly to be deplored that no record was preserved of what was said on this occasion.

In the evening a display of fireworks in the Exhibition grounds closed the proceedings of a long day; and on the following morning, at 11, the building was opened to the public, on payment of a franc (half a Netherlands florin, or 10*d.*), and the rapidity with which it was filled by eager visitors of all countries, ages, sexes, and conditions, may best be gathered from the following description of the crowds who thronged the streets of Amsterdam during July, August, and September last, extracted from a letter from the special correspondent of an enterprising British newspaper:—"Boors in long black frock-coats, buckled shoes, and bishops' leggings; women in all sorts of comical head-dresses, some with gold or silver skull-caps, others with horns of gold or silver-twisted wire sticking out from each side of their face, some with blinkers of the same precious metals, caps of wondrous design and manufacture, and dresses of every imaginable cut, colour, and texture—flaming scarlet, bright pea-green, black, white and grey;—while a goodly number, with the proverbial indecision of their sex, had compromised the matter by wearing gowns and mantles, red on one side from top to toe, and black on the other." This last statement is not exaggerated, such being the conspicuous and picturesque costume of a large and wealthy orphanage of Amsterdam.

As has been already mentioned, this Exhibition, the formal opening of which has just been recorded, was divided into seven classes. I shall now proceed to an examination in some detail of each class; of the most remarkable articles in each class; of those which figure in the final awards as obtaining medals or honorary mention; and of those which popularly attracted most attention.

HOUSES.

THE dwelling-house being the first requirement of civilized society, and the one which, in a well-organized community, it should be possible to accept as affording an index to the other conditions and requirements of its inmates—of their wages, their food, their clothing, their education—naturally ranks first. Class I was, therefore, shortly termed "Houses," but included institutions for the use of working-men, plans of dwellings for married and unmarried working-men, and agricultural labourers, plans of bedrooms, kitchens, boarding-houses, washing and reading-rooms, and places of amusement. It also included any portion of these buildings; model dwellings, materials for building, experiments with cheap materials, mortar, iron, concrete, &c., felt and other covering for roofs; foundations, means to prevent damp, &c.; in short, it included every element or component part of domestic architecture.

In considering Class I, two apparently conflicting interests have to be conciliated; the requirements of the proprietor, and of the inhabitant; the hygienic and the financial, or the moral and material questions.

The proprietor often only wants a good return for his money; i.e., a rent representing a fair percentage on his outlay. In towns where ground is costly and measured by the inch, the necessary reconciliation is often effected by the erection of many-storied barrack-like buildings, in which families are packed in layers, like herrings in a barrel. There is, indeed, much to be said in favour of this system. The bulk of the population of such houses is removed from damp cellar life and surface drainage into realms of purer air; but at what moral cost? At the cost of losing individuality and the sense of home, with all the attendant virtues such a sense brings with it. Habits of cleanliness, neatness and sobriety are not likely to be improved by daily and hourly contamination from the unclean, the untidy, and the unsober; and a percentage of such does exist in every class of our society. The tendency of such a heaping up of human beings is to force them to assume one level standard of a low average on the whole community. Each family is brought into immediate contact with the wants and misfortunes of its neighbours; the result is only too natural and inevitable. Among such a population there is at all times a certain amount of illness, of hunger, of drunkenness, of ruin, of despair, and other unhappy elements. These elements meet, on the stairs and in the passages, the redeeming elements of health, of sufficiency, of sobriety, of cheerfulness. The redeeming elements are seldom in a majority, and the result is the formation of a morbidly despondent colony of families and individuals, containing many families and individuals who might be happier and healthier, and better off, if not perforce compelled to mingle with their less fortunate or moral brethren. It has been well said that "the lower we descend in the social scale, the less is the self-restraint, the greater the passion and violence, and *the greater the need of a certain extent of separation.*"

Among the valuable evidence adduced on this subject at the Paris Exhibition of 1867, not the least important was the following statement of M. Veron.

when maintaining the superiority of the four-house block and garden system of Mulhouse, where practicable, over the *cités ouvrières*, or what have been termed perpendicular streets. "After due deliberation," said M. Veron, "the Committee unanimously rejected the principle of the great barracks which had so ill succeeded in Paris and elsewhere. If these buildings have the advantage of economy in ground-rent and cheapness of construction, they have, on the other side, in the agglomeration of the population, a crowd of inconveniences, the least of which is the repugnance of the working-classes to this sort of dwellings."

Mr. Edwin Chadwick, in his excellent Report on Dwellings, published in the 3rd volume of Reports on the Paris Exhibition of 1867, presented to Parliament in 1868, goes even still further. He practically rejects the four-house block and garden Mulhouse system, with the following remarks :—"In bl>cks of four contiguous houses, one morose owner, one shrew or common scold, or one set of ill-conditioned children, from whom there is no power of escape, may make the habitation of the other three unpleasant, and render most desirable the right of forcible eviction ;" and he tells us further how penal statistics teach that a too close aggregation of ill-trained people works badly ; how, in a court, a common pump has kept an attorney in good practice : —A little girl going to fetch water would be thrust aside by a big girl, and being saucy, would be beaten ; the mother of the little girl would come out, and beat the big girl ; then the mother of the big girl would come out and straightway attack the mother of the little girl ; then the husbands would come out to do battle for their wives and children ; and then, if Irish, sides would be taken by the other occupiers of the court, when a battle royal would ensue, ter-

E

minating in prosecutions for assault and battery, and work for the attorneys.

Though this is, no doubt, a lively picture of the evils of agglomeration, it does not touch the worst features of the case. Boys at school may form sides and fight without breeding bad fellowship or immorality, and it is only charitable to suppose that a court or alley population, especially with the introduction of a large Irish element, may do the same. The worst features in the *cités ouvrières*, or perpendicular streets, are the silent negative ones, that do not assert themselves, even on close inspection ; the callousness to suffering and misery bred by every-day and all-day contemplation of wants, physical and moral, which those who contemplate them have no means of adequately relieving ; the gloom engendered by the daily visit of the doctor to some inmate or other of the overgrown house ; the frequent visits of the undertaker ; and a thousand other occurrences incidental in a given ratio to the population, but which it is not healthful to have paraded constantly before the eyes of those whose turn has not yet come.

All this happens in such buildings in a time of health, and under normal conditions ; but it is under abnormal conditions, which will occur at intervals— conditions of contagion, of famine, of strikes, of fire, &c.—that the *cité ouvrière* is seen to its greatest disadvantage as an institution. On the horrors of such periods it is needless to dwell ; they appeal to the imagination with only too great readiness and reality ; but still it is necessary not to overlook them in an inquiry of this kind.

With these preliminary observations, which I am unwilling to extend, we shall turn to an examination of the phases of the dwelling question, as represented the other day at Amsterdam.

Probaly few towns in Europe stand more in need

of improved dwellings for the working-classes than
Amsterdam, and therefore it was natural that the
Dutch exhibits in Class I should be of an important
nature. No less natural was it that the British
exhibits in this class, crowned as England was with
laurels, at the great International fair of 1867, should
be somewhat scanty in number, and essentially practical in character, being principally confined to
improved articles of construction, or advance in
economy, or detail of execution. The bulk of the
wage class of Amsterdam inhabit cellar or basement
dwellings, varying in depth, but always some feet below
the water level of the inevitably neighbouring canal.
A fair average specimen of these dwellings, for which
at least 2s. a-week is paid, has been accurately
described as follows :—" I went down six steps, and
found myself in utter darkness. The weather was
very fine, the air was dry, but the brick floor of the
cellar was moist, and the walls reflected the light of
the candle, which was lighted in honour of my visit."—
Such dwellings are naturally liable to sudden inun-
dations from heavy rainfall at any season of the year,
and are especially unhealthy during thaw. In sharp
frost they are extremely prejudicial, owing to bad
ventilation and easy overheating beyond the sanitary
point. Taken altogether, they probably combine
most of the worst conditions of life, as judged by
modern science. Yet notwithstanding this, and notwithstanding the extreme difficulty in Amsterdam of
procuring ground area for horizontal streets of workmen's houses, the cités ouvrières are highly unpopular
in that commercial locality. Within the last fifteen
years, indeed, such buildings have been erected ; but
the leaning of the class concerned is towards isolated
dwellings and non-aggregation. This leaning, like
every other demand, is producing a supply ; and
among others a house has been produced and exhi-

bited in full size, of which the following is some
account :—

The cottage in which Prince Henry took luncheon,
as has been stated above, was erected in the grounds
of the Exhibition by an Amsterdam society for improving the condition of the working-classes, entitled
the *Bouwkas*, or building fund. So great has been
the demand for these houses, that 68 have been built
within the distance of a mile from the Exhibition ;
54 of them are single, and the remainder two-storied,
the rent being 2s. 6d. and 5s. a week respectively.
The single-storied dwellings are mostly inhabited by
artisans, whose annual wage averages 15s. to £1 a
week. The price of their construction is stated to
be 1,100 florins, or about £92. Each covers an area
of 31½ square mètres,* and has an open yard behind
of 13½ square mètres, containing a tub to catch rain
water, and an outhouse. The cubic contents of its
two rooms are 78½ mètres ; that of the loft, or garret,
43½ mètres. The double-storied house covers
38½ square mètres, and has on each floor a cubic
measurement of 103½ cubic mètres ; that of the loft
being 53½. In the single-story house there is a bed
recess in the room by which you enter, and two or
more in the garret. The roof, which is of tile, has
in it a window, which will open. A common complaint of such dwellings is, that too much has been
aimed at in their design. The accommodation is
diminished by being too much cut up. One good
room is sacrificed to two bad ones : a front room of
3 by 3·70, and a back one of 4·17 by 3·17 mètres ;
the height is 2·85 mètres. The front room is intended
for the sleeping place of the parents, the back for the
living room. Of its accommodation, however, 2 square
mètres must be deducted for the space taken up by
the ladder leading to the garret, for the stove, a chest,

* The mètre measures 39·371 English inches.

a stone sink, and a dresser. Complaints are made of the difficulty of keeping things tidy in so small a room, and the tendency is to stow everything not immediately required, or actually in use, in the loft where the children habitually sleep. This practice, extending to fuel, potatoes, preserved food, such as salt fish, &c., can but have a prejudicial effect on the growing generation. Still, as has been said, these dwellings are popular in Amsterdam; and those in use, to which a supply of excellent water from the dunes has been laid on, are proved by statistics to be more salutary abodes than either the *cités ouvrières*, or the cellar dwellings. The demand for them is, consequently, on the increase.

Models of workmen's houses on the scale of one-tenth were exhibited by a similar society at the Hague, and by Mr. Kleiweg Dyserinck, of Haarlem. These are blocks of four houses each, each house consisting of one room with an antechamber or wash-house, containing outhouse, stone sink, and cupboard. The inner room is 4·50 by 4 mètres, and there is a spacious cellar for storing fuel, &c. In one corner is the stove, with a chimney containing a very good parallel ventilating flue. In addition to this there are gratings close to the floor, which do no good, as the inhabitants invariably stop them up, on account of the draught they occasion. The cellar, to which access is obtained through the cupboard door in the antechamber, is airy and light. By an outer stair, under which is a small cupboard opening into the inner room, a second floor is gained, composed of two small rooms of equal aggregate size to the room below. In the smallest is a good sized cupboard, and an iron bed place attached to the wall. The larger room may be used as a drying place for clothes. The ceiling of both is formed by the wooden roof covered externally with zinc. The height of the

Class I.

Hague and Haarlem exhibits.

ground-floor room is 3·10, and of the upper floor 2·55 mètres. The windows open nearly up to the ceiling, and provide perfect means of ventilation. Each dwelling has a habitable area of 42 square mètres. Those facing the strect let at 2s. 11d., the others at 2s. 6d., a week. The society calculates on a return of 7 per cent. on its outlay for such cottages. They are very popular, and are considered exactly suitable for artisans earning about 1l. a week ; onc-seventh being the Dutch theoretical fraction of an income appropriate for house-rent.

The Haarlem model differs little from the above description of the Hague Society's cottages.

One of the best models for rows of cottages was supplied by the Dutch Carpenters' Society (*Tot Nut voor den Timmerman*). This represents a block of eight buildings, each with a separate entrance opening immediately into the living-room. This is 3·75 by 4·50 mètres, has a sleeping place or alcove of 2 by 1·25 mètres, a cupboard, and a stove. Each house has also a kitchen of 3·35 by 2·25 mètres, an out-house, a sleeping-room of 2·55 by 2·25 mètres, and under it a cellar. The kitchen contains a cooking-stove, a stone sink, a dresser, a cupboard, and a place for stowing fuel. Each house has its own stairs leading to a second story of three rooms of similar aggregate dimensions to those on the ground-floor, and to a loft or garret above. Every room in these houses has a ceiling ; the ground-floor rooms are 3 mètres, the upper ones, 2·85 mètres high. Ventilation is secured by air-holes or gratings opening into the space between the floor and ceiling, and by parallel flues in the chimney. This block, which covers 620 square mètres, costs 14,450 florins, or about 1,204l., not including the price of the land.

Some of the most generally popular workmen's dwellings, of which models and plans were exhibited, were a series of fourteen double cottages, erected at Dort by Mr. K. W. Veth in 1864–67. They face east and west, and have two fronts, one family occupying the ground-floor, and another the first story. Each family enters by a porch containing an out-house ; in the case of the first-floor family, this porch is reached by a broad solid stair springing from the garden of 50 square mètres, which each family has on its own side of the house. Each garden contains a pump and drying-ground. Each dwelling occupies 47·25 square mètres (is 7 mètres long and 6·75 broad). From the porch you enter a living room of 4·60 by 3·50 mètres, with two windows, a fire-place in the middle of one side of the room, having a cupboard on the one, and a sleeping alcove on the other side of it, and in the back wall two doors, one leading to a well lighted kitchen with a chimney and stove, two large cupboards, a dresser, and a small cellar for storing potatoes, &c. ; the other door opening into a sleeping-room 3 mètres by 2·60, equally well lighted, with two bed places. The internal arrangements of the upper and lower dwellings are precisely similar, except that the lower has an altitude of 2·80 and the upper of 2·60 mètres. The garret is wainscoted, and can be equally divided between the two families ; the upper one entering by an in-door ladder, and the ground-floor family by an out-door ladder, leading to an end gable window. The underground cellar can likewise be divided, and entered by the ground-floor family, if desired, from the inside of the dwelling, and by the upper-story family by some steps from their garden. Usually, however, the ground-floor family takes the whole cellar, and the upper family the whole garret. In either case the two families need never meet, and there need be no collision nor even communication between them if not desired by themselves.

These cottages at Dort are built of hard yellow brick; the walls of the ground-floor are about 9 inches thick, those of the upper story something less. They are roofed with blue tiles. The flooring of the living- and sleeping-rooms is of thick wood on strong beams, with good stucco ceilings underneath to deaden the sound of footsteps, voices, &c. The kitchens and cellars have tile floorings; the ground-floor is raised about 18 inches, to escape damp, and to introduce thorough ventilation. The use of wooden bedsteads is prohibited in these cottages; one iron bedstead is provided for each family, and more can be hired of the proprietor at 3 cents a week each. The rent of these dwellings is 2s. 6d. a week.

These fourteen houses for twenty-eight families cost in all £2,880 including pumps, wells, a bridge over a canal to reach the dwellings, laying out the gardens, hedges, supervision of work, &c.

The price of the ground was exactly £200, making a total cost of £3,080 for the fourteen double cottages; that is, £220 for each, or £110 for each individual dwelling. It is calculated that these dwellings will be occupied and bring in rent for fifty out of the fifty-two weeks in the year, and as yet they have done so. This would make the fourteen double cottages at half-a-crown a piece bring in £175 per annum, and deducting £21 for annual repairs (a sum which will accumulate for the first few years), £154 remain as net revenue return for the £3,080 invested, or exactly 5 per cent.

With suitable precautions in the selection of tenants, and possibly with a slight increase of dimensions for the living- and sleeping-rooms, there can be no doubt this model would prove a highly satisfactory dwelling for the artisan.

As has been said, Great Britain did not exhibit

any large models of houses or showy objects in Class I.
With the exception of articles of construction and
detail, to be mentioned hereafter, she only sent plans
and designs for detached cottages and *cités ouvrières*
or town blocks of dwellings. Among the most admired of the former ranked a set of plans exhibited
by the Central Cottage Improvement Society, of 37,
Arundel Street, London, and among the latter,
drawings of buildings erected by the Society for
Improving the Condition of the Labouring Classes.
Both these associations are already so well known,
and the work they perform is already so highly appreciated, both at home and abroad, that it is hardly
necessary here to describe in detail their exhibits at
Amsterdam. Both of them received the highest
order of award. On one point, however, it may be
well to touch, with reference to the Central Cottage
Improvement Society, especially in connection with
the description that has gone before of the workmen's
dwellings exhibited by Mr. K. W. Veth of Dort.
One of their latest models is of a dwelling one story
high, costing (it is not quite clear whether this is
without the price of the land it stands on, but it is
presumed that it is so), £100 single, or in pairs £170.
Now in a recent annual report, that society stated it
had received from the Royal Commissioners on the
employment of children, young persons, and women
in agriculture, an important communication conveying in unequivocal language the following expression
of opinion. " In reference to the question of designs
for cottages, the Commissioners desire to direct
attention to a point which has come before them
very prominently. A great preference appears very
generally to be given by the wives of agricultural
labourers to cottages having all the rooms on the
ground floor. They say they are better able to look
after the children or the sick where they are in rooms

adjoining the living room ; when the mother is upstairs for any domestic purpose the younger children
cannot be so safely left alone, and other obvious risks
and inconveniences are likely to ensue. Some influential landowners are therefore returning to the
plan of having all the rooms on the same floor,
although at increased cost to themselves." This view
is entirely corroborated by the popularity of the
Dort dwellings, which, though double-storied, are
practically one-floor cottages ; the only difference
between the two stories being the necessity of a gate
or half-door at the entrance of the porch of the upper
flat as a precaution against accidents to children.
This Dort model, therefore, appears at first sight to
be in several ways an advance in principle on the
Central Society's cottages ; and at any rate merits
particular study. It contains so many elements of
comfort and health, with its double front and garden
on both sides, with the possibility it affords of so
arranging the windows of each flat as not to overlook
the garden or approach of the other, as to comb'ne
to a great extent, even in its actual phase, the
desirable condition of economy with the comparative
isolation which is known to exercise so beneficial a
moral and physical influence on the well-being of the
working-man, and on the formation of habits of
respect for property, and for the laws in general.

I have said even in its actual phase, for the principle appears capable of further extension, and it is
probable that still greater results might be obtained
by the application of, for example, the Dort design
for double-storied but single-floor tenements, to the
well known Mulhouse block system. The two systems
are easily delineated thus :—

The Dort Double Dwelling.* (For two Families.)

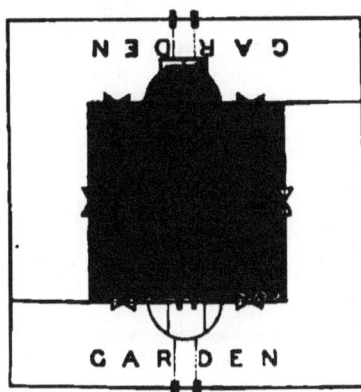

The Mulhouse Block.† (For four Families.)

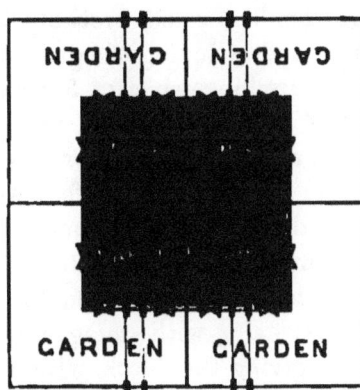

A combination of the two would produce the following ground plan, providing under one roof accommodation for eight families, four on the ground-floor, and four above, each having its own separate entrance and garden.

* The deep shading represents the porch, windows, &c., of the upper story tenement.

† These cottages are single or double storied, as required.

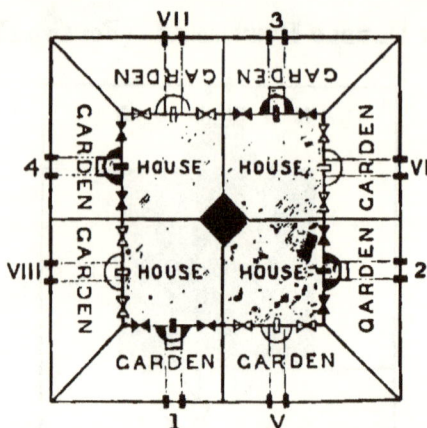

Nos. 1, 2, 3, and 4 represent upper story tenements reached by Swiss covered stairs.

Nos. V, VI, VII, and VIII are ground floor tenements.

Such a block, capable of accommodating eight working-men's families, could probably be built of good dimensions, and including the ground, for £400, that is, at £50 a dwelling, which at 5 per cent. would make the rent of each 50s. per annum, or say 1s. a week; allowing, as Mr. Veth of Dort does, for their being unoccupied on the average for two weeks in the year. Such dwellings might contain two rooms, each dwelling having its porch entrance with out-house attached, on Mr. Veth's model; the upper ones reached by Swiss stairs, with storage-room for coals, &c., underneath, giving the block, with slightly pro-jecting roofs, a very neat and pretty aspect. Each dwelling might have a window on each side of its door; one of the rooms (the larger one) would then have an outer door leading into the porch, and a window for light and ventilation; the other (the smaller one) would have a window, and a door into the larger room; or, if found desirable, the interior accommodation might be further cut up by the addition of a third room, lighted by half of one of the windows, which might be made to open cottage fashion. The kitchen stove might be placed at the back of the large room, so that one good chimney, with ventilating shafts or flues for each dwelling, would be sufficient for the whole block. Each dwelling would thus only overlook its own little garden ; and by placing the block diagonally to the points of the compass thus—

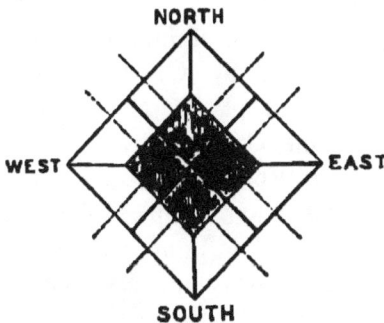

—no one dwelling would have a northern aspect, and each household would in turn be gladdened by the health-giving rays of the sun, to the enhancement of the value of its garden as a drying-ground or vegetable producer.

On the same pattern, but on a smaller scale, eight single-room dwellings for unmarried workmen might be constructed at a still more moderate cost, so as to enable their being profitably let at under 1s a week.

To the important points here touched upon, Captain Dashwood, who was Vice-President of the International Jury in Class I, and who is a member of the Council of the Central Cottage Improvement Society, will no doubt have turned his best attention; and I therefore deem it my duty to forbear from pursuing this interesting inquiry any further at the present moment, leaving to the public and to those

specially interested in these matters the task of
taxing the value of the suggestions I have hazarded,
and of working out the necessary details.

Mr. Watson's
designs.

In this class a bronze medal was awarded to
John Edward Watson, Esq., of 59, Grey Street,
Newcastle-on-Tyne, for six drawings of workmen's
dwellings strongly marked by the practical character
which pervades all the creations of the north country
whence they came.[*]

Mr. Hard-
ing's exhi-
bits, roofing,
&c.

Among the articles of improved and cheap construction exhibited by Great Britain in Class I,
roofing took a high place. Mr. James Harding, of
20, Nicholas Lane, Cannon Street, London, exhibited
from his steam works at Dod Street, Limehouse,
East and West Ham, samples of so-called " unin-
flammable roofing felt," of patent indestructible
carbon, metallic paint and dry colours, and of a
flexible floorcloth. For the first of these articles Mr.
Harding obtained a silver medal. This roofing
claims to be specially adapted for cottage use. Being
flexible, it can be stretched over rafters without preliminary boarding, as is necessary with asphalte. It
is cleanly, strong, and durable, is said to be free from
smell when exposed to the rays of the sun, it furnishes
a very suitable material for covering farm buildings,
railway carriages and trucks, and is even applicable
for sheathing ships. It is made in lengths of 25
yards, by 42 inches broad, and is sold at $1\frac{1}{2}d.$ the
square foot.[†] The paints combine the advantages of
rapid drying, and of being at all times ready for use.

---

[*] As these plans had to be sent in sooner than originally
intended, Mr. Watson was unable either to finish them as highly as
he had desired, or to send with them designs for baths, wastehouses,
&c., which he had in course of preparation. The plans exhibited
were presented by Mr. Watson to the Amsterdam authorities.

[†] Owing to its increasing popularity and extended sale, this
roofing is now reduced in price, and is sold at one penny the square
foot. It is largely used by the British Government at Woolwich,
Chatham, and other dockyards; it is also much appreciated on the

They are applicable to stucco, wood, iron, ships, &c. All colours are sold, pots included, at 1*l.* 8*s.* per cwt. This house also furnishes efficient waterproof lining for damp walls, floors, &c., at the very moderate rate of 1*d.* the square foot; carbonized oil dressing for roofing, tarpauling, &c., at 1*l.* per six gallons (or 3*s.* 6*d.* per gallon); a cheap, durable, and superior flexible floorcloth at 2*s.* the square yard, and a floor cloth for passages from 18 to 60 inches wide from 10*d.* a yard upwards.

Further exhibits in roofing included some good samples of English asphaltic roofing felt, by Messrs. D. Anderson and Son, of Belfast, which obtained honourable mention, and by Messrs. Engert and Rolfe, of Upper Barchester Street, Poplar New Town, London, who obtained a bronze medal.

Messrs. Anderson's exhibits.

This last firm also exhibited a fibrous asphalte for foundation walls, to prevent damp from rising. In Holland, where the foundations of all houses are literally laid in water, and where the common Archimedes screw-pump has to be kept constantly at work while digging and building foundations, this invention is likely to find a large sale. The system was well illustrated by a model house brick foundation with anti-damp courses, fixed in an iron cistern with water up to a given level to show effect. It furnishes an effectual and easily applied remedy for damp rising from foundations, and can be supplied in London at 1¼*d.* the square foot. In naming this house, one cannot omit a mention of their hair felts in long lengths for covering steam-boilers. This article, of which Messrs. Engert and Rolfe state themselves to be the only manufacturers, is a non-conductor of heat calculated to save 20 per cent. of fuel.

Messrs. Engert and Rolfe.

continent, and in North America. Its appearance, when dressed with a coat of the varnish supplied, nearly resembles patent leather, and combines ne ᵗ ᵗess with strength and other weatherproof qualities.

Drain-pipes were also strongly and well represented, and obtained for great Britain three awards in this class, viz. :—

1st. A *Diplome d'Excellence* awarded to Messrs. Joseph Cliff and Sons, of Wortley, by Leeds, for a magnificent display of huge salt-glazed fire-clay draining pipes, which " appealed not only to builders and engineers, but to all visitors, who regarded them wistfully as possible preventatives of those odoriferous breezes which furnish perpetual reminders that Amsterdam is not yet drained." This enterprising firm undertook to deliver this article at Amsterdam at the same price at which it supplies the London market.

2nd and 3rd. *Mentions Extraordinaires* were conferred on the monster firm of Messrs. Doulton and Co., of Lambeth, of Rowley Regis, in Stafford-shire, of Smethwick, near Birmingham, and St. Helen's, Lancashire ; and upon Messrs. Gallichan and Co., of London.

Gas-meters, cooking-stoves, and fittings generally, likewise showed well in the British section of Class I. *Diplomes d'Excellence* were awarded to Messrs. G. Glover and Co., London, for meters ; and to Messrs. W. Blews and Sons, of Birmingham, for fittings. A silver medal was granted to Mr. C. J. Philp, of 29, Caroline Street, Birmingham, for chandeliers ; and bronze medals were bestowed on Messrs. T. H. Phillips, London, for cooking-stoves ; and on Messrs. Partridge and Co., Birmingham, for gas-brackets.

The first-mentioned of these houses, that of Messrs. George Glover and Co., of Ranelagh Road, Pimlico, deserves especial praise for their 19s. working-men's dry meter. The value of gas as a light-giver and as a fuel both for heating and for cooking purposes, becomes every day more widely recognized. That the result has been an immense and continuous increase of consumption will surprise no one, though few will probably be prepared for anything approximate to the fact. It has been stated on authority that the gas consumption of about one-fifth of London (which was supplied by the Imperial Gas Company) increased from 216,000,000 of cubic feet in 1830, to 448,000,000 in 1840; from 898,000,000 of cubic feet in 1850, to 1,982,000,000 in 1860; and from 2,637,000,000 of cubic feet in 1865, to 2,838,000,000 in 1866: that is to say, roughly speaking, it has doubled itself each ten years. Meanwhile, the price of gas decreased from 13s. 6d. per 1,000 cubic feet in 1830, to 4s. per 1,000 cubic feet in 1866; thus bringing the article within the reach of every class of society. Another instance of this increased consumption is given by Mr. West Watson, the City Chamberlain of Glasgow, who stated, in a report printed in 1866, that the gas consumption of that city increased 50,000,000 of cubic feet per annum. All this means, in other words, that the artisan is now consuming gas. The want of a reliable yet cheap working-man's meter, to protect his interests and those of the company which supplies him, which last condition is of the utmost importance to him, as it regulates the supply price, had thus become manifest. How far this want has been appreciated by the enterprising firm now under review, may be gathered from the following memorandum, written for the Amsterdam Exhibition; how far it has been met by them, can only be measured by the sale of the article they have invented, and by the results of the competition to which it must be exposed :—

"Light is a primary object of importance to the working-man, and the economy of gas light is so obvious and generally admitted, that one or two illustrations will be sufficient. The cost of a sperm wax candle burning for 2¼ hours is 1d. The cost of the commonest dipped tallow candle is 1d. per 5½

F

hours. While common coal gas, at 4s. 6d. per 1,000 cubic feet, will give the same amount of light for 44 hours, and cannel coal gas, at 6s. per 1,000, for 55 hours for 1d.

" Gas is no mere luxury, but has become one of the necessaries of life to the manufacturing population. To the working-man its importance can hardly be over-estimated ; as an instrument in the acquisition of wealth every one admits its value ; and its relation to our domestic and social well-being, our manufacturing and mercantile prosperity, is too obvious to need further remark.

" And only second in importance to the gas itself is the question of its fair and equitable measurement, which in Holland has not received all the attention it deserves. But the Government are now making arrangements to provide standards of sufficient accuracy, so as to accomplish this very desirable object.

" The mere fact that gas is not a solid or liquid like candles or oil, but an aëriform body, makes it more difficult to measure ; but not less desirable that the seller should be paid for all the gas he delivers, and that the purchaser should obtain the full quantity he pays for. A correct gas meter therefore, which cannot be tampered with, gives mutual confidence to the buyer and seller of gas.

" The construction of such a meter involves a multiplicity of chemical and mechanical considerations, to each of which due weight must be attached. A subtle, invisible, elastic aëriform body, very complex in its chemical constitution, susceptible of change in condition and volume from slight variations in temperature and pressure, has to be accurately measured, and the result of that measurement must be accurately recorded. The instrument must be self-acting, and must act in a closed chamber, continually or at intervals, requiring no adjustment or interference of any kind. All its parts which come in contact with the gas must be made of anti-corrosive metal; while the materials, forms, and combinations, of its different parts must be so arranged and so adapted to each other, that when put together as a whole, it shall work easily, steadily, and correctly.

" In Glasgow and the West of Scotland, where there is a very large population of working-men, thousands of small gas-meters, sufficient for two or three lights, are used by them, in connection with fittings which can be purchased for a few shillings. The working man purchases his small dry gas-meter for 19s. 6d., and when he moves his residence takes it along with him. The meter is placed either on a shelf, or frequently hung upon the wall like a clock.

" There is great economy in the working-man's family where gas is used for heating as well as lighting. In a few minutes, at the most trifling expense and with no trouble, warm coffee or tea can be prepared. The convenience of this is apparent in the early morning, before he commences his daily work, or when he returns at night exhausted with his toil. Besides, if he has a wife, it is of great importance in preparing a little warm milk or food for her baby or sick children, when her numerous duties put it often beyond her power to kindle a fire, especially during the night, or in warm weather. The economy of time, money, and trouble, under such circumstances cannot be overstated, so that wo are justified in the statement made at the commencement, that gas has really become a necessary of life in the seats of human labour, and that every contrivance which cheapens the accessories to its use, brings it within the means of the working-man and confers on him a very important benefit."

Of this house Captain Webber and Mr. Rowden, in their report on the testing-house at the Paris Exhibition of 1867, spoke in the following terms of unqualified praise :—

"Mr. G. Glover, of Ranelagh Road, Pimlico, London, was the only manufacturer who sent meters to be tested.

"One may fairly suspect that a reason which influenced makers in refusing to send meters for trial was the undoubted laxity which prevails in gas measuring.

"In London alone about 14,000,000,000 of cubic feet of gas are consumed annually, for which a sum of 2,800,000*l.* is paid. It is therefore surprising that more care is not taken to provide reliable gas-meters.

"Mr. Glover is a manufacturer of dry meters only, so no opportunity presented itself of comparing their accuracy with that of wet meters under various circumstances ; but the perfection to which that maker has brought his meters prevents the possibility of those extravagant errors which are well known to exist where wet meters are used. The stamp on a dry meter is a guarantee of its accuracy, as nothing short of breaking into the instrument can alter its action ; but the stamp on a wet meter merely implies that if the instrument is perfectly horizontally fixed, and the water kept at a certain level, it will register accurately. Now, as neither of these conditions is attainable in practice, it follows that as a measurer of gas the wet meter is defective.

"The working parts of Mr. Glover's meters are constructed of anti-corrosive metal. Other improve-

ments in the valves, leathers, &c., he has secured by
a patent."

The important question of gas heating and cooking stoves was represented, as has been said, by
Messrs. Phillips and Son, of 25 and 26, Barbican,
London, on whom a medal was conferred. This firm
manufactures these articles in every size and at
almost every price, from 7s. 6d. up to over £50,
capable of cooking for one person or 300. Many of
the small models are admirably adapted for cottages
and dwellings of the poorest kind; in fact, it may be
said, that the poorer the household the greater the
advantages derived from gas under proper management and control, and the greater the importance to
both tenant and proprietor of its general introduction. In the present state of our civilization it is
indeed a matter of the utmost primary importance
as regards health, pocket, cleanliness, and as promoting, if well applied, conditions of improvement
both moral and physical.

While dilating on the advantages of gas, it must
not, however, be forgotten that a long time will probably elapse before this article is laid on generally
throughout the villages and hamlets of Great
Britain; and that even then there will still exist,
though on a smaller scale than now, a demand for
ordinary fuel stoves. The lonely English cottage by
the side of the wood, the Scotch shepherd's bothy on
the edge of the muir, and possibly the collier at the
pit's very mouth, will continue to find the fuel close
at hand the cheapest, and, for their purposes, the
best procurable. The wants of this class, very
numerous to-day, must not be forgotten, and were
not forgotten at Amsterdam. They were represented
by Mr. J. Sparkes Hall, of 308, Regent Street, London, who received an award in another class, and

CLASS I.

whose so-called "Plympton" cottage stove, presented by the inventor to his tenants and workmen as a suggestion for their increased comfort, convenience, and economy, is an open fire-place available for burning cheerfully wood, coal, or peat, and for baking, roasting, boiling, or frying, at the cost of a few pence. Complete with flues it costs 38s., and merits the attention of all concerned in the housing of the masses.

Messrs. Duley's kitchener.

A *mention extraordinaire* in this class was conferred on Messrs. Duley and Co., of Northampton, for a very practical and handy kitchener.

Remaining British exhibits in Class I.

Four more recompensed articles demand notice among the British exhibits in Class I. The first of these was the splendid display of iron and coal samples, exhibited by the celebrated firm of Messrs. John Brogden and Sons, of Tondu, near Bridgend, Glamorganshire, who rank high among the largest employers of labour in the United Kingdom, and to whom a gold medal was awarded. The second were exhibits of the well-known dry-earth system, patented by Messrs. Moule, of 29, Bedford Street, Covent Garden, London, upon whom a bronze medal was conferred. The third consisted in a choice collection of encaustic or mosaic tiles and terra-cotta, exhibited by Messrs. Maw and Co., of the Benthall Works, Broseley, Shropshire, who received a *diplôme d'excellence;* and the fourth, which claims more detailed attention, and obtained honourable mention by the Jury, was Messrs. Strangman and Walker's, (3, Railway Place, Fenchurch Street, London,) *Niagara* laundry boiler, soup kettle, &c., of which the sole manufacturers are Messrs. Griffiths and Browett, of Birmingham.

The Niagara boiler.

The *Niagara* patented invention is of a very simple character. It consists of an inner vessel or lining, made to fit into a laundry boiler, saucepan, coffee-pot, or cocoa-biggin, and so shaped as to divide the inner part of the boiler into two hemispherical chambers, which communicate with each other through round holes perforated in the bottom, and horizontal openings made in the top, of the inner vessel.

When the laundry-boiler is about half-filled with cold water, to which finely-sliced soap and the usual washing ingredients have been added in the proper quantity, and the clothing (having been soaked and soaped) is thrown in, and a brisk heat applied, the steam, generated in the bottom of the boiler, rises through the holes in the bottom of the inner vessel, and penetrates through the fabric in the boiler, loosening the dirt attaching thereto; at the same time numerous steamers of highly-heated water are precipitated through the openings at the top of the inner vessel, and maintained in circulation through the textile fabrics, completing the cleansing and whitening process without any manual labour or wear to the material and in half the time usually required for washing clothes.

The soup kettle is nothing more nor less than a small boiler or saucepan, with the inner vessel attached, where the water and steam are made to act on broken bones or meat. Every particle of valuable substance is extracted, after which the inner vessel is lifted out, taking with it the remains of the bones, &c., and leaving the soup clean and beautiful in the boiler.

The coffee-pot and cocoa-biggin act on the same principle, and require no explanation.

Boilers for dyeing textile fabrics are also made on this principle, and work to the greatest advantage. The boiler may be advantageously employed in cleansing rags, and in obtaining all kinds of extracts in chemical works.

The approximate retail prices are as follows :—
Circulators for coppers of the usual sizes—

    Made of tin or iron from .. .. 10s. to 20s.
      ,,   copper   ,, ... 20s. to 40s.

Oblong laundry boilers, with circulators complete—
    Tin or iron, from   .. .. .. 10s. to 20s.
    Copper   ,, ... 20s. to 40s.

Soup saucepans, coffee and cocoa pots from 3s.
upwards, according to size and material.

A system of house-heating combined with ventilation, by means of hot water, forwarded to the
Exhibition by Messrs. J. L. Bacon and Co., of Far-
ringdon Road, Holborn, London, unfortunately arrived too late to admit of its examination by the
International Jury.

The Belgian exhibits in Class I were both numerous and important. In addition, they were more
systematically arranged than those of Great Britain.
This was partially due, no doubt, to the contiguity
of the country whence they came, and to increased
facility of supervision ; but was due no less to the
classifying governing principle which the Belgians
have borrowed from their ethnological brethren the
French, and which they, like the French, apply
unhesitatingly to exhibition or railway arrangement,
and all details of life. Their exhibits in Class I were
consequently subdivided under four heads :—

    A. Plans and Models of Dwellings.
    B. Plans of Lodgings, Restaurants, Schools,
        Baths, Reading and Recreation Rooms.
    C. Details of Construction.
    D. Materials.

One of the first Belgian exhibits that caught the
eye on entering the building was a model of work-

men's houses one-fifth of full size. They are on the Mulhouse block system, and were erected by Messrs. Gustave Janssen and Co., of Brussels, for the accommodation of the families employed in their candle manufactories. Each dwelling consists of two good-sized rooms, one above the other, each opening into a small back room, equally situated, one over the other. The stair is between the two rooms. Each dwelling has, moreover, a cellar and a garret. Each dwelling disposes of 100 square mètres of ground. The hire is 2 florins a week. The rooms are somewhat larger than those of the Dutch models, but the out-house arrangements are not equally satisfactory.

Two models from the Association for Building Workmen's Dwellings of Antwerp were highly praised ; they were separate cottages, having one large room on ground-floor, two small ones over it, and over that a garret; a cellar, and an open yard behind, two or three times the area of the dwelling, containing an out-house and a pump. The rooms are lofty, and the rent 1½ florins a week.

One of the most pleasing designs for *cités ouvrières* was exhibited by Madame Cordeweener, and possesses to the least extent possible the barrack-like appearance characteristic of this class of dwelling. It is spacious and airy, and specially arranged with a view to maintaining the privacy of its inmates.

Many other models and plans of dwellings were exhibited by Belgium ; the cheapest of them all were some designs for cottages exhibited by Crombrugghe's Society, of Ghent. One of these represents a dwelling of two rooms, each 4 mètres square by 3 high, with garret and a small garden, for which only 6 francs per month is demanded. A smaller scale of this dwelling is offered at a rent of only 5 francs a month. These buildings are, as their

CLASS I. price sufficiently denotes, of an unsatisfactory nature, both of construction and material. A superior dwelling is, however, exhibited by the same Association, at 8 francs per month, containing on the ground-floor one good room and above it two smaller ones, a cellar, kitchen, garret, and garden. These dwellings are attached to different manufactories, and reserved for the hands therein employed.

Some plans of *cités ouvrières* exhibited by Messrs. Duyk, of Brussels, obtained a silver medal.

In details and materials of construction, Belgium exhibited some ingenious ventilating methods, and some good roofing and cements; but she failed to obtain from the International Jury any recompense in Class I, except for iron, zinc, window-glass, wall papers, nails, and casting. Cements were finally adjudged *hors concours*, owing to the inability of the Jury to test their durable qualities.

French exhibits in Class I.

The exhibits of France at the Amsterdam Exhibition were not marked by any appreciation of its special domestic and economic character. Under these circumstances it is not surprising that, with some few exceptions, France did not take a high place in Class I. Foremost among these exceptions ranks the well-known and honoured name of Jean Dollfus, of Mulhouse, to whom belongs the first place on the Continent among those whose thoughts, directed by the Exhibition of the Prince Consort's model dwellings in 1851 to the consideration of improved house accommodation for the working classes, have since borne practical fruit. His exhibits in this class were cottage and village plans on the four-block dwelling system, of which mention has been already made; but in another class he received the highest recompense the Jury could bestow for the manufactured goods turned out by his workmen who, well satisfied with their condition in his employ,

prove by enhanced zeal in his service their appreciation of the inseparable community of interest which
ever bind together the master and his men. Gold
medals in Class I were obtained by France for metal
castings by M. Ed. Zegut, of Tuscy, Meuse, and for
general excellence of plan and arrangement by the
De Blanzy Coal Mine Company, Soane et Loire, by
MM. Gemets, Fils, and Herrscher, Frères, of Paris,
for heating apparatus, by MM. Nent and Dumont, of
Paris, for centrifugal pumps, and by MM. A. Paillard,
of Paris, for mirrors.

From the North German Bund some very practical and beautifully executed models of peasants'
cottages, farm buildings, stables, &c., were exhibited;
among others, a remarkable model of a miner's dwelling, exhibited by the direction of the Prince Hohen-
lohe Works at Hohenlohehütte. Most of them,
however, only repeated features with which the
world was familiarized by the Paris Exhibition of
1867.

North-Ger-
man exhibits
in Class I.

In ground-plans and elevation drawings Germany fully maintained at Amsterdam her reputation
for technical educational development. In this
branch of skilled industry nine beautiful drawings
representing a workman's colony at Borsig, and some
designs for miners' hospitals exhibited by M. Scher-
benning, director of the Schorley Mines, both in
Silesia, were specially admired.

The three Northern Kingdoms comprising Scandinavia were distinguished in Class I for the solidity,
simplicity and practicability of their designs. Denmark, indeed, received two gold medals in this class,
both for plans of workmen's dwellings: the one exhibited by the Workmen's Building Association,
established at Copenhagen by the hands employed
in the factories of Messrs. Burmiester and Wains;
the other by the Managing Board of the Classen

Scandina-
vian exhibits
in Class I.

fidei-commis, also of Copenhagen. The special characteristics of these dwellings were, as has been said, solidity and simplicity; many of the walls being 50 centimètres thick, and two rooms and a very small kitchen being considered ample accommodation for one family. The kitchen of one Copenhagen plan is described as 1½ by 2 mètres, dimensions that even excited the wonder of the Dutch, as being still smaller than the too scanty kitchen accommodation provided in some of their own cottages.

Some good asphalte roofing was exhibited from Denmark by Messrs. Ericsen and Company, of Copenhagen ; and a preparation of paraffin oil for preserving timber, which obtained a bronze medal, deserves notice as an invention probably capable of still further improvement.

FURNITURE.

Class II was very voluminous, and comprised almost every article of domestic use excepting clothing, food, and implements or their component parts. It was briefly styled Furniture and Household Necessaries.

Beginning with pots and pans, which has been somewhat disdainfully termed the backbone of the Exhibition, the Dutch Province of Friesland was strongly represented in earthenware; and some exhibits of Mr. A. Coopman's, of Leeuwarden, attracted considerable attention. The quality was good and the price low; this exhibitor moreover responded to the demand made to give the wholesale as well as the retail price. It was on his exhibits, 12 florins the 100 pieces; thus putting ordinary jugs, cups, saucers, plates, &c., all round, at 12 cents., or about $2\frac{1}{2}d.$ a piece. Mr. W. T. Stam, of Sneek, in Friesland, exhibited similar articles at a cent the piece less for ready money, on wholesale orders. Mr. A. Andree, of Bois-le-Duc, exhibited earthenware at the following low retail prices :—

Milk-pots	..	..	..	from	3	to 18	cents.
Roasting dishes		..	..	„	4	„ 12	„
Hand basins	..	..	..	„	3	„ 6	„
Black pans	..	..	..	„	2	„ 4	„
Coffee-pots	..	..	..	„	4	„ 8	„
Dishes ..	..	..	..	„	3	„ 6	„
Milk jugs	..	..	..	„	2	„ 6	„

Class II. Sieves ..   .. from 3 to 6 cents.
Small pots ..   ..   ..   at 1   „
Coloured tiles ..   ..   ..   „ 1½   „
Flower-pots ..   ..   .. from 2½ „ 5   „
  „   saucers..   ..   .. at 2   „
(5 cents equal to 1d.)

A very complete collection of similar earthen-ware, porcelain, and glass was exhibited by the Brothers Sieberg, of Amsterdam, and priced as follows :—

	Fl. c.		Fl. c.
Tea-pots	0 17½	to	0 35
Milk jugs	0 12¼	„	0 61
Filter coffee-pots	1 0	„	1 15
Butter-boats	0 25	„	0 35
Mustard-pots	0 12½		
Pepper-pots	0 12½		
Soap dishes	0 25	and	0 30
Breakfast plates..	0 6	„	0 7
Dinner	0 9		
Sugar-basin	0 15		
Tea service (4 pieces)	0 80		
„ with 12 cups and saucers	5 50		
Tea-cups with handles	0 10		
Egg cups	0 6		
Glass sugar-basin	0 40	and	0 50
„ salt-cellar	0 10		
„ tumblers	0 6	to	0 18
„ wine glasses	0 20	„	0 45
„ decanters	0 15	„	0 60
Porcelain tea-cups	0 22½	and	0 25
„ mustard-pot	0 80		
„ breakfast plates (per dozen)	3 50		
„ butter-boat	1 0		
„ stand with 8 egg cups ..	2 80		

&c. &c.

One of the peculiarities of Dutch cottage pottery

is the prevalence on it of mottoes serving to convey Class II. salutary, even if somewhat trite and sorrowful, reflections. Such words as *De Dood komt Zeker,*— Death must come,—are very commonly found at the bottom of cups and dishes; and can hardly tend to raise the spirits of those using them or conduce to conviviality at table. This kind of ornament is probably a remnant of the stern views of life, engendered by their wars of independence, the crockery literature of Holland retaining the rude unpolished character of former centuries, in striking contrast with the more modern and cheerful aphorisms imprinted on French or English earthenware.

Belgium was also richly represented in this Belgian ex-hibits. branch of Class II; and a very complete display of Crockery. earthenware, fully within the scope of the Exhibition, made by Messrs. Boch, Frères, of Keramis, near La Louvière, obtained for that house the highest recompense the jury could bestow. The moulds of this exhibit were good in design, and the articles themselves were distinguished by successful regular colouring and workmanship, combined with strength and absence of all coarseness or heaviness. The prices were as follows:—

		Fl.	c.		Fl.	c.
Coloured toilet services ..	..	10	35	to	17	25
„ coffee „ ..	..	11	0	„	18	40
„ candlesticks ..	..	1	50			
„ tea-things, per piece ..		0	70	„	1	30
„ „ per half-dozen		6	0			
Yellow coffee-pots	..	0	52	„	1	50
„ beer jugs	..	0	69	„	2	7
„ milk jugs.. ..	..	0	17	„	1	44
„ filter coffee-pots ..	..	1	44	„	2	87
„ toilet service · ..	..	4	90			
„ butter-boats ..	..	0	75	„	1	32

			Fl. c.		Fl. c.
Yellow tobacco-box	..	..	1 27	to	2 0
Grey beer mug ..	..	..	0 80	„	2 10
„ mustard-pot	..	..	0 70		
„ match-box ..	..	..	0 52		
White sauce-spoon	..	..	0 25		
„ sugar-basin	..	..	0 32	„	0 38
„ coffee-pot..	..	..	0 63	„	1 44
„ salt-cellar..	..	..	0 14	„	0 25
„ soap-dish ..	..	..	0 44		
„ soup-tureen	..	..	0 80	„	3 56
Fine white sugar-basin ..	..		0 9	„	0 12
„ coffee service	..		6 30	„	8 78
„ toilet „ ..	..		5 40	„	7 0
Printed plates, per dozen	..		2 60	„	4 15
White „ „	..		1 55	„	2 7

French exhibits. Crockery. France displayed much pleasing porcelain and glass, but her exhibits in this branch were evidently selected more with a view to attract the attention of the richer visitors, than with a desire to meet the special aims of the promoters of the Exhibition.

Austria. Vienna porcelain has long enjoyed a large sale in the Netherlands, and was, consequently, adequately represented. Its good qualities are cheapness, lightness, and strength; its principal defect is great liability to chip.

Denmark. Denmark maintained in crockery the solid qualities which distinguished it in Class I. Its pottery was characterized by cheapness and strength, but was mostly somewhat clumsy in appearance. In glass ware Denmark displayed more taste.

Heating. Heating was recompensed by the International Jury in Class I, and has, for that reason, been considered in that class in describing the British awards. Yet as the exhibits themselves were principally catalogued in Class II, it is more convenient in the case of foreign countries, where it is not necessary to

follow closely the awards, to respect the original
classification.

Commencing with the Netherlands,—it was
natural that turf and peat should be largely represented among the exhibits of a country whose
consumption of that fuel is fifty times as great as of
coke and coal together, and exceeds 40,000,000 tons
per annum. This is a very large average over a total
population of 3,650,000 souls, and may be supposed
to secure, to some extent, the poor of Holland
against one great source of human suffering—insufficient warmth. The preparation of this fuel has long
been a subject on which so much chemistry and skill
have been expended in Holland, that it may be
regarded as filling one of the first places among
articles of domestic industry in that country. Rough-
dried peats are seldom used except by the very poor
inhabitants of the districts where they are cut; but
complicated processes are resorted to for the introduction of new elements of heat and light-giving
power, and of duration in consumption. Ordinary
turfs are capable of holding 90 per cent. of water;
if simply sun-dried, the turf therefore becomes light
and porous. The simplest style of preparation in
Holland is as follows :—The undried turf is put into
a cylindric boiler and ground fine by circumvolving
knives working like an Archimedes screw. At the
bottom of the cylinder is a square box-press, into
which the turf is worked and caked, and as it leaves
this box, it is cut by machinery into the various sized
bricks which find favour in the market, for heating
and cooking, and for different stoves and furnaces.
Thus prepared, it is known as *machinale turf,* but it
is still in its infancy as a prepared fuel. To perfect
it still further, it is put into retorts and heated to
the glowing point, as coke is prepared from coal;
and a fuel, comparable to charcoal, and styled "turf

coal," or carbonized turf, is thus obtained. Many good specimens of turf in its various stages were exhibited in the Netherlands Section of Class II ; and among the French fuel exhibits appeared a remarkable specimen of paraffine derived from turf. Turf, like coal, contains many chemical substances, such as paraffine, coal-tar, creosote, &c. All these valuable substances are now lost, whereas, if they were carefully extracted, the turf itself might be sold at a lower price, though how far they could be removed from the fuel without injuring its caloric power and counteracting the economy effected, is an open question. There is, moreover, a spirit which can be distilled from turf, and which is of great value as a substitute for alcohol in certain chemical and scientific preparations. How far this can be productively utilized is also an interesting question. *Machinale turf* is sold at Amsterdam for $4\frac{1}{2}$ florins, or 7s. 6d. the 1,000 bricks of medium dimensions.

French peat. The general outward excellence of the French turf exhibited at Amsterdam was much admired by Dutch connoisseurs. It is said to be prepared with great care, but on a different system from the Dutch. In the art of preparing turf so as to derive therefrom the greatest benefit as a fuel at the least cost, much advance remains probably to be made even in practically coal-less countries like the Netherlands, where the question appears at first sight to have met with more attention than in coal countries like Belgium or Great Britain. Still, the possession of gold should not make us careless of silver, and it is to be hoped that competent persons will ere long devote more study to the turf question, as this fuel is probably capable of being made vastly more available for the poor in London and elsewhere, and has thus no remote nor unimportant bearing on the momentous theory of our coal exhaustion.

Second only in importance to the fuel itself, comes the mode of its consumption, or place wherein it is burnt ; and it will now be interesting to see how this question was represented by continental exhibits at Amsterdam.

The best means of combining heat with economy is a desideratum in all households, to whatever social class they belong; but to the working-man and his family this assumes an importance beyond all proportion to the sum spent upon it as compared to his total income. What was stated as a want in 1867 remains a want in 1869, viz., a stove that will warm the living room, cook the food of a family, and supply abundance of warm water at a consumption of fuel at the rate of one penny a-day. It is probable that gas, on improved principles and under perfect control, is the only heat-giver capable of rendering this service to humanity. Let us hope that some inventive genius will direct his energies to the discovery of some system of circulating hot water and gas at a cost easy of accurate regulation. Such an invention, providing heat, light, and hot water at 2d. a-day, would entitle its author to the highest rewards a Government could bestow.

The lead taken by France and Belgium at Paris is 1867 in the solution of this difficulty was fully maintained at Amsterdam in 1869, though they cannot be said to have made any actual advance. Many small iron stoves were exhibited by Dutch makers, at prices varying from 5 to 85 or 100 florins, and adapted to the use of coke, coal, or turf, but none of them struck the eye as improvements upon the continental models generally known. The small dimensions of the dwelling-rooms of the Dutch poorer classes, combined with the general objection to proper ventilation, permit of their being warmed at a trifling cost, and by minute stoves. For this

reason, therefore, though many of the stoves themselves are very cheap, and an advance in economy,
both in cost of purchase and consumption of fuel on
what are used in Great Britain by the corresponding
classes of society, they cannot conscientiously be
recommended as any real improvement on the 40s.
(Government contract price) " married soldier's
stove," with its open fire and ventilating arrangement, as perfected by Captain Douglas Galton. This
affords, perhaps, the best means of cottage-warming
and cooking yet known for the man in receipt of
good skilled labour wages. Below this, the want of
a cheap stove still exists in all its gravity, a proof of
how far off we still are from a millennium for the
poorer class of working-men.

Hardware:
Irons.

As might have been expected, the Dutch section
of Class II was rich in kitchen hardware, laundry
irons, heaters, wash-tubs, mangles, &c. On the
merits of most of these articles, however, it is difficult
to form a positive opinion in an exhibition, owing to
the impossibility of testing the durable qualities
which enter so largely into the just appreciation of
their value. This is a difficulty, indeed, which presented itself more or less throughout all the jury
work at Amsterdam, and which must present itself
at any utilitarian exhibition. On articles of ornament or objects of art, on jewellery or statuary, even
on carved furniture or rich carpets, it is easier to
arrive at a just conclusion than on the durable
qualities of the furniture and appliances of the poor
man's home, on their health-giving and health-retain-
ing qualities and the like. Considering, however,
the nature of the opinion at which the Dutch public,
as distinct from the jury, may be said to have
arrived, there exist reasonable grounds for accepting
their decision as of value in this case ; for the Belgian
and French manufactures were generally admitted

to be as superior in quality as they were undoubtedly cheaper in price, than the productions of Netherlands industry in articles of ironmongery and hardware. To begin with hand-irons, notwithstanding the fact that Dutch medical men have universally condemned the use of box-irons as unhealthy for the ironer, who is made to inhale poisonous gases,—all the more poisonous from their being to some extent confined,—many specimens of this class were exhibited. This was attributed to ignorance of the best means of heating the solid irons. Some small stoves for this purpose were exhibited, and one very simple one among them deserves notice. It was so constructed as to be available for cooking, or for heating six solid irons of different sizes, and professed a great economy of fuel. Its price was 17·33 florins, or about 1l. 9s., and it was evidently popular amongst the Dutch visitors. It was exhibited by the Local Committee of Copenhagen, where these stoves are largely used. A French stove for this purpose, exhibited by Mr. Paul Chapel of Paris, designed so as to prevent the actual contact of the solid irons with the coal, which destroys their smoothness, also received a good deal of attention from the housewives of Amsterdam.

In tin-foil the Dutch held their own very well, Tin-foil. and still continue to undersell Great Britain.

Washing was largely represented in the Dutch Steam-washing establishments. and Belgian sections of Class II, by models or plans of steam-washing establishments for rich and poor. On the Continent the wash-tub has been termed the " housewife's rack," and great efforts have been made in many towns to organize cheap washing associations, relieving the poor from perpetual soap-sud life, and giving them time to devote to other domestic avocations of a less laborious kind. In Holland, the success of steam-washing establishments has been very great ; and no doubt the time will come when washing at home will be considered a process wasteful of both time and labour, and only suitable for the rich. The wash-tub, moreover, is one of the most powerful allies of the gin-palace and the beer-house ; many a poor woman is compelled to have recourse to artificial stimulants to enable her to toil through her daily washing, and many a working-man on a general holiday, or when out of work, is driven from his home by the discomfort caused by his only room being converted into a reeking laundry. The children also of the poor will not fail to reap sanitary benefit from the partial banishment of the wash-tub and the permanent damp floors which it entailed.

Soaps.

Soaps, both hard and soft, were well represented in this section. Mr. J. G. Brunett, of Amsterdam, exhibited a hard, white household soap, very well spoken of by those who use it, at 19 cents, or a trifle under 4d. the lb. This soap showed no signs of excess of " buck," suds, or grease. M. Frère, of Gilly, near Charleroi, exhibited soft white soap at 50 francs the 100 kilos, and a hard, white *savon de ménage* at the same moderate price. The cheapest soap exhibited by this house was soft brown soap at 40 francs the 100 kilos (or 200 lbs). Many of the foreign soap exhibits were rendered very interesting from their being accompanied by a display of the ingredients and of their proportions as used in the manufacture of the article.

The British soaps met with high approval from foreign technical visitors.

Bedding :—Kapok.

In bedding the Dutch Section exhibited a substance as yet little known,—*kapok*. Of this valuable material for the stuffing of mattresses, bedding, &c., two houses had interesting exhibits, viz., Mr. F. G. Kratzenstein, of Amsterdam, who obtained a gold medal, and the Messrs. Klutgen, of Rotterdam. That this article will ultimately find general favour in Europe little doubt exists. The silky fibre is obtained from the seed gourd of the kapok tree, which grows wild in the Netherlands Indies and only requires to be plucked when very ripe. From this seed a valuable oil is obtained, and the refuse is excellent food for cattle. The supply of this material is practically inexhaustible and it can be imported for the cost of its collection in the jungles where it grows, *plus* the transport home. No cultivation is necessary. The most remarkable of its qualities are :—

1. Its immunity from attack by moths and vermin.
2. Its lightness.
3. Its elasticity and softness.
4. Its medium warmth.
5. Its cheapness.

Its price as compared with feathers is as follows for a double bed :—

Kapok   ..   10 kilos. at 1·20 = 12 florins.
Feathers..   16 kilos. at 2· = 32 florins.

And as compared with horsehair, for a double mattress :—

Kapok   ..   15 kilos. at 1·20 = 18 florins.
Horsehair.   20 kilos. at 2· = 40 florins.

The beds being in each case equally well stuffed.

Showing a saving of, in the first instance, 20, and in the second 22 florins. The economy of the use of kapok is thus sufficiently remarkable to warrant a fair trial by the public of its other qualities. It is known as *kapok, Edredon des Indes*, and *Pflanzendaunen.*

Cheap as is *kapok* compared with feathers and horsehair, yet cheaper bed-stuffings were exhibited by many Dutch houses. Messrs. Valleggia, of Amsterdam, sell sea-wrack at 1*d.* a lb., and prepared grass from the dunes at even less. This house also exhibited white blankets at from 3 florins 50 cents (5*s.* 10*d.*) upwards, and other bedding at similar moderate rates. France, Belgium, and Germany made little show in bedding, and to whatever cause it is to be attributed, these countries manifested evident disinclination to compete in downy substances with almost the only land in Europe where the eider duck is still indigenous.

As the old system of bed-places in the wall of a cottage room is now condemned on sanitary grounds in many European countries, though it will probably long continue to hold its own in unsophisticated rural districts, and especially in cold or temperate climates, some new system of bed arrangements seem a growing requirement for the poorer classes, where a large family can ill afford during the daytime the space occupied in their moderate-sized apartments by even small metallic beds. Not impossibly, and at first sight it would appear that the plan might be recommended on sanitary grounds, this riddle may find its solution in the adoption or partial adoption for children, of cots or hammocks, removable by day and suspended at night by hooks to the beams over tables, dressers, or other available spaces. One merit arising from the invention and adoption of a working man's cot, apart from the economy of space both in the arrangement of the room itself, and in the number of rooms required, would be the freedom from contamination of the walls, that has been so much complained of in the dwellings of the very poor, and the enhanced security afforded against the inhalation of noxious substances from proximity to many cheap wall papers or damp walls. A greater freedom of circulation of air would also be obtained, while every room of the

Working-man's cot.

dwelling would be available for night as well as day accommodation. Benefit would indubitably accrue to the working-classes from the adaptation and practical execution of this idea by some well-known firm ;—for example, Messrs. Peyton and Peyton would deserve well of humanity if they could contrive what, for want of a better term, I will call a descending cot, to be lowered out of the ceiling at pleasure and hoisted up into a prepared receptacle for it in the ceiling, when not required, by means of ropes and pulleys. The frame of the bed should, of course, be of metal ; and it might, if desired, be provided with folding legs, so as to rest steadily on the floor in place of swinging. The space between the ceiling and flooring, which is often used as a means of ventilating workmen's houses by the insertion of gratings or perforated bricks in the outer walls, would not become unfitted for this use, but rather the reverse ; for the aperture caused by the bed when down at night would act as a perfect means of ventilation from the top of the room without draught, or the possibility of stopping it up, as the poor are always inclined to do when they detect a current of air or ventilating medium. In dwellings constructed with the intention of adopting the descending cot system, the space between ceiling and flooring might be made a few inches deeper than is now customary, so as to provide abundant room for the bedding, and even for its ventilation to a sufficient extent when hoisted up for the day. Another advantage of this system would be the additional deadening of the sound of footsteps, &c., caused by increased space between ceiling and flooring, and interposition during the day of beds and bedding.

Excellent petroleum lamps, both for domestic and workshop use, were exhibited by Holland at moderate prices, and met with much favour from the public, notwithstanding the well-known danger of explosion inseparable from their use, which is now beginning to render them unpopular, even in America, where accidents of all kinds are, as a rule, so little dreaded.

Miners' lamps.

Belgium exhibited some miners' lamps, on the celebrated Davy principle, but of singularly simple and cheap construction. It is doubtful, however, whether a trifling economy, at risk of efficiency, in an article of this vital importance deserves to be encouraged ; most people would probably prefer a lamp of, if possible, improved construction, even if of higher price, and agree that this affords a good example of a class of article in which economy is not the first consideration, even to the working-man.

Cheap furniture. Sweden.

In cheap chairs, tables, and other wooden furniture, Northern Europe took an undoubted lead at Amsterdam. The Society of Working Men of Gottenburg exhibited marvels of workmanship, of solidity, and neatness at fabulously low prices that attracted general attention. Chairs at 1s. 8d., tables at 3s. and 4s., a chest of three drawers, 9s. 4d. ; a shut-up bedstead, 12s. 6d. ; and very solid garden seats at 5½d. Mr. N. P. Matsson, of Gottenburg, displayed a full-sized chest of drawers of white pine, veneered with polished oak, with good locks, for 1l. ; a comfortable sofa-bed for 25s., and chairs of polished teak for 2s. 6d. a-piece.

Denmark.

After Sweden, Denmark ranked first in practical exhibits of this kind ; and Messrs. Severin and Andreas Jensen, of Copenhagen, exhibited excellent strong cottage furniture at prices higher, indeed, than those of Gottenburg, but far below the continental average. Very superior furniture, at extremely moderate cost, was exhibited by Mr. August Knoblock, of Vienna ; imitation walnut or rosewood chairs at 3 florins (5s.) a-piece, and tables, sofas, &c., at corresponding prices, being altogether an advance in

Vienna.

economy on any article of even inferior quality
obtainable in Great Britain.

Among the Belgian cheap furniture, of which
there was not a very remarkable display, the article
that attracted most attention was an exhibit by
Messrs. Duyk, of Brussels, of a cupboard 4 feet 6
inches high by 3 feet wide and one deep, into which
could be packed the whole furniture of a bed-room—
viz., bed, bedding, table, night-table, toilet-glass, four
chairs, and four *chauf-pieds*. This exhibit was a
great curiosity, and every article belonging to it was
well made, adapted to the working-man, and convenient for the frequent change of dwelling to which
he is liable ; but the price, 11*l.*, practically placed it
beyond his means. One more article in this section,
which was the subject of popular notice, was an iron
garden table with umbrella-shaped awning rising
from its centre, capable of being opened or furled,
and hoisted to any height as circumstances might
require. This, however, was a luxury, and clearly
without the scope of the exhibition.

There were good displays of wall-papers, carpets,
muttings, and stuffs for covering furniture from
France, Belgium, and Germany. Little advance in
cheapness, however, was observed in this class of
goods, with an exception in favour of Mr. J. Leroy,
of Rue Lafayette, Paris, on whom a gold medal was
deservedly bestowed for the manufacture of a selection of articles, pleasing to the most fastidious taste,
unobjectionable from a sanitary point of view, and
produced at a price within the means of any hard-
working artisan.

In clocks no country could compete, at Amsterdam, with England and the United States for cheapness and excellence combined ; and it will be seen
from a glance at the following brief statistics of the
clock importation into Great Britain in 1866 that the

days of Dutch clocks are numbered,—the article, though still endeavouring to hold its own, being rapidly replaced among the wealthy by French industry, and among the poor by the cheap productions of the great Republic :—

			Value.
			£
Holland	..	39,055	9,523
France	..	80,177	190,321
United States	..	134,510	54,353
Other parts	..	612	1,682

Algeria.

An interesting collection of the productions of Algeria, mineral, agricultural, and industrial, exhibited in Class II by the French Minister for War and the Colonies, attracted a good deal of interest and attention, but contained nothing of novelty to the practised exhibition eye, and was, in reality, little more than a small, though choice and varied, selection from the galleries of Oriental wares which dazzled with their exceeding brilliancy the crowds that flocked to Paris in 1867.

England.
Mr. G. Kent.

The British exhibits in Class II were, with few exceptions, of a very practical and satisfactory character. The only gold medal they won, however, fell to the lot of the veteran exhibiting house of Mr. George Kent, 199, High Holborn, London, who exhibited articles for promoting domestic economy in the dairy and the kitchen, and for household work generally. The articles sold by this firm are very various, and comprise soaps, cucumber and vegetable slicers, mincing and paring-machines, egg-beaters and decapitators, portable mangles, butter presses, the admirable so-called champion carpet-sweeper, shoe-cleansing machines, knife-cleaners, strainers, milk savers, portable revolving driers, clothes-wringers, mixing-machines, six-minute churns, jelly strainers, refrigerators, ice-safes, &c., &c. Most of the exhibits of this house came fully within the scope of the Amsterdam Exhibition, and were distinguished for cheapness and strength. Mr. Kent's wares are too well known in England to need description, and, thanks to his persevering attendance at foreign exhibitions (Nice, Cologne, Paris, Amsterdam, not to mention New Zealand and Berar), his practical inventions and time and labour-saving machines, are rapidly attaining equal popularity abroad.

Ten British firms reaped silver medals in Class II. They were :—

Mr. William Cooke, of Grove Works, Leeds, for paperhangings printed by machinery.

Mr. J. C. Davis, of 69, Leadenhall Street, London, for knife-cleaners. Mr. Davis also supplies mincing-machines, and opening-knives for tin cases.

Messrs. E. Martin and Sauteur Brothers, of 48, Hatton Garden, London, for clocks, and instruments of precision.

Messrs. E. Moore and Co., of the Tyne Flint Glass Works, South Shields, for cheap glass. This firm was established in 1820, has a very large home demand for its manufactures, which are distinguished for cheapness, durability, and beauty of design and exports very largely to every part of the world. Its collection of glass at Amsterdam was much admired by the Dutch, and it is to be hoped that the firm will reap in a practical shape advantage from their appreciation.

The Seth Thomas Clock Company, of 3, Leigh Street, Liverpool, for cheap clocks. This is an American firm, established at Thomaston, Connecticut. Mr. R. M. Marples, of Liverpool, is sole agent for Great Britain and Ireland, and can furnish a day cottage time-piece for 6s., and an eight day cottage time-piece for 7s. 3d.

Messrs. Tritton and Hoare, of Stoke-upon-Trent, for cheap earthenware, much admired by the Dutch.

Messrs. Isaac Ricketts and Sons, of Hull ;

Messrs. Edward James and Son, of Sutton Road, Plymouth ;

The London Starch Company, of Dod Street, Limehouse, London ; and,

Messrs. Parsons, Fletcher, and Co., of 22, Bread Street London :

The last four houses for rice starch, which promises to become a new industry in Holland, since the Amsterdam Exhibition took it by the hand, and introduced it to the general approval of the Dutch people.

Rice starch.   As the starch exhibits, not only British but Belgian and Dutch at the Amsterdam Exhibition, commanded a great deal of attention, and gave rise much public discussion in the Netherlands ; and as, moreover, this was a subject on which I did not deem myself competent to express an opinion on personal examination and inquiry, I availed myself of an offer of service from Mr. P. L. Simmonds, who had studied the subject technically and chemically, both at Amsterdam and at previous Exhibitions, and requested him to favour me with a brief paper, embodying the views and opinions of the experts whom the

International Jury had consulted in this matter. This he kindly did, and I am in consequence indebted to him for the following clear and concise report, which can hardly fail to be of interest to the several trades and branches of industry to whom starch is of more importance than is generally supposed by the uninitiated :—

"Starch manufacture is now a most important industry in Europe and America. And its progress and improvement may be watched with interest, for it is chiefly within the last quarter of a century that the various chemical and manufacturing improvements have been made, by working under new processes and upon new materials. With the progress of population, the diffusion of wealth, and the enormous increase in our textile manufactures, a greater consumption has arisen.

"For a long time wheat starch was the only one that entered extensively into commerce ; but in 1840 Mr. Orlando Jones patented a process which led to the introduction of rice starch, and other somewhat similar processes were adopted by Mr. Berger and Mr. Colman ; and now the manufacture of starch from rice is the rule rather than the exception in England, there remaining scarcely one manufacturer who uses wheat. The cheap price and abundance of rice has led to its employment now very generally in France and Belgium ; Italy, Prussia, and Austria, however, still cling to wheat.

"The high price of, and increasing demand for, wheat for food purposes in Europe, and the possibility of a return of the potatoe disease, or of that root being less extensively planted in Ireland and elsewhere, renders it probable that the price of starch will be maintained. It is, therefore, important to consider whether some non-edible root or substance may not be obtained, or some of the superior starch-producing plants of the tropics be cultivated to a sufficient extent to supply the wants of Europe. Rice and maize have been the latest articles resorted to, although attempts have been made to utilize the horse-chestnut and other substances.

" A few remarks on the different kinds of starch shown may not be out of place.

" *Wheat Starch.*—The wheats of rich warm countries contain more gluten and less starch than those of cold countries. The average of northern wheats bring about 70 per cent. of starch and 16 of gluten ; the less gluten there is the more starch will of course be obtained. The difference between starch and fecula is that the latter will not form, or with great difficulty, the long crystalline needles into which the wheat and rice starches break up on drying. By improved processes adopted in France, the gluten is now separated and utilized for food purposes.

" *Rice Starch.*—The production of rice is so extensive in the East, and there is so much broken waste or refuse available in the markets at a low price, that the manufacturer can almost always purchase and store large quantities at his convenience. It may be kept a very long period in the rough. As much as 80 or 90 per cent. of starch has been obtained from some kinds of dry rice ; but the average may be taken at 73, and there is about 13½ per cent. of water in the grain. The general appearance of the rice starch shown by British exhibitors was excellent ; the crystals fine and the colour good ; the same may be said of one or two of the Belgian exhibitors who compete creditably with England. It may incidentally be stated that the largest and best known British manufacturers, such as Messrs. J. and J. Colman, S. Berger, Orlando Jones, Messrs. Wotherspoon, and Joseph Lescher, Son, and Co., &c., declined to exhibit.

" *Maize Starch.*—The enormous production of Indian corn or maize in the United States, and the fact of its containing a less proportion of gluten than wheat, has led to its extensive utilization for starch manufacture, and also as a food product under the terms of maizena and corn-flour. For the last-named purpose it is working its way largely into use in Europe ; but it has not yet been able to contend successfully for laundry purposes with rice and wheat starch. The first cost and expense of manufacture must necessarily be less, but it does not form those fine crystals in drying which other starches do. As an alimentary product it received a silver medal.

" *Potato Starch.*—All bulbous and tuberous roots contain a very large proportion of water, which is subject to considerable variation, and hence the amount of starch which a manufacturer can obtain from a given weight of potatoes is widely different. While the manufacture of wheaten- or rice-starch may be carried on throughout the whole season, that of potatoes is confined to the period of the year commencing in October, and ending in February. The process by which potato starch is now so largely made on the Continent by improved machinery, is very perfect. Its hygroscopic properties are very great, even when sold in the form of dry starch. As a substitute in the shops for arrowroot, it contains 18 per cent. of water, and if placed in a damp atmosphere, it would rapidly absorb double that amount of water. Fecula of potatoes is at present employed for a number of purposes ; for the sizing of very fine papers ; for the manufacture of starch, sugar, imitations of tapioca and sago ; as an addition in the manufacture of vermicelli and semola ; and for roasted starch.

" The applications of torrified starch, known under the name of dextrine or British gum, are very numerous. Among them may be cited the following —for stiffening and making up tulles, laces, gauzes, &c., and in fact for all kinds of cotton and linen tissues. Sizing or preparation of linen or cotton warps for weaving, especially of the finer articles. For thickening of the mordants used in printing on silks, woollens, and cottons. In calico printing for thickening both mordants and colours, when the latter are employed in what is called padding. Liquid gum for fixing on labels, adhesive postage and receipt stamps, envelopes, &c. For thickening colours for printing paperhangings. As mucilaginous baths for block-printing on silk, &c. There are some print works in Manchester which use as much as a ton a-day for stiffening fabrics.

" The exhibitors of starch were not very numerous, consisting of three Dutch manufacturers, six Belgian, and five English ; one of the latter was, however, an American manufacturer. The starches shown by the Dutch were entirely wheat starches, whilst those shown from England and Belgium were nearly all made from rice. The starches were, under the Jury classification, shown in Class II ; but as they appeared to have been only superficially examined by the Jurors of that extensive class in their recommendation for medals, the Central Jury referred them all for careful examination to Class IV., on which there were a great many chemists and scientific men fully competent to form an independent judgment. Some careful experiments were therefore made by them at the laboratory of Professor Gunning, the Government chemist and analyst for the town, as to the density, hygroscopic properties, tenacity, and character of the jelly formed by each of the starches exhibited ; and upon the results of these experiments the awards were founded.

" As an article of diet, the most tenacious varieties of starch are preferred, on account of the economy of employing an article of which a less quantity will suffice ; and the same is true when applied to starching linen, provided the jelly be not deficient in clearness. When starch jelly is used for the purpose of starching or glazing linen or cotton goods, those varieties that are most transparent are understood to be preferred, if at the same time they possess the requisite tenacity. The jellies that are most tenacious are generally the least translucent.

" The exhibitors of starch were as follows :—

" *Dutch.*

" Gerrit Vis Albz., Zaandyk (honourable mention) ; A. J. Thys, Maastricht.

" Claas Honig and Son, Koognaa de Zaan.

" *Belgian.*

" B. Haussens and Sons, Trois Fontaines, Vilvorde (silver medal) :

	Per 100 kilos. Francs.
Amidon royal (wheat starch)	75
Ditto, second quality	65
Potato fecula	36
Ditto, in packets of ¼ kilogramme ..	53
Royal rice starch	33½
English national rice starch	28¼

" Th. Malengraux, Hornu (Hainaut), potato fecula, fit for alimentary or industrial purposes, 36 francs the 100 kilogrammes.

" E. Remy and Co., Wygmael, near Louvain, royal rice starch, white or blued, in packets

of 2¼ kilogrammes ; 70 francs the 100 kilogrammes, and the same in smaller sized
packets ; 75 francs wholesale for quantities
not less than 500 kilogrammes.   Silver
medal.

" Usine de Machelen, near Vilvorde (silver
medal) :

	Per 100 kilos. Francs.
Rice starch, 1st quality	70
Ditto, 2nd ditto	50

" J. Servais and Co., Antwerp (silver medal) :

	Per 100 kilos. Francs.
Rice starch, 1st quality	75
Ditto, 2nd ditto	65

" Ch. Vermiere von Geetcruyen, Hamme, near
Termonde :

	Per 100 kilos. Dutch florins.
Wheat starch, 1st quality	31
Ditto, 2nd ditto	29

" *English.*

" Glencove Company, London.   Duryea's
maize starch, for laundry purposes.

" E. James and Sons, Plymouth.   Starch for
laundry purposes, white and blue.

" London Starch Company. Rice starches and
finished starches for calico and linen printers,
as well as for paper-makers.

" Parsons, Fletcher, and Co., London.   Rice
starch.

" Isaac Recketts and Sons, Hull.   A fine
collection of starches obtained from various
plants, with microscopic representations of
the forms of the granules of different kinds

of starch. The wholesale price of English starch is about 34s. per cwt.

" France had also one or two exhibitors of potato starch, and its subsidiary products.

" The British exhibitors received a collective silver medal, and the Gleucove Company, United States, a silver medal for maizena as food."

Little doubt exists that one of the results to Holland of the Amsterdam Exhibition will be the general introduction and use of rice starch. Considering the enormous quantities of rice annually imported into the Netherlands from their East Indian possessions, it is strange that the manufacture of starch from the damaged rice, of which little other use can be made, and of which a certain large percentage exists in every cargo, should not before now have become a national industry. Yet, whatever the cause as regards the past, Holland must ere long become a large exporter of rice-starch, instead of being, as now, a small importer of wheat, potato, and other starches for domestic use.

The bronze medals earned by Great Britain, in Class II, were bestowed upon the following six houses :—

> Messrs. Chorley and Debenham, of Avenue Road, Camberwell, London, for floorcloths. ·
>
> Messrs. James Hartley and Co., of the Great Wear Glass Works, Sunderland, for glassware.
>
> Messrs. G. B. Kent, and Co., of 11, Great Marlborough Street, London, for brushes of all kinds.
>
> Mr. A. Lyon, of 32, Windmill Street, Finsbury, London, for time and labour-saving domestic articles, viz. : sausage-machines,

bean-cutters, pea-shellers, &c. This last patent invention proved a great favourite with the Dutch.

Messrs. W. Taylor and Co., of Leith, for soap and candles. The paraffine candles manufactured by this firm are warranted not to bend in warm weather, nor in a temperature of 90 degrees Fahrenheit. Though dearer than stearine, paraffine candles have been calculated to give out 48 per cent. more light, a circumstance which reduces their practical cost by all but half, and brings them within the range of the poorer classes; their brilliant and cleanly qualities are well known.

The paraffine oils of this firm claim an extraordinarily high igniting point in relation to their respective gravities, a feature of the greatest importance in forming an estimate of their economical value, which generally suffers from their too dangerous nature.

Their crystal oil is warranted not to ignite under 135 degrees Fahrenheit; their paraffine oil under 145; and their "People's oil" under 170. These oils are produced from shale, by processes which Messrs. Taylor and Co. have patented.

Messrs. Simpsons, Payne, and Co., of Millwall, London, for candles. The advertised wholesale prices of this firm are:

	s.	d.	
Pure paraffine candles	11	0	per doz. lbs.
Transparent mixed candles of pure paraffine and stearine	9	6	„

	s.	d.	
Pure stearine or sperm candles	9	3	per doz. lbs.
Best composite candles	8	6	,,
Second quality ditto	8	0	,,
Cheap ditto	6	6	,,
Family night lights	4	9	per doz. boxes.

They also supply grey sulphate of ammonia at 16*l.* 10*s.* per ton ; and white sulphate of ammonia at 17*l.*

This firm possesses special claim to favour for the leading part taken by them in the first processes for the aqueous decomposition and distillation of fatty matters in 1854 ; and, a year later, in processes for distilling glycerine, and in its original pure chemical manufacture, to which services rendered both to science and to humanity, Dr. Abbott Smith has done justice in his interesting little work entitled " Notes on Glycerine," reprinted from the " Technologist " in 1868.

Honourable mention by the International Jury was obtained by the following British firms, in Class II. :— Honourable mention in Class II.

Mr. John Adams, of Victoria Park, Sheffield, for furniture and plate powder, polish, and paste.

Messrs. Osborne, Bauer, and Cheeseman, of 19, Golden Square, London, for soap. The cheap soaps manufactured by this firm for the working classes are as follows :—

	Per cwt.
	s.
Honey soap (in 1 lb. bars, or tablets, 3, 4, 5, 6 to the lb.)	84

	Per cwt.
Glycerine soap (in 1 lb. bars, or tablets)	*s.*
Oatmeal (ditto)	
Glycerine and almond (ditto) ..	
Oatmeal and glycerine	
Almond meal (ditto)	84
Sunflower (ditto)	
Elderflower (ditto)	
Brown Windsor (ditto)	
Ditto (ditto) .. .. 112 to 190	
Petroleum soap (for skin eruptions, in 1 lb. bars)	
Petroline ditto	112
Sulphur ditto	

Messrs. Piesse and Lubin, of 2, New Bond Street, London, and of Mitcham Road, Surrey, for soaps and perfumery.

Mr. John Anthony Pols, of 5, Pancras Lane, London, for refined oils. This house also exhibited cotton-seed, ground-nuts, and lubricating oils; foots from oil; carbonate of potash and vegetable charcoal, &c. It is distinguished for zeal and enterprise in the invention of improved processes for cleansing and crushing seed, and refining oils, either medicinal, vegetable, or animal, and intended for heating, cooking, or burning, or for lubricating machinery. An analytical chemist of considerable repute, Mr. A. Phythian Tarner, by whom the processes of Mr. Pols and their results have been carefully analyzed, strongly recommends his mustard oil, castor oil, and cod-liver oil, as being of the finest quality, and as tasteless to the greatest extent possible, without impairing their specific character. He also reports very favourably on Mr. Pols' system of flavouring with the essential oil of bitter almonds, especially as the oil for this purpose has had the hydrocyanic acid previously separated from it. One remarkable proof of the value of Mr. Pol's processes is the fact of his oils and cotton-seed cakes commanding a considerable advance upon the ordinary market prices.

Messrs. Wilson, Turner, and Co., of Burdett Road, Limehouse, London, for nickel silver, electro-plated spoons, forks, &c.

The six diplomas of excellence, ranking with gold medals, obtained by British houses in Class II, were :—

Messrs. Napoleon Price and Co., of Bond Street, London, for perfumery.

Mr. Thomas Spencer, of 32, Euston Square, London, for domestic purifying filters. This house makes filters at 10s. a-piece (wholesale price), which will purify from six to seven gallons of water daily ; this is 25 per cent. less than the published price list. The patent enjoyed by this house specifies the filtering or purifying agent to be magnetic protoxide of iron, in chemical combination with a small portion of carbon ; it dates from 1858. Both Houses of Parliament, and the Peninsula and Oriental Steam Ship Company use these filters, as 1 am informed.

Messrs. F. C. Calvert and Co., of Gibbon Street, Bradford, Manchester, for carbolic acid, for medicinal, agricultural, and disinfecting purposes. Dr. W. A. Miller, F.R.S., of King's College, reports that with 1 per cent. of Calvert's carbolic acid disinfecting powder he kept blood perfectly free from decomposition for a month : a stronger proof of its power could hardly be given. In addition to its powerful antiseptic qualities, it must be remembered that, according to the high authority of Mr. W. Crookes, F.R.S., the disinfecting substance is a clean white powder, devoid of any unpleasant smell, has no irritating action on the fingers, is easily brushed off anything on which it may accidentally fall, is not deliquescent in the slightest degree, and has for its basis an absolutely inert, insoluble, and non-poisonous body. It will thus seem to be pre-eminently adapted for domestic purposes. Calvert's carbolic acid disinfecting powder was strongly recommended by the Royal Cattle Plague Commissioners in 1866, as superior to many others, and was used with good effect in subduing the too celebrated outbreak of typhoid fever at Terling, in 1868 ; yet it is well to bear in mind that this disinfectant only suspends the decomposition of animal or vegetable accumulations of filth or drainage, which should never have been allowed to accumulate—and which, so surely as they are allowed to accumulate, will inevitably produce typhoid results ; and an official report on its use at Terling concludes with the following clear and practical remark, which all who have occasion to employ it should bear in mind : " However powerful may have been the action of carbolic acid at Terling, its use as a disinfectant can only be looked upon as a temporary expedient for holding pestilence in check, until the contemplated and much-needed sanitary improvements have been carried into effect."

Messrs. Peyton and Peyton, of Bordesley Works, Birmingham, for iron and brass bedsteads. The value of these articles as preventive of vermin and conducive to cleanliness in the poor man's home, can hardly be exaggerated ; and manufacturers should consider it a duty not only to bring them within the range of the poorest in the land, but to supply them cheaper than any wooden bedsteads can be obtained. Properly constructed they are stronger and cheaper, and take up less room than wooden bedsteads. They are doubtless destined to universal use among rich and poor alike, so soon as all the existing wooden bedsteads in the world have done descending in society, by means of auctions and the pawn-broker, and been finally consumed as fuel, the only purpose to which they can be hygienically applied. Messrs. Peyton exhibited at Amsterdam metallic bedsteads at 14s., which should find favour abroad as a marked advance in economy on continental goods of this description ; and a bedstead at 18s. 4d., after paying 5 per cent. import duty, and 30 per cent. discount to retailers, was, when delivered in Holland, generally admitted a superior article to a Prussian metallic bedstead costing £5.

Messrs. Powell and Bishop, of Hanley, Staffordshire, for china and stoneware. The wholesale prices of this firm are moderate, and the articles first class. They are very large employers of labour.

Mr. Eugene Rimmel, of 98, Strand, 128, Regent Street, and 24, Cornhill, London, for perfumery.

Extraordinary mentions were conferred on seven British houses in Class II. They were :—

Messrs. Bollman, Condy, and Co., of Battersea, London, for their fluid for purifying water, and general disinfecting purposes. This is a most important article, and one of equal value to every class of society, while, at the same time, within the reach of all. The price of a gallon of strong disinfecting fluid, made by mixing one-part of Condy's fluid with 200 or 300 parts of water, does not exceed 1*d*.

Messrs. Condy also supply cheap filters for 2 francs, which, with the aid of a minute quantity of their fluid, will purify from 10 to 20 gallons of water daily. The filtering medium can be renewed for a few centimes. These filters are equally available for brightening turbid water, and are said to have the effect of removing lead from water containing that dangerous metal. This last is a very important point, where good water is not easily procurable, as in some parts of Holland, where these articles should be in daily domestic use on a greater or smaller scale, according to the water consumption of the household.

Messrs. Crichley, Wilde, and Co., of Cannon Street, Birmingham, for umbrella-stands. This firm also produces superior stove-grates, fenders, and general ornamental casting.

Messrs. J. C. and J. Field, of Lambeth Marsh,

London, for candles. This firm claims, among other inventions, that of the plaited-wick for candles, and has obtained prizes at the Exhibitions of London, 1851 and 1862; Dublin, 1865; York, 1866; and Paris, 1867; for supplying the brightest quality and the cheapest kinds of wax, stearine, sperm, composite, and paraffine candles, night-lights, and soaps.

Messrs. Mander, Brothers, of 17, Gracechurch Street, London, and of Wolverhampton, for resins and varnish. (Established in 1803)

The Silicated Carbon Filter Company, of Church Road, Battersea, London, for filters. The claims of this firm to eminence are great and varied. The Commission appointed by the "Lancet" to inquire into the subject of drinking-water and filtration, adopted a very severe test for the purpose of proving the capabilities of a filter for removing organic matter from water, viz., the use of water mixed with milk, which represents, chemically, all the organic impurities usually found in water. From this test the Silicated Carbon Filter emerged triumphant, the milk being effectually eliminated from the water. The Company supply pocket filters at 2s. 6d.; filters for the bedroom at 5s.; for the kitchen at 14s. 6d.; and for the dining-room at 30s. They also supply what are really more valuable, as tapping and purifying the poisoned stream before it effects an entry into the house, main-service filters at £6 6s. and upwards, besides high-pressure filters, refrigerative filters, ship filters, &c.

This firm claim for themselves the merit of standing alone in supplying filters which do not render the water flat and insipid, but impart carbonic acid instead of withdrawing it from the water.

The following is stated as the effect of the Silicated Carbon Filter upon Thames water obtained near Battersea Bridge at high water :—

	Unfiltered.	Filtered.
	Grains.	Grains.
Total solid contents of an Imperial gallon.. ..	33½	8·7
Hardness, as determined by Clark's test	Degrees. 13	Degrees. 6
Earthy carbonates deposited by boiling.. ..	Grains. 11	None.
Organic matter contained..	3·8	Grains. 0·6

" The unfiltered was of a greenish yellow colour, and during evaporation gave out a most offensive odour, the residue being a dark brown mass of organic and saline impurities. When passed once through a Silicated Carbon Filter it became perfectly colourless, sweet, and drinkable ; during evaporation not the slightest odour was perceptible, and the residue was quite white, and consisted of little more than chloride of sodium (common salt)."

Mr. Henry Stephens, of 171, Aldersgate Street, London, for ink. To Mr. Stephens belongs the honour of standing in the front rank of those who have applied chemistry to atramental fluids. His black, blue, and red writing inks, his copying and marking inks, are justly celebrated and widely used.

Messrs. Shaw and Fisher, of 43, Suffolk Road, Sheffield, for electro table services.

To two British houses only, in Class II, was the highest award of all—*Diplôme d'Honneur*—given, viz., to—

Price's Patent Candle Company (Limited), of London.

And to—

Young's Paraffine Company, of Glasgow, both for candles.

The firm of Messrs. Price supplies night-lights, soaps, oils, glycerine, paraffine, &c., as well as every description of candle. It obtained a gold medal at Paris, in 1867, and is too widely and well known to call for more remark. Price's solidified glycerine soap, may, however, be mentioned as a great step in advance in the application of chemistry to every day life.

The second of these distinguished firms, Young's Paraffine Light and Mineral Oil Company (Limited), sell hard paraffine candles at 1*s.* per lb.; sulphate of ammonia at £16 10*s.* per ton; and burning and mineral oils at 1*s.* 7*d.* the gallon, and £16 the ton, respectively. These are wholesale prices, on which a further reduction is made of $2\frac{1}{2}$ per cent. for cash payments.

CLOTHING.

Class III was devoted to clothing, and included every article connected therewith, or entering into its manufacture. Cottons, linens, woollen and mixed stuffs, garments of all kinds, waterproofs, leathers, hats, caps, thumbstalls, boots, buttons, pins, needles, purses, scissors, rings, bracelets, and other cheap trinkets; and, oddly enough, tobacco-boxes. Comprising so great a variety of articles, it was not surprising that Class III ranked second in number of exhibits among the classes at Amsterdam.

Dutch cloth exhibits.

A glance at this section was enough to prove that times had changed since Holland held an important place in the cloth market of the world. The decline of the Dutch cloth manufacture since the seventeenth century, when Steel Street in Amsterdam, where the cloth merchants congregated, was one of the sights of Europe, inspiring Rembrandt with the subject of one of his most celebrated pictures, "The Steel Masters," is attributed by the Dutch themselves to an early Treaty made by the first Napoleon with Spain, one Article of which permitted the exportation from Spain into France of merino sheep, which, crossed with the French breeds, produced the best results in wool. About the same time, during the reign of George III, the merino sheep was likewise introduced into England; but there it was found that, though the wool did not deteriorate, the meat met with little favour in the market, and ultimately farmers contented themselves, as in France, with judicious crossings with the Southdown and other breeds. The farmers of the Netherlands do not appear to have realized the importance of this subject until about thirty years ago, when English sheep with longer and finer wool were introduced for crossing purposes with good effect. From that date the Dutch wool market began to revive, though it will probably never recover its lost pre-eminence. Woollen manufactures of all kinds are now largely on the increase in the Netherlands.

Notwithstanding this improving state of things, Dutch woollen exhibits at Amsterdam were by no means what they ought, or might reasonably have been expected to have been. In successful dyeing, indeed, they held their own ; but in the manufactured article, that from the earliest period to the present day has continued to be of primary importance, as forming the principal part of the clothing of mankind in the temperate zone, Holland was but feebly represented in her own Exhibition. In fact, in cloth the honour of the Netherlands may be said to have depended on the efforts of one house, Messrs. Cruhay and Co., of Maastricht, who exhibited a fair show of coloured cloths and buckskins at the following prices :—

	Fl. c.	Fl. c.	
Brown duffle	4 40 and	5 50	per 7 palms.
Blue „	5 0		„
Buckskin	3 30		„
Grey Molton	3 30		„
Brown reps	3 30		„
Black cloth	3 85		„
Red flannel	2 0		„
Blue „	1 40 and	1 90	„
Light blue military cloth	4 15		„
Dark blue „ ..	4 35		„

I

Belgium was as strongly, as Holland was weakly represented in cloth manufactures at Amsterdam, and most of her exhibits in this branch of industry possessed the special merit of coming strictly within the scope of the Exhibition, being remarkable for cheapness and solidity. A gold medal was awarded to Messrs. H. Rolin, Fils, and Cie., of St. Nicholas, for an assortment of their stuffs ; and a collection of articles exhibited by M. Wynandy-Venster, of Dison, attracted particular attention for their general excellence, taking into consideration the low price at which they were ticketed :—

		Mètres.	Fr.	c.	
38,000	Coteline ..	2·40 at	6	70	the mètre.
50,000	„ ..	„	7	10	„
60,000	„ ..	„	8	45	„
55,000	„ ..	„	8	25	„
45,000	„ ..	„	7	55	„
40,000	„ ..	„	6	90	„
35,000	„ ..	„	6	45	„
25,000	„ ..	„	6	0	„
55,000	Satin ..	„	6	90	„
48,000	„ ..	„	6	45	„
37,000	„ ..	„	5	60	„
44,000	„ ..	„	6	0	„
40,000	„ ..	„	5	35	„

The North German Bund made little show in articles of this class except in buckskins, of which Mr. Christian Sauer, of Hersfeld, Hessen, exhibited some good qualities ; and in trouser stuffs, of which some popular cheap sorts, varying from 2 to 3 thalers a piece, were displayed by Messrs. Aug. Zchille and Müller, of Grossenhaim. Some of the Saxon thick woollen cloths should likewise be mentioned favourably among the exhibits of this class.

An interesting exhibit in this section was one
made by the Schmidtsche "forest wool" (*Wald-wol*) manufactory, at Remda in Thuringia. This article, which is of a rusty colour and smells strongly of turpentine, resembles flannel in texture, and is made in different thicknesses. It is said to be woven from the fresh needles of the fir-trees of the Thuringian and Black Forests. It is considered a specific against gout and rheumatism, and is very much used by the poor and middle classes in the Netherlands, where many leading physicians regard it with favour, and where there are agencies for its sale in every considerable village. The process of its manufacture was first perfected, after many years of study and labour, by Herr Josephus Weiss, who established a factory of it in Silesia as much as twenty years ago; but so great were the prejudices against which he had to contend, that it is only quite of late years that the faculty on the continent have deigned to examine into its merits, and give it a fair trial.

Other articles besides clothing are produced from the fir-needles by the manufactory at Remda; a spirit is distilled from them which is said to be very efficacious in friction; and an oil obtained from the same source is much recommended for soaking the flannels, &c. in, previous to their application to the rheumatic parts in acute cases. Lozenges are also made, of which the chemical basis is said to be derived from the same abundant source of health and wealth—the pine forest. As this subject is of special interest in connection with the latest practice of some of our leading medical men of sending consumptive patients to pine woods, whereby the curative, or at least health-giving qualities of the raw material of which these goods are made, would seem to be recognized, either on scientific principles or on practical experience, I annex a price list of the different

CLASS III. articles procurable from the Schmidtsche Forest Woolware Factory at Remda :—

	Fl.	c.
Knitting thread, 4 skeins	3	0
Wadding, per packet	0	50
„ „ small ..	0	25
Twilled flannel, per ell	2	0
Flannel, per ell	1	30
Twilling	0	80
Sleeves, per pair	1	40
Socks, No. 1	1	20
„ No. 2	1	35
Men's stockings, No. 1	2	0
„ No. 2	2	30
Ladies' stockings, No. 1	1	50
„ No. 2	1	75
Knee cap, No. 1	1	40
„ No. 2	1	60
Soles for shoes, No. 1	0	50
„ No. 2	0	55
„ No. 3	0	60
Muffatees	0	60
Half socks	1	0
Blankets	10	0
Pillows	3	0
Mattresses (according to their size).		
Fir-needles, per 5 ozs.	0	30
Back protector	2	0
Chest „	2	0
Bands	2	0
Scarfs, No. 1	0	50
„ No. 2	0	60
Chest-protector (ladies')	1	30
Caps..	1	0
Under caps, No. 1	0	70
„ No. 2	0	80
Under waistcoat (ladies') No. 1 ..	4	0

		Fl.	c.
Under waistcoat (ladies) No. 2	..	4	50
„ (men's)	.. 3 60 to	4	50
„ „	.. 4 75	5	75
Drawers	.. 4	0	4 55
„	.. 4 75	5	75

These articles will all wash.

	c.	c.	Fl. c.
Oil, per half, whole, or double bottle, at ..	35	70 and	1 30
Extract, per half and whole bottle ..		.. 75	1 50
Elixer, per bottle ..	..	..	0 75
Pomatum	..	..	0 60
Spirit	..	..	0 50
Syrup	..	..	0 60
Soap, per piece ..	..	..	0 25
Bonbons, per box ..	..	..	0 30

The Austrian and French cloth exhibits possessed great beauty of colour, and were of fine quality, though for the most part somewhat dear in price, and thus beyond the pale of the Exhibition. One remarkable exception to this general rule was rewarded by a well-merited gold medal bestowed upon Mr. E. Couchon, of Périgeux (Dordogne), who exhibited some strong woollen stuffs at 92 cents the mètre.

In linens and cottons generally, Holland in some measure made up for its deficiency in cloth exhibits; yet here again Belgium had an undoubted precedence, while North Germany, with the Elberfeldt industry, was meagrely represented. Notwithstanding the fact that Dutch flax cannot compete with the flax of Flanders or Great Britain in whiteness, it retains its ancient popularity on the Continent for durability, and specially for superiority in design of damasks. In linens Holland may be said, on the whole, to have been respectably represented, though little more; while in cottons and calicoes the absence of many of the largest manufacturing houses of Overyssel and Haarlem deprived the collection of completeness as a national display. To this fact, among others, must be attributed the paucity of awards given in this class to Dutch exhibitors as compared with some foreign countries, which constituted so honourable and novel a feature in the Amsterdam exhibition as compared with previous occasions of a similar kind, and notably with Paris in 1867, where nearly one-half of the total recompenses were bestowed on French houses. A little reflection will show that this neglect of the Netherlands to be adequately represented at their own Exhibition, which would at first sight appear so remarkable, considering their large fabrication of linen and cotton goods for export to Java, &c., is probably to be traced to this very cause; their principal custom for these goods is in Asia, not in Europe, and perhaps on the whole they are wise in not caring to exhibit side by side with other countries, and invite invidious comparisons between goods destined for the Eastern market and those intended for the more fastidious taste of European communities. Whether this suggestion be just or unjust, it is one they have themselves provoked in the necessity for seeking obscure motives for their allowing foreigners, and especially the neighbours of whom they are so jealous—Belgians—to carry off the palm in the branch of industry now under review.

Leather.

Of leather, worked and plain, one of the most difficult articles to judge by the eye, the touch, or any test short of actual wear and tear, there was a handsome show from several countries.

Made-up clothing, Dutch.

In made-up articles of clothing, upper and under,

for the working-man, there was no lack in the Amsterdam Exhibition ; indeed this may be said to be one of the departments most fully represented from every country. One of the most complete collections of underclothing in the Netherlands section was that of the Evangelical-Lutheran Sisterhood of the Hague. It was composed as follows :—

	Fl.	c.
Layette (complete)	24	0
Linen aprons	0	90
Coloured aprons .. ∴. ..	0	75
Jackets	2	25
Red pocket handkerchiefs	0	45
Coloured dusters	0	25
Linen shifts..	2	5
„ shirts..	2	20
White neckerchiefs..	0	32
Long drawers	1	60
Short „	1	50
Waistcoats	1	95
Girls' shifts..	0	95
Boys' shirts..	0	95
Sheets	2	10
Small sheets	1	35
Petticoats	2	25
&c., &c.		

Another collection of similar articles, priced somewhat lower, apparently of equally good material, but not quite such fine workmanship, was comprised in the exhibits of Mr. F. L. Van Deth, of Dort. The prices were :—

	Fl. c.	Fl. c.
Children's vests		0 35
Girls' „	0 55½ to	0 90
Women's „ large		1 55
„ „ small		1 15

				Fl. c.	Fl. o.
Boys' vests		..	..	0 75	1 10
Men's „ large		..	..	..	2 0
„ „ small		..	..	..	1 55
Boys' drawers	..	..	..	..	1 0
Men's „	..	..	..	..	1 65
Nightcaps		..	..	0 22½	35 0

The cloth clothing for the working-man which Holland exhibited at Amsterdam was not so much characterized by cheapness as by solidity and good workmanship. Among the most interesting objects in this section were the complete dresses for a labourer and his wife exhibited by Baron Mackay van Ophemert. They were composed and priced as follows :—

WORKMAN'S DRESS.

				Fl. c.
Cloth blouse ..	..	..	..	4 80
Waistcoat	..	..	..	1 50
Trousers	..	..	..	2 90
Jersey ..	..	..	..	1 95
Drawers	..	..	..	1 40
Shirt ..	..	..	..	0 80
Neckcloth	..	..	..	0 25
Stockings	..	..	..	1 0
Shoes ..	..	..	..	2 20
Cap ..	..	..	..	0 60
Pocket-handkerchief ..		..	..	0 35
		Total	..	17 75

DRESS FOR WORKMAN'S WIFE.

			Fl.	c.
Short gown	..	..	1	80
Upper petticoat	..	..	2	90
Under „ ..	..	..	2	85
Jersey ..	..	..	1	20
Shift ..	..	..	0	80
Neckerchief	..	..	0	37½
Apron ..	..	..	0	72½
Stockings	..	..	0	90
Shoes ..	..	..	1	40
Cap ..	..	..	0	27½
Pocket..	..	..	0	17½
Handkerchief ..	..	..	0	20
	Total	..	13	60

The Brothers Offermans, of Bois-le-Duc, also exhibited complete suits of clothing (consisting of coat, vest, trousers, shirt hose, neck-tie) of different qualities, but all good and solid of their kind, at 18·42, 15·82, 9·85, and 7·98 florins each.

Several Belgian houses displayed collections of **Belgian.** made-up clothes, most of them, however, of too high a price to be available for the working-man, and more adapted to the wear of his employer. Of the few Belgian clothing firms that did come within the scope of the Exhibition in this respect, the prices did not transpire ; and comparison with the productions of other countries is thus rendered impossible.

The made-up clothing exhibited by the North **North-** German Bund was principally composed of woollen **German.** articles of good quality, and very moderate in price.

Linen clothing was well and tastefully represented **Austro-** in the Austro-Hungarian section, which was indeed **Hungarian.** one of the most pleasing and characteristic portions of the Exhibition. In colouring, no other could compare with it, and the articles exhibited were of a singularly *bond fide* character, and mostly within the prescribed utilitarian conditions.   Thus Messrs. Hönig, of Vienna, showed excellent linen shirts at 2s. 6d. a-piece, and Messrs. Lichtner, also of Vienna, displayed other ready-made underclothing at equally moderate price.

Wooden haber- dashery.

A novel feature among the Austrian exhibits in this class was their *wooden haberdashery*, neck-ties, collars, cuffs, shirt-fronts, &c., being made of beautiful white wood shavings.   Hats and caps are likewise made of this material.   The exhibitor of these articles was Carl Viol, of Vienna ; and from the rapidity with which they disappeared, as they were bought up for keepsakes, it is probable that he, for one, was quite content with the results of the Amsterdam Exhibition.   The Austrian articles generally, indeed, met with much appreciation from the Dutch, who are greatly interested in everything that concerns that empire, from the fact of their being such large holders of its national obligations.

"La Belle Jardinière."

The first place among French ready-made clothing was incontestably filled by the Parisian house *La Belle Jardinière*, established under the management of Messrs. Bessand.   According to the advertisements of this Parisian Moses and Son, *la spécialité de cette maison est qu'on y entre tout nu et qu'on en sort tout habillé*.   This house professes to sell from £4,000 to £6,000 worth of goods daily.   Each article it displayed was remarkable for having appended to it an elaborate tariff of the prices of its component parts, and of the profit anticipated on its sale.   Thus a pair of fine cloth trousers gave the following explanation of its total cost :—

			Fr.	c.
Stuff ..	..	..	14	41
Silk ..	..	..	0	93
Lining	..	..	0	48
Coarse linen ..	..	..	0	7
Buttons	..	..	0	15
Buckle	..	..	0	4
Ribbon	..	..	0	45
Cutting out ..	..	..	0	50
Wages	..	..	4	0
Profit..	..	..	3	17 = 16 per cent.
Total	..		24	25

One item in this tariff is of interest, as being the
only one probably that is strictly reliable. I refer
to the last but one—wages, which are here seen
avowedly to represent a trifling fraction, under one-
sixth, or about 16 per cent. on the cost price of the
manufactured article. This speaks volumes for the
effect of our European civilization upon the wage
classes of society, if compared with the custom still
prevailing in India and other Oriental countries, of
estimating the labour in many trades at the same
price as the raw material. For example, a native,
requiring a dozen pocket-handkerchiefs or a silver
bangle, would buy the raw material, the cambric or
the silver, in the neighbouring bazaar, and call into
his verandah such labour as was needed to complete
its manufacture. In such cases the silver-workers
are paid in silver for the weight of their workmanship,
and the *durzees* (or tailors) would receive in wages
the value of the material.

La Belle Jardinière received a well-deserved gold
medal, for its handsome display of goods, combined
with this innovation in price lists, which rendered it
plus royaliste que le roi in responding to one of the
most important of the avowed objects of the Amster-

dam Exhibition, viz., procuring an analysis of the
price of production of articles of a first necessity for
daily use.

The wooden sole figures largely in Dutch working-
men's boots, and the English invention of the division of the wooden sole into several pieces corresponding with the movable portions of the sole of the
foot when walking, is largely copied.   In this section
Mr. P. J. H. de Ruyter, of Utrecht, displayed
wooden-soled boots and shoes at the prices given
below :—

	Fl.	c.
Sabots, or garden shoes, with wooden and leather soles	3	0
Ditto, with gutta-percha soles	3	25
Ditto, with wooden soles	2	0
Ditto, for over-shoes	1	75
Women's ditto..	1	75
Ditto, for over-shoes	1	40
Children's ditto	1	0
Girl's ditto	1	10

Mr. J. H. de Lang also exhibited a collection of
solid boots and shoes at the following low prices :—

	Wholesale.		Retail.	
	Fl.	c.	Fl.	c.
Mud-boots (high)	5	0	6	0
Ditto (ankle high)	3	5	4	0
Calf-skin ditto, with double soles and nails	4	0	4	50
Ditto, single soles	3	0	3	50
Ditto shoes	1	75	2	0
Ditto boys' shoes	1	25	1	50
Ditto children's ditto	1	0	1	20

One of the most interesting boot and shoe collections from Belgium was that furnished by the Co-operative Society at Cureghem. Among these were strong boots for iron-workers at 4·50 florins, for miners at 5 florins, and for carters at 4·12 florins. All these appeared to be of excellent manufacture, and represented a decided advance in economical construction.

The boots and shoes exhibited in the Austrian Austria. section were more remarkable for beautiful workmanship than extreme cheapness.

In *chaussures*, as in all articles of clothing, France France. exhibited a rich variety, and obtained no less than four gold medals. These exhibitors were great Paris houses, well-known to the shoe-making world since 1867, and call for no special comment.

Denmark had three exhibitors of boots and shoes. Denmark. Some of these, made of pig's leather, attracted a good share of general attention.

It is not my intention to describe the miscel- Miscellane- laneous articles exhibited in this class, which always ous exhibits. form so popular a portion of every exhibition. Cheap finery of various kinds found ready purchasers, and the Amsterdam utilitarian Exhibition of 1869 furnished no exception to the rule laid down by previous experience, which numbers such stalls among the most attractive to the bulk of human nature out of which exhibition crowds are made.

Two British firms received gold medals in British exhibits in Class III, viz. :— Class III.

> Messrs. W. Bliss and Son, of Chipping Norton,
> Oxford, for woollen fabrics ; and,
> Messrs. Ermen and Engels, of Manchester, for
> sewing cotton.

It was on the former of these firms, Messrs. Bliss Messrs. Bliss. and Son, that the Emperor of the French was prepared to bestow in 1867 the new order of reward, if Her Majesty's Commissioners could have overcome the difficulties which beset its acceptance by British subjects; and the circumstances on which their claim to that distinction was founded, afford a sufficiently striking illustration of the inseparable nature of the interests of the workgiver and of the workman to warrant their being quoted in connection with an Exhibition whose main object was to contribute to the general knowledge of this fact. To their honour then let it be again recorded that the firm of Messrs. Bliss and Son was founded in 1757, and that in 1867 it could be proved that during the 110 years that it had flourished, no dispute had ever occurred between the masters and the 500 hands they had continually employed; that during that time none of the workmen had joined Trade Unions, nor had unions had any effect on their wages. There had been no combination; no hands had been allowed to go to the workhouse—families had worked for three generations—the duration of life had been above the average; workmen had saved money and bought life insurances; children had never been employed under 13, and married women employed had not been required to work before breakfast in the winter. Schools, reading-rooms, lectures, concerts, cricket, football, had been liberally promoted. That a gold medal should fall to such a firm, and that their tweeds and cloths should be both cheap and excellent, and not suffer in repute from Continental competition cannot excite surprise; but the fact is none the less a source of international gratification, conducive, let us hope, to the promotion, the continuance, and the adoption by others of the most remunerative and the only Christian treatment of workpeople by their employers.

The second British gold medallist in Class III,

Messrs. Ermen and Engels of Manchester, cannot boast of such an ancient lineage as Messrs. Bliss, of Oxford, having been established at Eccles and Pendlebury in 1837. They employ, however, 1,000 hands, and produce immense quantities of most superior cottons and threads, both for the home and export trades.

The following nine British houses received silver medals in Class III.

Thomas Ainsworth, of Cleator Mills, Whitehaven, for linen-thread for sewing-machines, tailors, &c. This house also exhibited linen tapes and towels. Some of the merits claimed by these threads are, that they are cable-laid and back-twisted, are round and smooth, and have these advantages over silk for sewing leather :—1st. Stronger, size for size, than silk. 2ndly. More durable, resisting wet and exposure to the weather better than silk. 3rdly. Make closer work, because not elastic, like silk. 4thly. Cheaper, because there is a greater length in a given weight, size for size, than in silk.

Messrs. Anderson, Abbott, and Anderson, of Dod Street, Limehouse, London, for india-rubber and oil-skin clothing. This firm produces :—

	s.	d.
An oil-skin jacket at	3	8
„ trousers	2	8
„ sou'-wester hat ..	0	10
Or, complete waterproof suit	7	2

7½ per cent discount is allowed on wholesale orders, with a further reduction of 2¼ per cent. for cash payments.

Messrs. Cow, Hill, and Co., of 46 and 47, Cheapside, London, for patent india-rubber sponges, glove-cleaners, printers' rollers, serrated mats, &c.

Messrs.] Day, Watkinson, and Co., of Huddersfield, for Bedford cord.

Messrs. Robert Jeffrey and Sons, of Brunswick Street, Glasgow, for linen and cotton twilling, ticking, and sheeting.

Messrs. W. and C. Kesselmeyer, of 1, Peter Street, Manchester, for cotton velvets, velveteens, moleskin, Genoa cords, &c. This house claims credit as the original inventors and patentees of velveteen, a material which strength, durability, warmth, and good outward appearance has justly rendered an especial favourite with the working classes.

Messrs. McIntyre, Hogg, and Co., of 122, Brunswick Street, Glasgow, for shirts and woollens.

Messrs. Thomson and Dodds, of the Priest Royd Mills, Huddersfield, for fancy trouserings.

The North British Rubber Company (Limited), of Edinburgh, of 4, Cannon Street, London, and of 8, Spring Gardens, Manchester, for india-rubber shoes, clothing, and waterproof goods, machine-belting, hose, washers, &c.

Bronze medals in Class III.

Seven bronze medals were conferred upon British exhibitors in Class III, they were :—

Messrs. J. Buckley and Son, of Leeds, for hats and caps.

Messrs. D. McArthur and Co., of 26, Bothwell

Street, Glasgow, for linen sets. This house also exhibited embroidered muslins, ties, robes, &c.; embroidered shirts, crape collars, and lace goods.

Messrs. Charles McDonald and Co., of 60, Ingram Street, Glasgow, for shawls.

The Paisley Co-operative Manufacturing Society, established at Paisley, for cheap shawls.

Messrs. B. Vickerman and Son, of St. George's Square, Huddersfield, for woollen and mixed cloths, &c.

Messrs. Wadkin and King, of Chepstow Street Mills, Manchester, for cotton twines. This firm claims the credit of being the first makers of net-twine from cotton, an invention which they perfected about twenty years ago. These twines are now in general use for fishing-nets, &c., being more durable and economical than those made from hemp. This exhibit was of great importance to the Dutch.

Messrs. H. Monteith and Co., of 11, St. George's Square, Glasgow, for corahs, bandanas, and fancy pocket-handkerchiefs.

Diplômes d'Honneur, which ranked above gold medals, were awarded in Class III to the two following distinguished British houses :—

Sir Elkanah Armitage and Sons, of 48, Mosley Street, Manchester, for cotton-sail, canvas, cotton-duck for manufacturing into india-rubber belting, American leather-cloth, &c. This great house, which employs an average of 2,000 hands, was established in 1829, and is one of the great cotton-spinning firms of our cotton-spinning country. Their

"Diplômes d'Honneur.

Sir Elkanah Armitage.

K

manufactures may be described as embracing every description of cloth made of yarns dyed in the skein or hank. There is a large and growing demand for them on the Continent, where their excellence is fully appreciated, and obtained for them a gold medal at Paris in 1867. Their goods are not actually the cheapest made, but from their durability and superior qualities they are great favourites with the working-man, and largely consumed by the class for whom the Amsterdam Exhibition was specially intended.

The second house thus rewarded was that of—

Mr. Robert Thatcher.

Mr. Robert Thatcher, of Oldham, Lancashire, for cotton-yarn produced from waste, cotton-twines for netting, cotton-banding for machinery, and the manufactured goods for which the yarn is used. This house has been established about fifty years, and, I believe, never exhibited at any previous Exhibition. The departure from its practice in favour of the Working-Men's Exhibition at Amsterdam must, therefore, be regarded as stimulated less by the hope of individual gain, than by the generous desire of entering into friendly rivalry and competition with other manufacturers in the supply of articles of a quality and price calculated to render them a boon to civilization and society at large.

" Mentions honorables " in Class III.

Four British firms received honourable mention in Class III. They were :—

Messrs. Arundale and Co., of 257, Argyle Street, Glasgow, for Scotch hats and caps.

Messrs. R. and T. Grimstone and Co., of Clifford Mills, near Tadcaster, for shoe-threads, shop and netting twines.

Messrs. Howden and Wade, of Millshaw Mills, near Leeds, for pilot cloth.

Messrs. William McLaren, Sons, and Co., of 5, South Hanover Street, Glasgow, for cambrics and tweeds. Shawls and woollens were also exhibited by this house.

All these houses complied with the request for information as to wholesale prices, but as these prices are constantly fluctuating with the price of the raw material, no quotations can be of practical utility.

Five diplomas of excellence, ranking with gold medals, were conferred on British exhibitors in Class III for articles not strictly coming within the declared scope of the Exhibition. Their recipients were :—

"Diplômes d'excellence" in Class III.

Messrs. Brough, Nicholson, and Co., of Leek, Staffordshire, for silk.

Messrs. Hitchcock, Williams, and Co., of St. Paul's Churchyard, London, for waterproof mantles. This firm exhibited a 7s. 11d. waterproof cloak, in great favour among the working classes in Great Britain; and there can be no doubt that this article entitled them to compete within the scope of the Exhibition. Theirs, however, is one of the many cases referred to in the official letter of the President of the Exhibition, forwarding to the Home Minister for publication in the "Gazette" the ultimate awards of the Central Jury. In this letter it is stated that the awards must be regarded as having reference to the general

character of exhibits, and that being judged
hors concours as regards the special objects
of the Exhibition, by no means implies that
the firm concerned exhibited nothing for
the use of the working classes. Some firms
deemed this ruling hard,—and it had, indeed, a harsh effect as applied to this particular exhibit,—but such cases of isolated
individual hardship must occur where it is
essential to adopt a general code of procedure applicable to all classes and to every
country. *Contretemps* of this description
are a necessary evil to which every Exhibition is liable, and constitute, in regard
to Exhibitions, a portion of the alloy
which it is impossible to eliminate from
all human undertakings, however sterling
and genuine.

Messrs. E. Posselt and Co., of City Road
Mill, Derby, for elastic boot-webbs.

Messrs. W. Salmond and Sons, of Arbroath,
Forfarshire, for sail-cloth.

Messrs. Morton and Sons, of Kidderminster,
for carpets.

"Mentions extraordinaires" in Class III.

The five following British houses received extraordinary mention in Class III :—

Messrs. Waldemar Lund and Co., of 60,
Chandos Street, Strand, London, for ivory
and gold studs.

Mr. Samuel Wills Norman, of Grosvenor
Gardens, S.W., and 116, Westminster
Bridge Road, London, for boots and shoes.
These are for wear in a very low tempera-
ture, and are porous, not waterproof.

Mr. Edwin Wilks, of the Promenade, Chel-
tenham, for portmanteaus, remarkable for

lightness, strength, and convenience, some being air-tight and others water-tight. This firm takes off 40 per cent. discount on large orders.

Messrs. Henderson and Co., of Durham, for carpets.

Messrs J. Wilkinson and Son, of St. Helen's Mills, Hunslet, Leeds, for carpets.

If many of the British exhibitors in Class III failed to obtain awards to which they deemed themselves entitled, from the well-known excellence of their wares and manufactures, not a few of them have only themselves to thank for the result, in not having taken the pains to be adequately represented at Amsterdam. Exhibitors should bear in mind that an Exhibition, to succeed, must be made attractive to the eye, and that the mere display of a small sample of their goods, such as they would send round for the inspection of retail dealers, even though such specimen may, strictly speaking, be sufficient to enable the examining Jury to arrive at a just decision on its merits, cannot be held to constitute a perfect claim to the highest order of award if compared with more important exhibits, of perhaps equal intrinsic merit, from other countries. A Jury in great part composed of jealous Frenchmen, Belgians, Germans, &c., requires to be satisfied and convinced of the rank the exhibitor holds among his rivals, as well as of the actual excellence of his often very limited exhibit, and considers, *cæteris paribus*, that the firm which is well represented by handsome cases, is more worthy of a great recompense than the house that has gone to little trouble or expense, taken no interest in the undertaking, and displayed no public spirit of laudable national emulation or honest pride in its own representation. Even as a

Importance to exhibitors of being well represented.

soldier who appears untidy on parade is an unpleasant object for the eye of his commanding officer to dwell on: so an exhibitor who appears in callous attire at an international industrial tournament is an eye-sore to the jury and the public, and cannot expect his foreign judges (for to every country represented the bulk of the jury is foreign), to take for granted, or be anxious to be convinced, that a shabby exterior is a necessary criterion of internal merit. In the particular instance now under consideration, I have no hesitation in attributing many of the superior awards obtained by France and Belgium to this cause, which contributed not a little to the facility with which British interests were outvoted and disposed of in the International Jury at Amsterdam. It is to be hoped that the lesson, there somewhat rudely taught, may be turned to future account by British exhibitors remembering that a respectable show of goods, on a scale commensurate with their importance, is the first element of success at international exhibitions—of success to the exhibitor himself, and to the exhibition as a whole; further, that those the British manufacturer ventures to compete with, when he sends his goods abroad, are, as a rule, by no means ignorant of the advantage of display, or wanting in good taste to enhance the general effect of their endeavours. How far such causes contributed to the non-satisfaction of the claims of the unsuccessful British exhibitors in Class III it is needless to inquire in detail, but no doubt some, if not many, will be able to lay to their hearts the flattering unction, that, had they striven, they would have reaped their reward.

These remarks apply of course chiefly to great manufacturers, of whom there were many in Class III at Amsterdam, who were represented by most insignificant exhibits. Great Manchester houses

serve their country better by abstaining from exhibit- Class III.
ing at all, if they do not deem it worth their while to
exhibit well, and by staying at home where they are
known and appreciated, rather than by sending a
few square feet or yards of their manufactures, to
render them an object of derision to the Jury, and
of no interest to visitors at large. With inventions
the case is different; and though the advantage of a
showy exterior should never be neglected, even at
exhibitions of a utilitarian character, exhibits of this
description are able to stand more exclusively on
their own merits than ordinary manufactured goods.

FOOD.

Wie der mensch iszt so ist er was the motto of Class IV, which was devoted to food, and included all kinds of edible, agricultural, and industrial productions and preparations. Flours of all kinds, oils, vinegar, and other condiments, coffee, tea, chicory, and all sorts of sweets. It also included tobacco and snuff, both of which are chewed largely in Holland. It is perhaps worthy of incidental remark that Holland is the only country besides China in which the habit of taking snuff with a small spoon has come under my personal observation; and it would not be without interest to know whether this is a remnant of a once universal custom, or whether it has been imported into that country by sailors and other roving Dutchmen, who from time immemorial have visited the East in such numbers. Class IV also contained collections of dried and salted meats, extracts of meat, milk powder, canned and bottled vegetables, fruits, &c.; drinks of all kinds, beers, spirits, wines, and, lastly, every variety of preserved and smoked fish, which forms so large a staple of the people's food in that amphibious country.

The food question in Holland is one of importance not only to Netherlanders, but also to ourselves, who are at present such large consumers of what under the existing *régime* of the Dutch people is considered superfluity, and is thus available for foreign markets. To prove this it is only necessary to draw attention to the following brief column of statistics which may be taken as a sufficiently accurate, though of course only an approximate Table of the principal food exports of Holland during 1869, of which Great Britain has taken, roughly speaking, all the live stock and meat, and by far the greater part of the other articles :—

240,040 sheep and lambs.
98,240 horned cattle.
32,304,000 lbs of butter.
34,400,000 ,,   cheese.
4,400,000 ,,   mutton and pork.
132,000,000 ,,   sugar.
24,000,000 ,,   rice.

Now this large supply of meat, which we draw from Holland, principally for our London market, would, if divided among the adult males of the Dutch population, be little more than enough to provide them with an additional weekly dinner of meat, so that our retention of this source of feeding the metropolis is dependent on a very precarious tenure—namely, the absence of increased meat consumption by the bulk of the Dutch people themselves; and a very small increase in such meat consumption (which is actually nil among the poorest classes), would be sufficient to cut it off entirely. From this point of view it is evidently of great interest to inquire how the Dutch are fed at present, and what chance exists of the extension of meat diet in that country.

In the first rank among substitutes for meat in Holland stands fish—both sea and river, fresh and salt. The herring fisheries along the coast, for participating in which, until a few years ago, a Government licence was required, are now open to every coasting craft without exception, and it is asserted

that the herring banks are being overfished, and that
the supply is consequently falling off. The same
source of danger to the fish supply has been detected
at the mouths and estuaries of the Rhine, where
salmon-netting has hitherto been pursued in the
most reckless manner, the annual close time being
limited to *one month*, and no weekly slaps being
prescribed by law. To such an extent, indeed, has
the salmon been overfished by the Dutch, as to
render necessary an appeal by the upper proprietors
or riverain states—Prussia, Hesse, Baden, and
Switzerland—to those doctrines of international law
which deny the right of a country, into whose hands
geographical accident has thrown the command of
resources extending beyond its own national limits,
to use or abuse such resources to the detriment of its
neighbours. After much tedious and protracted ne-
gotiation, this appeal has at length been listened to,
and a Treaty was signed the other day at Manheim
between the parties concerned, laying down a code of
laws for the preservation of the Rhine salmon, and
prescribing a fairer annual close time. The weekly
slap, after many vain attempts of the upper States
to induce Holland to accept it, had finally to be
abandoned in order to allow of the Treaty being
signed before the expiration of 1869, on which some
international obligations of Switzerland towards the
German powers were said to be dependent.

Still, salmon is mainly an article of export, or of
consumption by the rich alone in Holland, and is
thus of less real importance to the country, nation-
ally, than the millions of herrings which take the
place of meat in the food supply of the peasantry,
and it is sincerely to be hoped, both for the Dutch
and for ourselves, that some means may be found
ere long to again limit the coast-fishing to the
number of nets the banks can carry without injury

to the future supply. It should be known, however, that this is a subject which has not yet
received a sufficient share of public attention in the
Netherlands.

Of the consumption of fresh-water fish in Holland, no statistics are procurable, and it is therefore
impossible to decide whether the supply is threatened
with exhaustion; it is probable, however, that it is
not, or at any rate not to the same extent as salt-
water fish, for the fresh waters are private property
and jealously preserved, which the sea is not. Eels,
pike, roach, perch, &c., are, however, in daily use as
food among large classes of the population, and the
seasons are but little regarded in connection with
their consumption.

But apart from the question of the probable
decrease of certain food sources in the Netherlands, there exists a growing demand for supplying
the people with more meat. A comparison has been
attempted between the meat consumption of the
masses in Holland and in the neighbouring Kingdom of Belgium, and roughly and imperfectly as
the inquiry has been made, no doubt exists as to
the Belgian consuming the more meat. Some Dutch
political economists, forgetting the mineral resources
of their neighbour, and the absence of fish, which
lie doubtless at the bottom of this consumption of
a more expensive diet, have apparently mistaken the
cause for the effect, arguing that the consumption
of meat has made the Belgian richer than the
Dutchman; whereas the truth evidently is that increased prosperity has been the forerunner of more
meat. To console themselves for their deficiency in
the matter of meat diet, the Dutch next undertook a
series of inquiries on the average of human life, and
the progress of diseases among the meat-eating and
non-meat-eating classes of the population of the

CLASS IV. Netherlands. How accurately this was conducted I cannot say, but it was publicly announced, at the time, that the results were by no means unfavourable to abstinence from meat. The highest and most unfavourable figures are stated to have occurred among those who, leading irregular lives, sometimes well off and sometimes in want, are in the habit, after long abstinence from meat, of eating perhaps little else for a week or so at a time. Whether or no these inquiries were accurately conducted, and the results deserve to be regarded as reliable, for they were prosecuted chiefly by private hand, and not under the authority of Government, a growing demand for meat diet exists in Holland, notwithstanding the increase of that article in price; and sooner or later this demand will infallibly begin to tell on our meat importations.

Grains.

Of grains and flours a rich collection was exhibited at Amsterdam. Messrs. Bouwman, of Rotterdam, exhibited a case containing nearly 250 different kinds. Of their comparative merits it is of course impossible to speak without extending this Report beyond its legitimate limits. English seed is very popular in Holland, and many of the best exhibits in grain and flour were especially advertised as originally grown from English seed. In all these cases the grain was remarkably heavy and full. Peas, beans, canary, &c., also abounded in the Dutch section. The size attained in some specimens of the horse-bean attracted the attention of foreign visitors, and many fruitless inquiries were made as to how the result was obtained. Oats were not well represented. A prejudice exists in Holland against the use of this meal for food, and the little grown is exclusively used for horses and fattening cattle.

Tobacco.

Of tobacco there were plentiful exhibits, both in the leaf and in every stage of preparation. The

Dutch tobacco was pronounced of good quality;
better than the ordinary German, but inferior to the
best French kinds.

Of hops there were none exhibited of Dutch
growth, the plant being little cultivated in the
Netherlands, and an article of importation from
abroad. In the Belgian exhibits they were well represented, though the quality of some cases challenged
the adverse criticism of brewers and other experts.

In dried fruits the Belgian were held to surpass
the Dutch collections.

Among the French agricultural exhibits were
some wheat sheaves and bundles of hemp grown on a
very limited extent of poor ground at Vincennes,
and exhibited by the well-known agriculturalist
Mr. George Ville, as a specimen of what can be done
by artificial and natural manures. A small book
accompanied and explained these interesting exhibits.
It was entitled *Conférences Agricoles faites au Champ
d'Expérience de Vincennes*, and, being in the trade, is
readily procurable by any who do not disdain to inquire whether we have anything to learn from
French science in the art of farming and of adding
by the application of various phosphates to the
weight of corn, length of stalk, and other elements
of rural wealth.

M. Ville also exhibited specimens of the artificial
and natural manures, of the results of which he exhibited the fruits; but the Jury rightly declining to
judge objects, the merits of which are only practically
tested by the ensuing crop, a test for which an Exhibition Jury cannot wait, these interesting and
valuable exhibits were adjudged *hors concours*, and
left to the enterprising agriculturists to test for
themselves. In Holland, where high farming is daily
gaining ground, this test will not be long in being
applied.

Although these remarks have been called forth
by a French exhibit, I should say that we have more
to learn in manures, especially probably in liquefied
farm yard manures, from the Dutch than from the
French; and in my opinion the husbandry of the
Netherlands has not yet received the study it deserves.

Several other countries sent specimens of cereals,
but none of them appeared to call for special notice
or remark, unless, indeed, it be that the bulk of the
exhibitors evidently piqued themselves upon the
extreme whiteness of their flour, in seeming ignorance
of the well-known fact, that perfect purity is alone
attainable by the elimination of the coloured particles
nearest the husks of the grain, which chemists have
declared to contain the largest percentage of pure
albumen.

Maccaroni.

In maccaronis and vermicellis, France was pre-
eminent. First-class collections were displayed by
the great houses of Messrs. J. Brun and Co., of
Lyons, and of Veuve Majuin et Fils, of Claremont-
Terrent. This last is a veteran exhibiting house, and
boasts no less than sixteen gold medals for previous
exhibiting campaigns. It was established in 1820,
and is worked by steam representing 135 horse-
power.

Biscuits.

In fancy biscuits, France was equally in advance
of other Continental nations, though England carried
off the palm in all the plainer sorts.

Drinks.

As might have been expected in a country where,
as a rule, there is,

"Water, water, everywhere,
And not a drop to drink,"

owing to the pollution of canals and the absence of
sweet springs, potations of all kinds and strengths
were largely and well represented : to the dissatis-
faction of many, who would fain have obtained their

exclusion on the ground of the impropriety of giving Class IV. them a diploma as recognized articles of necessity for the working-man. Though not strong enough to obtain their total exclusion, the temperance influence succeeded in getting wines, spirits, and even medicinal cordials adjudged *hors concours;* a decision of some injustice to the working-man, to whom it is undeniably a matter of importance to know where to get a little generous stimulant in cases of ague or more serious illness, without exposing himself to the risk of imbibing liquid fire or absolutely poisonous decoctions. This decision had, indeed, something positively quaint about it, when contrasted with the liberal adjudging of gold medals, &c., within the scope of the exhibition, and consequently for the working-man, to snuffs, tobacco, &c., in all the stages of subtle preparation of which that popular though noxious narcotic is capable.

Although strong drinks were thus under an Beer. official cloud on this occasion, beer was far from being included in this category ; and the high awards conferred upon the exhibits of the Great Royal Netherlands Brewery of Amsterdam, and upon Messrs. Heineken and Co., who resorted to a novel and practical method of advertisement, inserting in the catalogue a printed cheque bearing their official stamp, and worded, " Good for a glass of beer on presentation at the refreshment stall," afforded ample evidence of the very proper preference which those who ruled on this occasion accorded to the use of sound and wholesome ale over intoxicating and spirituous drinks, as a suitable article of consumption for the labourer and artisan.

Another Dutch brewery demanding notice is that of Messrs. Lans and Son, of the Hague, whose barley beer at one penny the three pints, is for its price unsurpassed in Holland.

Breda beer and Maastricht ale, both justly celebrated on the Continent, and exported even to
Germany, the land *par excellence* of beer, were duly
represented and appreciated.

In this connection it remains to mention, in terms
of well-merited praise, the exhibits of the successors
of the great Vienna house of Anton Dreher, of the
Royal Bavarian Breweries, of the great Strasburg
establishment of Messrs. Wagner, and of the far-
famed Lager beer and Koppel beer of Messrs. Ahrens
and Co., of Berlin. All these beers have their merits,
and combine innocence of manufacture with modera-
tion in price.

Taken as a whole, the continental collections in
Class IV, though covering a great deal of ground,
presented little variety of appearance. France, Italy,
and Germany, all had their rows of preserved fruits
and vegetables; lines of oddly-shaped bottles, containing their well-known wines and liqueurs, but
little or nothing calling for remark on the ground of
its originality. Altogether I should be inclined to
say that of all the classes into which the Amsterdam
Exhibition was divided, Class IV exercised least
influence on its visitors, from the absolute impossibility of forming, by inspection, a judgment on any
other quality of its exhibits than their price ; and
this, taken by itself, without the most perfect analyses
and application of tests (to discover, for instance, their
retention of freshness and flavour under various conditions of temperature and keeping), might almost as well,
for all practical purposes, have been written in Runic
characters, or in Cuneiform hieroglyphics. Of all the
countries represented, Denmark was, perhaps, most
worthy of attentive study, on account of the novelty
of many of her smoked and dried provisions, as well
as for the perfect appreciation of the character of the
Exhibition which rendered the Danish Court in

general a model of what the whole Exhibition should have been, but unhappily was not.

The British exhibits in Class IV were of a very high order of excellence, and universally admired. The highest award they gained was a *Diplôme d'Honneur*, conferred upon the renowned firm of Messrs. Allsopp and Son, of Burton-on-Trent, for pale ale, a cosmopolitan drink, the consumption of which is rapidly becoming universal.

The second award in order of rank, a gold medal, fell to Messrs. W. J. Coleman and Co., of 13, St. Mary-at-Hill, London, for Liebig's extract of meat. This house also exhibited Harding's cattle food, mustard, vinegar, and isinglass. Their extract of meat is manufactured on the establishment of Robert Tooth, Esq., of Sydney, Australia, and is used by the Government of India. According to the high authority of the "Lancet," it compares as follows with other similar preparations:—

	Tooth's: Coleman and Co.	Ramornie.	Liebig's Extract of Meat Co.
	Grains.	Grains.	Grains.
Water	17·06	17·83	18·56
Organic alcoholic extractive matter, containing creatine, creatinine, inosic acid, &c. ..	51·28	47·93	45·43
Organic extractive matter insoluble in alcohol	•10·57	•12·92	•13·93
Mineral matter	21·09	21·32	22·08
	100·00	100·00	100·00
•Containing gelatine	7·87	9·63	8·56
„ albumen	0·19	0·62	0·29

Purchasers are warned to beware of having extract made from wild cattle in South America substituted for Tooth's Liebig's extract, which is made in Australia from cattle of English breeds, for this is said to be one secret of its success.

"Diplômes d'excellence." *Diplômes d'excellence*, ranking with gold medals, were conferred on the two following British houses, whose exhibits were deemed beyond the scope of the Exhibition :—

> Messrs. Batty and Co., of 15 and 16, the Pavement, Finsbury, and 8, Finsbury Place, London, for pickles ; and
> Messrs. Peter Rappolt and Co., of 367A, Strand, for gin and liqueurs.

The first of these firms, Messrs. Batty and Co., stands so high as to render comment on their goods superfluous. I annex, however, an interesting memorandum on the pickle trade, by which their exhibits at Amsterdam were accompanied.

Memorandum on the pickle trade. "About fifty years since a great impulse was given to the pickle and provision trade in England by the abolition of the duty on salt, which had previously been £36 per ton, and which was reduced to 30s. per ton. A very increased consumption of all salted and cured provisions immediately ensued ; and a very increased supply of vegetables for pickles, in the preparation of which a large quantity of salt is used, resulted. This increased demand continued steadily for twenty years or more, till at length the English market gardeners were unable to keep pace with the demands of the trade, and prices rose so high as to threaten a reduction of the consumption to its former limits. Under these circumstances Messrs. Batty, accompanied by Mr. Blackwell, of Soho Square, made a voyage to Rotterdam, for the purpose of opening the supply of cauliflowers, gherkins, onions, walnuts, and other vegetables in brine from Holland. Great difficulties were encountered in opening this trade, the chief of which arose from the high price of salt in the Netherlands, which would have precluded a profitable business, the Government being unwilling to permit the use of salt in bond, and, moreover, very suspicious of what uses might be made of it. A specimen of cauliflower was prepared by Messrs. Batty, and after a very lengthened period, during which it was proposed to resort to Belgium in case of refusal, the scruples were removed, the use of salt in bond was granted, and a large trade has ensued, and millions of pounds have passed into the hands of Dutch agriculturists. This trade has been jealously watched by both French and Germans ; but the low freight for these bulky heavy goods has at present prevented any other country competing successfully with Holland. Messrs. Batty alone use, at a low estimate, about sixty hogsheads of vegetables a month, and one house in London a still larger quantity ; and it appears, as English tastes are becoming more and more universal, still larger results may be expected."

Messrs. Batty and Co. further exhibited preserved fruits, jams, jellies, marmalade, and preserved fish. Amongst these there was a novelty demanding notice, viz., strawberries preserved in syrup made from potatoes ; the price is about one-half of what they can be supplied at if preserved in any other manner.

Three silver medals awarded next demand attention. They were bestowed upon— *Silver medals in Class IV.*

> Messrs. Tomlin, Rendell, and Co., the London Agents for the Glencove Company, of Long Island, New York, for maizena.
> Messrs. John Aitcheson and Co., of Edinburgh for Scotch ales ; and
> Messrs. George Borwick and Sons, of 24,

CLASS IV.

Chiswell Street, London, for baking-powder, by means of which it is said that puddings can be made without eggs, bread without yeast, and pastry without much butter.

Bronze medals in Class IV.

Bronze medals fell to—

The Banbury Brewery Company, for brown stout.[1]

Mr. John Green, of 12, Graham's Terrace, Ridley Road, Kingsland, London, for sheet gelatine. This house has a largely increasing Dutch connection, and French gelatine is annually becoming less and less imported into Holland.

Mr. John McCall, of 137, Hounsditch, London, for preserved provisions; and

Mr. Thomas Amey, of the Rushes Farm, Petersfield, Hants, for desiccated and condensed milk.

"Mentions extraordinaires."

Mentions extraordinaires, without the scope of the exhibition, were awarded by the International Jury to the seven following houses :—

Mr. Patrick Auld, of Walbrook House, Walbrook, London, for Australian wines.

Mr. J. Gilbert, of Pusey Vale, South Australia, also for Australian wines.

Messrs. Henley and Son, of Joiner Street, Tooley Street, London, for cider.

Messrs. Huntley and Palmers, of Reading and London, for biscuits. This firm employs upwards of 1,500 hands.

Mr. John Mackay, of 119, George Street, Edinburgh, for quintessences.

Mr. J. T. Morton, of 107, 108, and 109, Leadenhall Street, London, and of Aberdeen, for preserved provisions; and to,

Messrs. Peek, Frean, and Co., of London, for their biscuits, which command an almost universal sale in Holland.

In cooking-stoves Great Britain made on the whole a creditable display, and took undoubted precedence of other countries in this regard. Although some of these stoves and ranges have already received cursory attention in dealing with Class I, which embraced heating generally, I deemed it right to solicit a few notes on the subject from an expert who was in charge at Amsterdam of a large collection of food and cooking exhibits, and who, as a former cookery instructor to the British Army, was entitled to speak with some authority upon various practical points of which I myself was naturally ignorant, and unable otherwise to acquire equally reliable information. As these notes appear to be sufficiently explicit, and not yet too discursive, I beg leave to append them *in extenso*, without further comment.

" The cooking apparatus exhibited in the English Section consisted of—

1. Captain Warren's Army Cooking Stove.
2. Captain Warren's Navy Ship's Hearth.
3. Captain Warren's Domestic Cooking-Stove.
4. Messrs. Duley's Cooking-Stove.
5. Mr. Sparkes Hall's Cottager's Stove.
6. Weygood's Camp Stove.
7. Phillips's Gas Cooking Stove.
8. Hen's, New York, Petroleum Stove.
9. Hepburn's Spirit Stove.

" The only trials that took place were with Nos. 1, 6, 7, 8, 9. They were made under the superintendence of Mr. George Warriner, late Instructor of Cookery to the Army. The trials made with Captain Warren's Army Stove were similar to those so ably described by the late Captain Webber in his report on the testing-house in the Paris Exhibition, with the exception that the various kinds of fuel exhibited were tried, in order to test their quality. It was found that in this stove coke would not answer, wood and turf together did very well, but took a large quantity. Newcastle bituminous coal quickly choked the flues with soot, and even impeded the cooking before being finished. The best coal tried was a steam coal (inland) exhibited by A. Bannister, Esq., of Hull; this gave hardly any smoke, and the cooking was well done; 200 lbs. of potatoes with roast meats being done better than by any other fuel; but as the apparatus was in the open air no satisfactory statistics as regards quantity could be arrived at.

"No. 6. Weygood's Camp Stove is a small stove intended for camp or cottage use. Its peculiarity consists in its having an oven, in which, when required, on removing the cover over the fire any article can be boiled. The top of the stove holds a stewpan or a strainer, and the front of the fire a stand for a Dutch oven. The following were the objects cooked by it: A fruit pie was placed in the oven, it was cooked in 32 minutes. It was removed, the oven door opened, and the boiler put in, with 6 lbs. of salt meat, which took 1 hour 45 minutes. At the expiration of 1 hour 6½ lbs. of dumplings were added. At the same time that the pie was placed in the oven a small plum-pudding was placed in the stewpan on the top, with 3 lbs. of carrots, and within 30 minutes of the meat being ready, 6 lbs. of potatoes were placed on the steamer over the pudding, and were well done in 30 minutes. On the oven, in front of the pie were placed 3 pigeons, with toast, these also took 30 minutes. The period taken to cook the above was 2½ hours, with 10 lbs. of coal;

but it was considered that if the weather had been favourable, or if it had been under cover, $2\frac{1}{2}$ lbs. per hour would have been sufficient.

" No. 7. Phillips's. This stove is described in the reports on the Paris Exhibition, which give an exact description of it; only in the baking I placed the pie over the top burner for 10 minutes so as to cook the interior; the crust got done by the time the fowls were done. I cooked a dinner, with fish, fowls, cutlets, 3 vegetables, and omelette for 6 persons, in 1 hour with 65 feet of gas.

" 8. Petroleum Stove. This is a small cast-iron iron ring 9 inches in diameter and 4 inches deep, with a tin lamp of the same diameter 1 inch deep, having two felt wicks 3 inches long, worked by a small pen and pinion to control the flame. This lamp holds the petroleum, and rests on a small ring or stand. Three pints of water in a small kettle boil in 15 minutes; 6 mutton cutlets are fried in the same amount of time ; a thick beef-steak also in about the same time. It consumes 1 gill of petroleum per hour.

" 9. The Spirit Stove, known as the Rob-Roy, but called in the catalogue " Velocipede Stove," is a small portable copper stewpan, which holds every article required for use, as well as the can to hold the spirits. The heat generator consists of a small circular boiler in copper to hold the spirit ; under this a small quantity of spirit is placed, which, when lighted, quickly heats the spirit in the boiler, the vapour of which passes out through a small pipe that acts as a blowpipe ; the heat from it is excessive, and quickly cooks the object required. This stove is well adapted for travellers in places where a fire is not quickly obtainable.

" No other apparatus was tried. No. 4, Messrs. Duley's Kitchener, is similar to that known as the

Leamington Kitchener, with the exception that a flue passes through the oven. This kind of stove or kitchener is only adapted to burn smokeless coal; bituminous coal quickly fills the flues, and all advantages resulting from them is thereby lost. One has been in use in the Guards' Hospital, Rochester Row, London, for some years with very little repair."

Infants' feeding bottles.
One last article connected with the food question, and exhibited at Amsterdam, calls for some remark, although, and indeed chiefly because, it did not find favour with the chemical members of the Jury to whose examination it was submitted. The article referred is the feeding-bottle, sold by Mr. William Mather, of Manchester, and of 14, Bath Street, Newgate Street, London, at 3s. the dozen. This infants' feeding-bottle meets with so much demand in Lancashire, where I am told its sale is counted by several hundreds of thousands each year, and indeed on the Continent, wherever it has been introduced, that I could not but regard it as my duty to inquire of Professor Gunning, the Government Analyst at Amsterdam, the reasons which had led to its condemnation. These reasons were kindly given to me, promptly and without reserve; and the question being one in which it is of the first importance to challenge criticism, and by all means to arrive at the truth, I do not hesitate to quote them in translation, leaving the further discussion of the knotty points involved to the scientific world. With these objections, which probably apply more or less to all infants' feeding-bottles made upon the same principle, I shall close this review of Class IV :—

" I object to the 'infants' feeding-bottles' in all instances when any part of them is composed of caoutchouc, or any like material.

" There is nothing so ill-suited to the constitution of the human body as the material in question. Milk, which by contact is only slightly tainted with the smell thereof, although this is, perhaps, imperceptible to the keenest sense, must have lost a portion of its quality of quick and easy digestion.

" When, in consequence of suction, the pores of the caoutchouc are enlarged, some portion of milk always remains behind in them, which cannot, or at least cannot without great difficulty, be removed. This milk quickly becomes bad, and spoils the fresh milk with which it comes in contact.

" The caoutchouc material in question is made up of several ingredients. White zinc or white lead is very commonly employed, which are very poisonous.

" My objections are not founded exclusively on à priori conclusion. In this country many fatal cases have happened among infants, which, on solid grounds, may be ascribed to the use of these bottles."

IMPLEMENTS.

Class V was devoted to tools for working-men, by which was principally meant tools to economize time and labour in any trade, or in domestic arrangements. This included tools for gardeners, farm-labourers, and dyke-workers; agricultural implements of all kinds; nets and tackle for fishermen; and sewing-machines. Steam machinery was practically excluded.

These articles, great as is their variety, are capable of classification under one or other of three heads, and thus formed three distinct groups, viz. :—

Implements for field-work.
Implements for the workshop.
Implements for household use.

In this last category many articles would naturally occur that have already received consideration in Class II.

Taking Class V as a whole, it was a collection which contained much that was good, but little that was new, and was consequently of more interest to the Dutch themselves than to foreign visitors. The prejudice existing in Holland against the use of improved implements is so great that one generation of carpenters, gardeners, &c., succeeds another in the use of the homely tools to which they had been bred, and which they regard with affection as the arms borne by their ancestors in their battle through life. Thus the Dutch exhibits in this class were largely composed of models, many of them beautifully executed, of domestic, field, flood, or household equipments. Among them were repre- sentations of the modes pursued in the several provinces comprising the kingdom of the Netherlands, for capturing the scaly population of the deep, which enters so largely into the food-supply of the lower classes. Taking into consideration the limited area of the Netherlands and waters in which the originals of these models are in use, they manifested a remarkable variety both of material and construction, and were by no means capable of being simply divided into the two great varieties one would have expected to find clearly defined, viz., salt and fresh-water fishing gear. There were drag, stake, hand, and casting nets of all sizes, strengths, and shapes; some heavily weighted for deep-sea fishing; others less weighted for shallow waters like the Dollart or the Friesland *Wadden* ;* some of hempen rope, with meshes suitable for monster cod; others of cotton twine, with meshes small enough to hold anchovies; some for salt and some for fresh, some for rapid, some for stagnant, waters; nets for seas, nets for rivers, nets for lakes, —nets, in short, of suitable variety for all the fish that swim.

It might, indeed, be instanced as a striking proof of the self-reliant and self-contained character of the Dutch peasant, be he a ploughboy or a fisherman, that almost every province of Holland, from Groningen in the north to Zeeland in the south, has its own special characteristics in agricultural and piscatorial pursuits to a much greater extent than is the case in England, Scotland, Ireland, and Wales, which form the component parts, on a much larger scale, of the sister kingdom of Great Britain. Each province of Holland has not only its peculiar crop rotation, and mode of draining, cultivating, and enriching the soil,

* Shallows.

but also its own style of architecture, both for dwellings and farm-buildings. In one province the cottages rise like pyramids from the grounds, and at a little distance the walls can hardly be discerned, so low is their perpendicular elevation and so overlapping is the roof. In another, perhaps adjoining, province, the roof is so flat as to be hardly perceptible or distinguished at a distance from the outline of the house itself. The farm-buildings in one province are invariably laid out in a square, of which the dwelling-house forms one side; yet, five minutes' walk from the door, you may cross a canal, constituting, perhaps, a provincial frontier, and you will find the dwelling-house detached from the farm-steading, and at some distance from it; and this with equal invariability and without any apparent cause. In one

Hay.

point only do they all agree, and that is a point of agriculture, in which they are in advance of us, and which British farmers would do well to imitate; it is the universal pyramid thatched roof with protruding eaves with which they protect their haystacks from the rain by day, and from the dew by night. These roofs are suspended between four (or eight if required) strong upright poles, and can be raised or lowered according to requirement, and as the stack, which is begun from the top, is gradually consumed. Who can tell how much of the fine quality of Dutch dairy produce is due to this system, which insures a dry and sweet supply of hay for the cattle throughout the wettest and most inclement winter, and, doubtless, renders service likewise during heat by preventing the hay from getting fiery and brittle. In the Haarlemmer-meer polder, many of the provincial characteristics of Dutch agriculture may be studied side by side; M. Gevers d'Eendegeest, M. Verschuur, and other large landowners, original proprietors from the date of its draining, having erected samples of each for the purpose of comparing results under CLASS V. similar conditions ; the only point in which one and all agree, being the suspended and sliding thatch-roofs for their magnificent stacks of hay.

Among the Dutch agricultural exhibits, one of Madder. great interest was contributed by Mr. Johannes Van den Berge, of Colynsplant, in Zeeland. It consisted of a complete set of the implements used in the cultivation and preparation of madder, an important staple of produce among the southern Dutch peasantry.

Another interesting exhibit was a collection of Dyke-worker's tools. dyke worker's tools and materials, for which the Exhibition was indebted to M. Conrad,* the able head of the Waterstaat Department, on whose exertions the physical existence of the Netherlands is dependent.

Messrs. Pietersen and Co., of the Hague, exhibited Kilns. models of the so-called Hoffmau circular kilns, or ovens for baking earthenware, porcelain, and for burning lime, &c. Their great merits are :—

1. That they allow of uninterrupted use.

2. That they burn any fuel ; coal-dust, saw-dust, or even straw, or dried cow-dung.

3. That the heat, on one oven being let out, is not lost, but passes into the contiguous ovens.

4. That experience of them shows a breakage of only 2 or 3 per cent. on the articles baked, instead of 10 per cent. as in other baking-ovens.

Next in the order of arrangement came book- Bookbinding. binding. This is an industry that has attained considerable development in the Netherlands. The work is always excellently executed, and from 20 to 30 per cent. cheaper than English prices. Utrecht is celebrated for its bookbinding. Dutch books, as a

* Since this was written death has deprived the Netherlands of the invaluable services of this great engineer.

rule, are seldom as sumptuously bound as English library editions, but are invariably solidly sewn, and open much freer than most cheap English bindings of the same class. A book cheaply bound in Holland is usually much more convenient in daily use than a similar English bound book.

Sewing-machines.

Of sewing-machines there was a rich collection at Amsterdam, most of the best known makers being represented. Messrs. Petit, of Brussels, exhibited various cheap models for the working-classes, to whom they are supplied on the building society's principle. For 10 per cent. above the ordinary retail price he furnishes a machine to any working-man of good character, to be paid for in ten monthly payments. By this system the firm of Messrs. Petit boasts that it has raised hundreds of families from actual want to the position of regular investers in a savings' bank.

Knitting-machine.

Messrs. Stokvis and Son, of Rotterdam, exhibited an American knitting-machine capable of making eighteen pair of socks in eight hours' time. Hose, and other articles of under-clothing can also be made by this machine, the cost of which is £14.

M. Citroen's gold chains.

The most important process of construction actually at work within the Exhibition where the lookers-on could trace the various stages of a manufactured article, was a work-table exhibited by Mr. Jacob B. Citroen, of Amsterdam, at which sat five young women engaged in making gold chains by very simple and light hand machinery.

M. Citroen claims credit for having thus discovered an additional industry to which female labour may be advantageously applied. He has been six years in perfecting and simplifying the appliances to this end, and now states himself able to undersell the great German factory of gold chains at Pforzheim. He states, moreover, that he can only attain this result by the employment of female labour, which, while cheaper, is at the same time much more delicate, accurate, and active in all its manipulations. Trusted hands are permitted to take their work home, where, with the aid of a small vice, an oil lamp, and a blow-pipe, a corner of an ordinary deal-table, can be easily converted into a perfect workshop. The girls employed by M. Citroen range between 13 and 18 years of age.

Many of the mats and mattings made by the inmates of the pauper colonies of Frederiksoord, on the borders of the Provinces of Drenthe and Overyssel, were much admired, but were by no means below the ordinary market price.

Though the Dutch pauper colonies are comparatively speaking well known, and though they are not remarkable for their financial success, a brief account of them will not probably be deemed out of place. They date from 1817, in which year, as well as in the previous one, all the crops failed in Holland. Bread attained a fabulous price, the small cultivators were completely ruined, the working-classes starved. Begging assumed such proportions as to constitute a public danger. Relief from such a condition of affairs was sought in the establishment of pauper colonies on the cheapest land procurable ; and Prince Frederick of the Netherlands became President of a society for their organization. Speedily, about £5,000 was collected, and a tract of country purchased, comprising 1,300 acres of fairish land, and 2,600 acres of unreclaimed heath. On these lands four colonies were established ; two called Fredericksoord and Willemsoord for *bond fide* paupers and impoverished families, and two called Veenhuizen and Ommerschans for street beggars and destitute orphans, and to serve as a penitentiary for such of the inhabitants of the former-named colonies as would not work. To support these four establishments a subscription list was opened and signed by 20,000 persons, who agreed to contribute 3½ florins a year a piece.

From 1818 to 1840 it has been calculated that each inhabitant of these colonies has cost, every expense included, 70 florins (say £6) per annum. As, however, the urgent necessity for their support happily disappeared with the return of good harvests, subscriptions fell off. The 20,000 signatures of 1818 dwindled down to 10,666 in 1839, to 7,300 in 1847, and are now represented by a mere nominal roll of a few of the original projectors, meantime the subscription itself has been reduced to 2½ florins.

The objects of the society were :—

1. To support, not in ease but in labour, such poor families as might obtain (on payment of 1,700 florins, £142, spread over sixteen years, and advanced by the parish or individual relieved from the maintenance of the pauper family) eight acres of ground, a house, a pig, agricultural implements, free schooling for children, and medical aid gratis, from the Society. At the expiration of the sixteen years a small rent, representing interest on the capital expended, was to be demanded.

2. To reform beggars, and to instil a love of labour and a desire to better themselves into those who refused to work and were convicted of mendicancy. This class was to undergo a course of training in agriculture, or any trade they might select.

Notwithstanding all the advantages these poor colonists have thus possessed, in having the idle eliminated from their ranks, and all their wants at the commencement supplied, the scheme has not succeeded as a self-supporting institution. Weaving has been introduced, and the cloth sold in large quantities ; yet each year a new demand is now made

on the States-General for money to enable the
Society to make both ends meet, and to pay the
interest on the not inconsiderable debt it has incurred.

Previous to 1864 (when the States-General
assumed the right of disposing of the Java surpluses)
the finances of the Society were kept tolerably well
balanced by subsidies made them now and then by
the King from the Dutch East Indian Revenues, of
which he could practically dispose to the extent of
over £2,000,000 a year by a stroke of his pen. But
times have changed in Holland as elsewhere; and
since the passing of what is known as the Indian
Comptability Law in the session of 1864-65, there
has sprung up among the majority in the Lower
House a constantly growing jealousy of the appropriation of Indian revenues to other than Indian
uses; and letting alone this somewhat tardy growth
of a knowledge of the position colonies should occupy
relatively to the mother-country, the ample means
and surpluses of former years are no longer there to
be disposed of right and left as temporary pressure
might dictate; so that practically the action of the
Second Chamber in this matter, while taking credit
for high philanthropic principles, and sound doctrine
in finance, amounts to little more than making a virtue
of necessity.

However this may be, an item of charge in support of these pauper colonies (established in 1818,
and meant to be self-supporting) is now of annual
occurrence in the Budget of the Dutch Minister for
the Home Department, and amounted in the Estimate
for 1869 to 322,000 florins. For this sum are practically maintained in forced or voluntary labour, in
sickness or in health, about 2,000 orphans and abandoned children, 1,950 bachelor and spinster paupers,
1,250 married paupers, with their families, 4,000

M

beggars, and 650 superannuated soldiers ; that is to
say, 5,850 persons in all, men, women, and children,
being 55 florins, or £4 11s. 8d. a head. Taking into
consideration Drenthe prices, and the indifferent,
or rather what we in England should consider very
indifferent, food supplied, this is far from being a
successful financial result, since paupers are maintained by ordinary machinery at about £5 a year in
Great Britain, where prices range higher, and a more
expensive diet is given. Moreover, if remission of
certain taxation, and some other indirect costs to the
country are taken into consideration, this annual
charge of £4 11s. 8d. a head is raised to £6 13s. 4d.

As a means of reforming mendicity, and of raising
the condition of the small occupiers, the result has
not been more successful than from a mere financial
point of view. Barely 5 per cent. of the small occupiers are stated to have cleared themselves from the
debt they incurred (on entering the Colony) to the
Commune they came from and to the Society, and
have been able after the first sixteen years to pay a
moderate rent ; while discharged beggars, after under-
going their term of reformation, varying from three
months to three years, rapidly fall back into their old
habits of life, many from desire to be reconvicted, and
again find all their wants supplied.

By some, the failure of this laudable attempt is
attributed to too much being done for the Colonists
—their not indeed being allowed to starve. No
habits of self-reliance are created ; and as it is many
years before they can hope to pay off their debts and
really begin to improve their condition, the impetus
acting on them is so remote as to be insufficient to
impel them forwards. Thus we have in Holland a
striking illustration of the fact that, in relieving the
poor, it is better to do too little than too much ; and
better to begin at the top of the ladder of distress

than at the bottom ; relieve those who ordinarily
employ labour, but are temporarily prevented by some
cause from so doing, and the labour-market is itself
again ; but the sudden creation of means of permanent relief, be they *ateliers nationaux* or pauper
colonies, is the planting of a cancer in the body corporate of society—an institution of artificial origin,
requiring artificial support, and representing ultimately purely artificial charity.

In Class V Belgium was meagrely represented. Belgian
One of her exhibits, however, was of so great interest exhibits.
Parachute
to coal-producing countries as to merit particular for coal-pits.
notice. It consisted in models of some improvements
made by M. Nicolas Libotte, of Gilly, in his well-
known *parachutes* for the prevention of accidents in
coal-pits. The principle on which it acts is as follows :—the cage in which the miners ascend and
descend runs between four close-fitting wooden per-
pendiculars. At the top or bottom of the cage are
four claws attached to a very strong spring beam,
which is bent by the weight of the cage to a bow
sufficient to cause the claws to run clear of the woodwork. If the chain or rope by which the cage is
suspended should break, the weight of the cage is
removed from the spring beam, which straightens,
and the claws immediately protruding fix themselves
in the woodwork to the depth of over an inch, and
arrest the further downward rush of the cage. This
principle, subject to some variations in constructive
detail, is in general use in the numerous Belgian
coal-pits, and has saved hundreds of lives in that
country. It is found in practice that when the cord
that suspends the cage snaps, so instantaneous is
the straightening of the spring-beam and the firm
burying of the claws in the woodwork, that the cage
has no time to descend a sufficient distance to
acquire momentum.

Another exhibit demanding attention was a machine for grinding millstones, shown by M. de Marie, of Marchienne-au-Pont. The cost is 400 francs, and it is intended to perform by machinery a process hitherto laboriously performed by hand with great prejudice to the health of the workmen so employed. It obtained a gold medal.

Messrs. Kockeril of Seraing, exhibited an ingenious hydraulic propeller for fishing or other vessels. The propeller is a fly-wheel under the bottom of the vessel, worked by a water-wheel, which is turned in the hold by a simple system of ingress and egress of the motive power—water.

M. Casterman, of Antwerp, exhibited a model oven, heated externally, for rapid and economical bread-baking.

The leading characteristic of the exhibits from the North German Bund in Class V was agricultural. Cheap farm tools were displayed in great profusion ; of hay forks and rakes alone there were upwards of twenty varieties, with wooden, iron, or steel prongs, differing in number, and priced from 1s. 8d. to 5s.

In shoe-lasts Germany was considered by the trade to excel any other competing country at Amsterdam, both in make and cheapness. M. Jos. Knettlmayer, of Passau, exhibited full-size rights and lefts at 36 kreuzers (1s.) the pair, and for ladies at 18 kreuzers (6d.) each.

Mr. Joseph Miles exhibited spectacles and goggles made of glimmer (mica) for protecting the eyes of persons engaged in hurtful occupations. They cost from 8d. to 1s. 1d. a pair, according to finish, and can be had in white and blue. Similar spectacles are in general use in Holland among iron-workers and founders ; and though young hands on entering these establishments are generally prejudiced against their use, this prejudice soon gives way. One great advantage which mica possesses in addition to economy is its value as a remarkable non-conductor of heat. The mica lenses are found to be most popular, and to wear best when set in leather rims of sufficient depth to rest upon the face, and thus completely shield the eye from the possible approach of obnoxious particles.

The exhibits from Baden in this class were confined to some glazed beer barrels, displayed by Jno. Werner and Co., of Mannheim. Some very good manufactured parchment paper or imitation parchment, exhibited by Mr. Carl Brandegger, of Ellwangen, Wurtemberg, attracted a good deal of attention and admiration.

Perhaps the most remarkable among the Austrian exhibits in Class V was a display of india-rubber and caoutchouc articles in all stages of their manufacture, which was traceable from the raw material through the several degrees of vulcanization, required for the various and variable purposes to which it is applied; viz. :—children's playthings, household uses, clothing, chemical processes and a thousand other requirements of our daily lives which render gutta-percha one of the most valuable inventions of, and one of the richest contributions to, modern civilization. A gold medal was bestowed on Mr. J. N. Reithoffer, of Vienna, by whom these articles were exhibited.

The only other Austrian exhibit in Class V to which I shall allude was of great interest to the real working-man, and perhaps more admired and envied by him than any other object in the whole exhibition. I refer to a full-size beech-wood carpenter's bench, exhibited by M. Franz Ritter Von Wertheim, of Vienna, which, with most of the essential tools for common work, was priced at 20 florins, or £1 13s. 4d. This bench was fitted with wooden screw vice and sliding planing-block; and combined great solidity with neatness. It was, I should say, about 7 feet long by 3 wide and 3 high. Numbers of such benches and sets of tools have been ordered from Vienna by the carpentering population of Amsterdam and other Dutch towns in consequence of this exhibit ; and it is believed and hoped that its popularity among those best able to judge of its merits will conduce not a little to promoting the custom of working at home by the piece, instead of working by time in unhealthy workshops, which in Germany has been considered to be an element of such importance in the moral and physical condition of the working-man.

In punches and shears for use in working by the hand metals even of considerable thickness, France had several very good and cheap exhibits, and in one magnificent collection of circular saws, morticing-machines, chisels, and other tools for carpentry on a large scale, she ranked second to none at Amsterdam, and was indeed only equalled by one exhibit from Great Britain, that of Messrs. Dodge, of Sheffield. The display referred to was made by M. Paul Gérard, of 32, Avenue, Daumesnil, Paris, on whom a gold medal was justly bestowed. Its arrangement was such as to show off each article to perfection, and to admit of tangible examination. It certainly sufficed to prove that neither England nor Belgium can calculate with any certainty, or even probability, on permanently supplying France with superior hardware of all kinds. The tools displayed by Mr. Gérard were quite equal to our own in finish and solidity of appearance. Carpenters and shipwrights at Amsterdam, who use these tools, testify moreover to the hardness of their steel, and to their durability in use.

A second collection of carpenters' tools, files, and steel implements in this section, exhibited by

M. Goldenberg, of Le Zornhoff, près Saverne, Bas
Rhin, was equally remarkable for its low prices and
the excellence of its articles, which many Dutch
experts deemed the equals of our own best kinds, and
far superior to the average of Belgian manufactures
in this important class of goods. In short, though
sorry to confess it, I deem it my duty to state that
England could boast of no undoubted lead over
France at Amsterdam in steel and hardened iron.

One article in this Court that attracted a fair
share of attention from the Dutch, to whom it was
quite novel, was a sewing-machine, of which the
motive power was electricity. It was exhibited by
M. Jean Henri Cazal, of 5, Rue de la Chaussée
d'Antin, Paris.

Electric sewing-machines.

An ingenious, but rather too complicated, needle-
threader, exhibited by M. Texier, of Colombes-sur-
Seine, at 1 franc, was also the centre of much
curiosity.

Needle-threader.

The highest order of award, *Diplôme d'Honneur,*
was only conferred on two British houses in Class V.
These were :—

English exhibits in Class V.

> Messrs. Joseph and Robert Dodge, of the
> Continental Works, Sheffield, for tools and
> cutlery.
> Messrs. Kirby, Beard, and Co., of 18, Cannon
> Street, London, and of Birmingham and
> Redditch, for fish-hooks and needles.

The firm of Messrs. Dodge, which has been established for upwards of a century, is too widely and
well-known, both at home and abroad, to need much
remark. Their exhibits at Amsterdam were strictly
within the special scope of the Exhibition, comprising
all the steel tools required by the working man, to
which were added some beautiful specimens of ornamental cutlery; and they afforded a striking proof

Messrs. Dodge.

of the possibility of applying the important accessories of a handsome exterior and attractive appearance even to a purely utilitarian exhibition. Taken altogether, as combining in the highest degree the qualities of which successful exhibits and successful exhibitions are made, the grand octagon display of Messrs. Dodge at Amsterdam deserved all praise, and showed that the firm in question has nothing to fear from the strict application of its own trade motto *Juste Judicato.*

The second of these distinguished British houses, Messrs. Kirby, Beard, and Co., have long been celebrated for their needles, and have lately registered an invention, which they deem important, known as the "indented eye." The advantage gained by this invention is, by flattening the eye, to prevent the bulk of the eye, when threaded, exceeding that of the body of the needle, thus necessitating a jerk to extricate the needle after each stitch. This jerk has hitherto only been avoidable by using a larger needle than the thread requires, and unnecessarily perforating the work with unsightly holes, which the thread inadequately fills up. Another, and perhaps more important invention, is their improved needle for the blind, the aged, and the weak-sighted. The method of threading it is as follows :—The thread, held fast by three fingers, is extended by the forefinger and thumb of the left hand (forming a triangle as it were), the side of the needle (firmly held in the right hand) is pressed along and across the thread, until the opening is found, when the thread passes in at a slit, and is perfectly secure to work with. The Kirby bend fish-hook is too favourably known to need a special notice.

The only gold medal carried off by the exhibits from Great Britain, in Class V, was won by the American firm of W. Lamb, established at New York, for sewing-machines; but two *diplomes d'excellence*, ranking with gold medals, but without the scope of the Exhibition, were obtained by—

Messrs. Johnson, Matthey, and Co., of Hatton Garden, London, for chemical apparatus; and by, The Patent Plumbago Crucible Company, of Battersea, London.

One of the most remarkable objects exhibited in the whole Exhibition was a platinum still and syphon, to concentrate 75 cwts. sulphuric acid per day, displayed by the first of these houses, Messrs. Johnson, Matthey, and Co. The price of this still was £1,240; it was made of chemically pure platinum, and combined all the most recent improvements in construction. The joints were autogenously soldered; the superiority, and indeed absolute perfection, of which process has been fully proved by the results of working more than sixty concentrating boilers, of capacities varying from 150 to 650 litres, in various large and well-known manufactories. Messrs. Crosse and Blackwell are said to use a similarly expensive platinum apparatus for the preparation of their pickles, thereby avoiding all danger from verdigris and other poisonous elements, inseparable from the use of cheaper metals. Messrs. Johnson, Matthey, and Co., further exhibited—

A condenser for syphon of improved construction.

Platinum distilling apparatus.

Platinum tubes, sheet, wire, dishes, crucibles, pans, lightning-conductors, capsules, gauze, &c.

Platinum assay apparatus, by the use of which gold assays can be made with greatly increased accuracy, rapidity, and economy.

Iridio-platinum gun-vents, for heavy ordnance.

Platinum in various forms—native, sponge, alloy, salts.

Nugget of native platinum, weight 4,728 grammes, of very perfect form (only one larger specimen known to exist).

Precious and rare metals—iridium, osmium, rhodium, ruthenium, palladium.

Ingot of pure palladium, value 48,000 francs, extracted by Messrs. Johnson, Matthey, and Co. from native platinum and gold, of the value of 26,000,000 francs.

Palladium—wire, sheet, foil, sponge.

Pure distilled magnesium — wire, ribbon, powder, &c.

And other chemical and metallurgical products.

Plumbago Crucible Company. The second of these firms—the Patent Plumbago Crucible Company—exhibited Morgan's patent crucibles for melting gold, silver, copper, brass, iron, steel, &c.; clay crucibles for refining the precious metals, portable smelting furnaces, portable muffle furnaces, scorifiers, roasting dishes for assaying silver, lead, &c.; porous battery cells, &c. These articles have been in use for many years in the English, Colonial, French, and other mints and arsenals, and have been adopted by most large engineers, founders, and refiners. They claim uniformity of quality, and power to withstand the greatest heat. Their average durability for gold, silver, and ordinary pourings is stated at 45 pourings, though they sometimes endure 100. This is a matter of great importance to manufacturers in estimating their value, since every new crucible entails heavy loss on the founder, owing to the quantity of metal which adheres to and impregnates them, rendering the loss on the first twenty pourings in a new crucible much greater than

on the pourings that follow, so that the older the
crucible the less the loss.

Silver medals in Class V were bestowed on no
less than eleven British houses. They were :—

Messrs. Ashby and Jeffery, of Stamford, Lin-
colnshire, for agricaltural implements. The
articles exhibited comprised portable mills,
wheel hand-rakes, turnip-cutters, chaff-cut-
ters, and oil-cake breakers. It is probable
that ere long, as high farming is on the
increase in Holland, there will be a large
demand from that country for articles made
by this firm.

Messrs. Wm. Hounsell and Co., of the North
Mills, Bridport, for fishing-nets. This house
also sells hemp cod, log, clothes, and other
lines, at very reasonable rates.

Messrs. Woods, Cocksedge, and Warren, of
Stowmarket, for agricultural implements of
various kinds. The agricultural steam-
engines, from 1 to 10 horse-power, made
by this house, are justly popular both in
England and abroad, as they require no
fixing, burn any fuel, are easily made portable, and are fitted with hot-water tanks
and other improvements. Their prices
are :—

Horse-power.	Diameter of Cylinder.	Stroke.	Price.
	Inches.	Inches.	£
1	3½	7½	45
2	4½	9	60
3	5¼	11	80
4	6	13	100
6	7¼	14	130
7	8	14	150
8	8½	15	175

If fitted with hot-water tank, 3 horse-power, £2 10s.; 4 horse-power, £3 10s.; 6 horse-power, £5, extra. Larger sizes made to order.

Messrs. D. F. Tayler and Co., of the New Hall Works, Birmingham, for pins and needles. This house also exhibited pearl buttons, and iron and steel wire.

Messrs. W. Woodfield and Son, of the Ease-more Works, Redditch, for needles.

Messrs. Hayes and Crossley, of 150, Cheap-side, and of Alcester, also for needles. Besides ordinary needles, sharps, blunts, &c., this firm has a large business in machine-needles of all kinds.

Messrs. W. Warne and Co., of 9, Gresham Street, London, for india-rubber goods.

Messrs. Sellers and Co., of 12, Walbrook, London, and Keighley, Yorkshire, for sew-ing-machines. These are made on the Wheeler and Wilson principle, with patented improvements, and their sale has already reached half-a-million. They are largely used in Ireland, as well as in England. The retail price is £7 10s.; and when it is considered that the wholesale price is £4 10s., it will be seen at a glance what benefit might accrue to the working-classes from the establishment of a society on the Belgian principle previously alluded to, for purchasing such machines wholesale, and distributing them among deserving families at their cost price; *plus*, if necessary, the cost of management, which would—or, rather, should—be a mere trifle.

The North American Sewing-machine Com-pany, New Brunswick, Canada; Agency, 5,

Falcon Square, London, also for sewing-machines. This is the original and improved "Weed," with the lock-stitch.

Mr. John J. Rollins, of Old Swan Wharf, London Bridge, for tools and implements.

Messrs. Wheeler and Wilson, of London, also for sewing-machines.

The one bronze medal bestowed on British exhibitors in Class V fell to—

Messrs. Allen and Cragg, of Lowestoft, for fishing-nets. This house does a very large business, and is especially famous for its mackerel and herring-nets of every sort, size, and weight, made of the best American cotton.

Honourable mention by the International Jury was bestowed upon—

Mr. Joseph Sparkes Hall, of 308, Regent Street, London, for a shoemaker's upright bench, price 25s.

As this is a matter of vital importance to a considerable section of the great community of working men, I shall allow Mr. Sparkes Hall to tell his own brief but interesting tale by transcribing the following memorandum which fell into my hands at Amsterdam. To many readers other trades will no doubt occur in which the posture during work has not received sufficient consideration. Let us hope that all employers of the most precious raw material that any country can possess—labour—will imitate the example thus set them by a thoughtful and practical cobbler :—

" Boys should be taught to make and mend boots

and shoes in an upright posture. The trade is by no means an unhealthy one, and it is only necessary to adopt a proper position of the body and a suitable bench to render it one of the most useful, remunerative, and pleasing of occupations.

" The fact is notorious that more mind has been manifested among the humble fraternity of shoemakers than has been found amongst any other equally humble class of the community.

" John Pounds worked at shoemaking while he conceived and practically carried out the first ragged school, and those celebrated shoemakers, Carey, Gifford, Bloomfield, Drewe, Kitts, and Devlin, all taught the necessity of 'sticking to the last,' as boys, and, of going beyond it as men. Even Lord Byron praises the occupation :

> " ' Ye tuneful cobblers, still your notes prolong,
> Compose at once a slipper and a song.'

" It is, however, generally known that the bent, sitting posture in which shoemakers work is highly injurious to health. The posture is maintained for generally 12 or 14 hours in a confined atmosphere, the spine, stomach, and bowels become disordered ; and, at a comparatively early age, numbers of this class solicit from us admission to the Hospital for Consumption.

" The Society of Arts, always the first in promoting the welfare of the industrious workman, thirty years since turned its attention to a remedy for this evil, and encouraged several ingenious contrivances which were successively brought out, exhibited, and rewarded, but never adopted.

" Ingenious as they were, and made generally by scientific men and engineers, I believe they failed simply because they were not practically useful, and because they were too expensive. My attention was directed to this subject some months since, on visiting some of my workmen in an attic near Soho Square, where I found one young man bending over his work, with a bright eye and a flushed cheek—indications which I knew too well of rapid decline, caused, I have no doubt, by the posture of his body and close application. I suggested an upright posture, and asked him if he had ever seen a bench that would enable him to stand at his work. He replied that he had seen some contrivance at Mr. Dennis's, in Pulteney Street, and would most willingly accompany me there. We went together, but found that the bench had been for some time past sold, or, as Mr. Dennis said, almost given away to get rid of it.

"Shortly after this, Dr. King Chambers delivered his lecture on 'Industrial Pathology' at the Society of Arts, and I was the more impressed with the importance of a reform in the manner of shoemaking. He said:—'Shoemakers and bootmakers suffer equally from a constrained position, and also from the pressure of the last against the stomach. A patient of mine, now in St. Mary's Hospital, has a hollow big enough to put one's fist into from the pressure inwards of the breast-bone by the last; of course his lungs and heart are diseased by such distortion. Cannot some one devise a new sort of last which will not drive its tap-roots into people's lungs?'

"I immediately turned my attention to an upright bench, and having met with an ingenious and practical shoemaker (Mr. Herapath), who had recently returned from America, and, being in delicate health, had adopted the standing posture with great advantage. Together we contrived a really useful, practical, and cheap bench, which will meet all the requirements of the juvenile as well as of the adult shoemaker.

"The work can be carried on, on the whole, better in a standing than sitting posture; but that certain parts of rounding the soles, lasting, or fitting may be done on the knees, a stool is added to the bench, which enables the workman to sit as long as he likes, and resume his standing position immediately after. I may, however, repeat to the young shoemaker advice which, perhaps, he has often heard before—

" 'Stand and grow good.'

"It is very desirable that boys in industrial schools should be taught to take casts and models of the feet in plaster of Paris ; it is soon acquired, and will give them a good idea of the true form of the human foot. This should be followed by last-making, which is a very important branch of trade, and is seldom conducted properly.

"The form of the foot must be studied from nature, and not from lasts made from old and useless patterns, which, in ninety-nine cases out of a hundred, had better have been burnt. The public have a right, now they are about to pay for industrial education, to demand a good industrial understanding."

In addition to this bench, Mr. J. Sparkes Hall exhibited excellent specimens of good and cheap boots and shoes for the poor. Among them is a cheap waterproof shoe, composed chiefly of felt and india-rubber. It requires little cleaning, is neat in appearance, and sells at 30s. the dozen pairs in sorted sizes. A stouter kind is sold at 35s., and children's boots at 24s. the dozen pairs. A still more economical article is sold for indoor wear—the old-fashioned list shoe, valuable for people obliged to stand much on stone floors. These are made up by industrious poor women in London, and are sold at 20s. the dozen pairs. The Crown Princess of Prussia is said to have introduced these cheap articles among the poor at Berlin, where they are very popular. Mr. J.

Sparkes Hall is also inventor of a patent sanitary ventilator for dwellings, price 20s.

Four British exhibiting houses in Class V received extraordinary mention, viz. :—

Mr. John Hynam, of 7, Prince's Square, Wilson Street, Finsbury, London, for plumbago crucibles for melting steel, malleable iron, copper, brass, zinc, antimony, &c. Mr. Hynam further exhibited, in Class II, Fuller's earth in lump and powder for manufacturing and domestic use, and an anti-friction powder.

Messrs. J. B. Brown and Co., of 90, Cannon Street, London, for wire-netting. This firm also exhibited their new patent B B lawn mowing-machines, garden-seats, &c. These articles were all of excellent quality, yet though it is alleged that the galvanized wire-netting is much used by the rural working man for confining poultry, &c., it will probably be generally deemed to have been rightly adjudged as without the scope of the Exhibition, and thus the exhibits of this firm afford an example of a class of article which, had the original purely utilitarian point of view been maintained, it would have been difficult to admit, and perhaps hard to exclude.

Messrs. Clarke and Dunham, of 48, Mark Lane, London, for articles for flour and rice-mills. This house further exhibited their patent needle lubricator, of which over 2,000,000 are said to be in operation; and a great variety of oil-testers, presses for stamping metal, belt-fasteners, smut-clearing machines, pressure and vacuum-gauges, and a fire-proof corn-

N

scouring engine, for preventing the dust from injuring the sight or entering the lungs of the workman, without creating the friction that compels insurance offices to make such heavy charges.

Mr. William Robinson, of Bridgewater, Somerset, for a cask-cleaning machine. The merits of this patent are sufficiently well known. It has received prizes at many previous exhibitions, and though an object of interest to the Dutch at Amsterdam, had little or no connection with the objects there aimed at.

INSTRUCTION AND RECREATION.

CLASS VI was set apart for means of moral, physical, and intellectual development. It included
within these elastic limits all principles and theories
of education, especially technical education, and of
recreation. Under the former heading ranked
principally school books and educational methods;
and under the latter were to be found popular
romances, gymnastic exercises, music, singing, games,
and toys. Lastly, Class VI included secondary
trades, things to be done in spare time, and employments for women and girls at home. Of the 256
exhibits composing this class, the Netherlands counted
113; and thus their collection wore an aspect of completeness to which no other country in Class VI could
compare. For this reason Holland will occupy the
first and largest share of our attention.

Of objects made in leisure hours, there was a
great variety of models in various materials, wood,
cork, cardboard, metal, &c. There were models, more
or less well executed, of many of the celebrated
buildings, and of most of the historical monuments
of the Netherlands; but it was mainly in practical
modelling—models of steam and water mills; of
locks, docks, and shipping; in raised models showing
the drainage of a town or district; and models of
foundations, staircases, or other architectural and
building details of construction, in which the mor-
ticing, courses, &c., were accurately pourtrayed—that

N 2

Holland excelled, and in these the industrious and
practical spirit of the people was conspicuous. Especial attention was attracted by a very complete model
$\frac{1}{15}$ of real size, of the diamond-cutting and polishing
machinery used in the celebrated establishment of
Mr. E. Coster, at Amsterdam. The whole of this
model was made by the exhibitor, Mr. N. Engel-
brecht, in spare time ; and its engines were wonderful
specimens of handiwork ; another striking model of
machinery was a perpendicular steam-engine, with
parallel action, entirely made by hand (with the exception of the cylinder), of hammered iron and copper, and
exhibited by Mr. D. C. Endest, of Amsterdam. A third
hardly less remarkable exhibit was that of Mr. G. H.
Kerbel, also an Amsterdam mechanic, of a low pressure steam-engine. A fourth deserving notice was a
hand-made horizontal engine, made and exhibited by
Mr. H. G. Theys. Fifthly, and lastly, there was a very
perfect and satisfactory model of a machine for doing
heavy boring work in metals by the hand. Among
these and other exhibits of the same description,
medals and awards were freely distributed.

Anna Paw-
lowna Infant
School.

Turning from the perfection of workmanship displayed in the above articles, mostly made by adult or
at least adolescent labour, some exhibits of a different
order demand attention. These were as remarkable
for want of finish and beauty, as the first mentioned
were conspicuous for those qualities, but they were
none the less interesting or praiseworthy on that
account. They were rude models, and drawings of an
elementary order, executed, under the direction of the
attendant nurses, on the well-known Fröbel method,
by the children of the Anna Pawlowna *bewaar* or

Amsterdam
Industrial
Girls' School.

infant school at Amsterdam. Ascending in the scale
again, there were objects, some in straw-plaiting, but
most of them in needlework, exhibited by an Industrial Girls' School at Amsterdam, established in 1865,

mainly by the efforts of the (in Holland) ubiquitous Society for promoting the public weal. *Maatschappy tot Nut van't Algemeen.* It is difficult to describe these exhibits in detail, but those who best knew the circumstances under which they had been produced, and the ages of the hands employed, deemed them satisfactory proofs of the practical nature of the instruction which, under what is really a compulsory educational law, is imparted to every child, male or female, in the Netherlands.

King William's House.

Next in order came exhibits from the King William's House at Amsterdam. These were principally books and methods of teaching in use in this institution, of which the first stone was laid in the name of the King in 1863, by its projector, the practical philanthropist, Mr. C. A. Adam Van Scheltema. This institution is as nearly as possible a copy of the Working-Men's Hall established at Shrewsbury by Mrs. J. B. Wightman, to whom Mr. Van Scheltema acknowledges himself indebted for the idea. Its functions are various : to promote and disseminate education among adults as well as among the young, and to reclaim habitual drunkards ; it has also a reformatory attached, and has Bible-meetings, singing-classes, public kitchens, &c. Its activity does not even stop here, for it has agents to visit the poor and make suggestions to their landlords and others, respecting domestic arrangements, drainage, good drink-water supply and the like. This last element of health it has introduced into 608 households in Amsterdam alone.

Noordwyk WorkSupply Association.

A third institution demanding notice on account of its exhibits at Amsterdam, is the Work Association of Noordwyk, established in October, 1868, for the purpose of finding work when labour is in excess of the demands upon it, or when the labour-market is temporarily overstocked, owing to the cessation of

CLASS VI. some industry or the closing of some manufactory, Its exhibits were remarkable alike for variety, good quality, and cheapness. They consisted in school-knapsacks, leather slippers, hassocks, trunks, purses, linen and cotton balls for gardeners, cushions, potato-sacks, hat-boxes, and many other articles of small carpentry or constructed of wood, leather, canvas, cloth, paper, &c. Though this Society has hardly been in activity a year, it has already rendered great service to the labourer, and has paid its own expenses, thus taking rank among the most valuable of philan-thropic inventions, those that are self-supporting, and even capable of paying a dividend if required.

Nut Van't Algemeen Society.

Lastly among this class of associations comes the parent, one may say, of them all—the *Society tot nut Van't Algemeen* (for the Public Weal). This insti-tution was established in 1784 by Pastor J. Nieu-wenhuizen, Protestant Minister at Monnikendam. It soars above the petty differences of politics, sects, and denominations, and bestows charity wherever it is most needed. This element of its constitution proved sufficient for its success in a country torn by dissentient creeds, as the Netherlands had been. It spread throughout the country, and established branches in every community where eight paying subscribers could be found. These now number up-wards of 15,000, each paying 2½ florins per annum. This sum is raised by communal contributions to 100,000 florins, and with these small nominal re-sources (I say nominal, as other sources of revenue exist, legacies, donations, &c.), more real good is done in Holland than can possibly be expressed on paper. The society makes it a duty to look after the educa-tional and other moral and physical requirements of those, whoever they may be, that most need assist-ance ; and exercises, under a perfect system of cen-tralized as well as local administration, a power and influence for good greater than can easily be imagined or expressed. I infinitely regret that neither time nor space allow of my following out in more detail the thousand ramifications of this magnificent monument of human charity. The matter is too large to be satisfactorily discussed in a cursory way, and is well worthy of being made the subject of separate study and report.

Of illustrated and popular works for imparting knowledge, there was a rich profusion headed by some beautiful and cheap editions of the "Wonders of Knowledge," and other books bearing the well-known name of the historical publishing house of Messrs. Belinfante, of the Hague.

The state of middle class and technical education in the Netherlands was well represented by a good collection of drawings, busts, models, &c., displayed by a large number of schools, and was singularly complete and satisfactory. This collection was well arranged by itself in a long gallery, and formed one of the most striking departments of the Exhibition. The three Government inspectors of this class of instruction in Holland, Drs. Steyn Parvé, Bosscha, and Staring, had invited all the schools under their control to exhibit specimens of drawing. In this way was established a close competition of upwards of 40 schools that had responded to the invitation. Of these, 4 were day and evening schools, 16 were evening schools, 5 were drawing academies, and 15 were drawing schools; besides this there were the various trades and industrial schools of Amsterdam. All of these drawings were divided into four classes :—

(a.) Drawings from nature.

(b.) Drawings from copies.

(c.) Rectilinear, architectural, and technical drawings, both from copies and from models.

(*d.*) Designs of buildings, &c., made by the scholars themselves.

The number of drawings sent up for exhibition was so great that the inspectors were compelled to undertake the arduous task of making a selection of the most remarkable, to hang on the walls and place upon the tables, and in conspicuous places; the remainder being left in portfolios and boxes piled under the tables. For a detailed description of the schools themselves, of the school-money demanded for this class of instruction, of the ages of the scholars, &c., I would refer to an excellent Report on middle-class education in Holland, communicated by Baron Mackay to Her Majesty's Commissioners, and published among their Reports on Technical and Primary Education presented to Parliament rather more than a year ago. As regards the results exhibited, however, I must venture to express the opinion that technical and rectilinear drawings seemed in many schools to have been less studied than classical drawing; and that much of the scholar's time is evidently wasted on very fine shading which might probably have been better utilized in rough outline and perpendicular work.

The original designs for buildings exhibited under head (*d*) were not so numerous as might have been expected, but would have elicited the approval of Mr. Ruskin for the appreciation manifested of the superior importance of practical architectural requirements over barren ornament and fictitious display.

The models exhibited (such as are in general use) for teaching rectilinear and perpendicular drawing deserve all praise. They were of the solid and outline kinds, and made of wood, iron, card, &c. Some of the most successful are those with a narrow metal outline, intersected by strings or wire attached to the different points and angles, thus visibly cutting up the solid body into several parts, the respective outlines of which, and their mode of cutting one another, are even more clearly thus defined than they are in the glass or other transparent models sometimes used. Of plaster casts there was a rich collection. Each school receives a donation of these from Government on its original opening. The drawings from them exhibited by one or two Girls' schools were admired for freeness of pencil and successful colouring.

As a branch or basis of technical education the practice of drawing from nature, from models and plaster casts, followed in these middle-class schools, is probably carried as far as is desirable in this country. There is great danger, when the scholars of some one school have attained a high degree of excellence in shading, say, or even in perspective, of pushing the ordinary standard too high for general purposes. The object is, after all, not so much to make a nation of artists as a nation of skilled artisans, capable of building the best houses, doing the best carpentry, ironwork, &c., and mixing the best colours in painting, in carpets, in prints, or in wall-papers. To the more gifted scholars, born to reach the higher realms of art, a comparatively low standard will suffice to indicate the right track ; while to society at large, how heavy a percentage of school time, which is a given and a small quantity in a workman's life, may be wasted in bringing the majority up to the level of the few in any one single branch. This is a pitfall into which many German Trades' schools have fallen. In many of these the higher branches of physics and even of metaphysics, as taught by Pouillet-Müller and Fichte, are studied by future carpenters and glaziers. I speak not from hearsay but from personal experience, as when young I attended more than one such *Gewerbeschule* in

CLASS VI. Germany, and the evil of over-education has certainly not decreased since those days. Speaking generally I should say, that in this matter, the importance of which to the bulk of the population it is impossible to exaggerate, Holland has chosen a medium and a happy compromise between the excessive course of instruction given in Germany and the less pretentious national education of France, which, with all its defects, is sufficient to produce skilled labour of the highest class to such an extent as to have awakened jealousy in the hearts of most of the British artisans deputed by the Society of Arts and Manufactures to visit Paris in 1867.

To return to details, the drawing academies of Rotterdam and Groningen were conspicuous on account of their satisfactory exhibits. The latter displayed landscape drawings from nature of a high order, and the former was remarkable for its representations of industrial appliances.

The schools of Rosendaal, Roermond, Deventer, Kampen, Zwolle, Hoorn, the Helder, Haarlem, Alkmaar, Zaandam, Utrecht, Arnheim, Zeist, and Gouda, also contributed drawings and models to compete in what was really a valuable national collection of methods for instilling technical education, and of the results with which the efforts of the Government and the public of the Netherlands in this matter have been crowned.

Mathesis Scientiarum Genetrix of Leyden. To complete a very cursory and insufficient review of this section, it is necessary to mention the portfolios of drawings exhibited by the Society *Mathesis Scientiarum Genetrix* of Leyden. This society was established so early as 1785 by the Brothers Van Campen, Pieter Rÿk, and Bartholomeus Van den Broeck, all architects, land-measurers, and practical men, to whom belongs the honour of having first detected the necessity of technical education in the Netherlands. From the path of utility traced for this institution by its founders, successive governors and patrons have never swerved, but constantly introducing every novel educational appliance, such as the Dupuis or Pestalozzi method, &c., this school has persevered for eighty-three years in its endeavours to create good citizens and skilful artisans ; and at this honoured work it still continues to labour with success.

The Dutch law provides that there shall be at least one technical school (where drawing, modelling, &c., shall be taught) to every 10,000 of the total population.

Among the most complete of the Belgian ex- hibits in this class were those sent by the *Crèche Ecole Gardienne* of Saint-Josse-ten-Noode-Lez-Bruxelles. This establishment has just entered on its twenty-third year of usefulness. It takes charge of every baby brought to its doors, from the ninth day after its birth to its thirteenth year, and is divided into three departments ; first, the *Crèche*, in which babies are kept on payment of 6 or 12 cents a day, according to age, or gratis if indigent, until they attain the age of thirty months ; secondly, the *Ecole Gardienne*, to which they are then transferred, and where they are attended to gratis, or for an additional one or two cents a day. This branch of the establishment takes in children by the day at similar rates. Here they remain until their seventh year, when they are transferred to the third and highest division, the *Section Professionnelle*, either gratis, or on payment of an additional two, four, or six cents per diem, according to their age. On attaining their thirteenth year, the boys are apprenticed to trades, and the indigent girls are put into Government schools of extended primary instruction, whence they take service, or are provided for as school-mistresses, &c. In the medium division from thirty months to six years of age, straw-plaiting, twisting paper, folding and cutting paper, and rough drawing and modelling in clay after the Fröbel method are taught. In the *Ecole Professionnelle*, reading, writing, the elements of arithmetic, grammar, and European geography, with a little natural history, are taught. In the case of girls, needle-work of different kinds is added, with boys, drawing, modelling, &c., are pushed to greater perfection.

The Budget of this valuable institution, which is one of the best in Belgium, and equal to the requirements of a large and average poor faubourg of 21,000 inhabitants, was as follows for 1868 :—

RECEIPTS.

	Frs.	c.	Frs.	c.
En caisse au 1 Janvier ..	..		10,260	58
Souscriptions	4,526	0		
Subsides de l'Etat ..	1,000	0		
„ de la Province ..	750	0		
„ de St. Josse-ten-Noode ..	1,500	0		
„ de Schaerbeck ..	500	0		
Rétribution de la Crèche ..	641	88		
„ de l'Ecole Gardienne' ..	579	96		
„ de la division supérieure ..	223	48		
„ du gardiennât..	308	9		
Rétributions des soupes ..	2,011	50		
Recette brute des fêtes ..	5,167	12		
Dons	3,368	41		
Legs de Mme. Rose ..	2,179	80		
			22,756	24
Total			33,016	82

EXPENDITURE.

	Frs.	c.
Loyer	2,906	40
Contributions, &c.	196	60
Entretien de l'immeuble	126	87
Ménage journalier	4,633	90
„ des soupes	2,157	10
Lingerie et entretien de la Crèche ..	311	30
Chauffage	604	20
Eclairage..	419	25
Frais de recondrement	452	60
Frais des fêtes	3,315	94
Traitements et salaires	3,528	45
Médicaments	26	70
Frais de la distribution des prix ..	364	89
Entretien du jardin	42	89
„ du mobilier	238	8
Impressions	349	35
Objets classiques	177	14
Divers	53	6
En caisse au 31 Décembre	13,111	80
Total	33,016	82

When established in 1848 this establishment had only 35 regular inmates; it now counts nearly 300.

A gold medal was awarded in this Section to Mr. J. S. Van Doosselaere, for publishing 220 educational works in Flemish and in French. IIis press is established at Ghent, and is open to all concerned in educational literature on the lowest possible terms. As a successful disseminator of knowledge, Mr. Doosselaere deserves the highest praise.

The Communal School of Ghent made a good display at Amsterdam of its books and working models. It further exhibited specimens of forms and benches with backs and writing-desks attached, varying in size and design according to the age and sex of the children for whom they were intended. Considering that, at 8 hours a-day, at the estimate of 250 days in the year, deducting Sundays and holidays, a child, in the course of 8 years' schooling, from 5 to 13, would spend 16,000 hours, or two-thirds of the best of its growing days, in a fixed position, it is certainly desirable to insure that position being the least harmful attainable.

Two more Belgian exhibits call for notice ; those representing the *Ecole Professionnelle des Jeunes Filles* at Brussels, and the *Ecole Industrielle et Communale* at Verviers. Both these were remarkable : the first for the taste displayed in designs for needle, worsted, and other work ; the second for excellent drawings of machinery and industrial processes, well calculated to leave a lasting impression on the scholars by whom they have been so skilfully executed, with a demand for further knowledge.

The Prussian exhibits in the class devoted to education, recreation, and improvement, moral and physical, were few, and were, with two exceptions, confined to school books. The first exception was a collection of the well-known and excellent *Kindergarten* toys ; and the second, suggestive of the real game for which the German youth is being educated, was a well-executed model, made in spare time, and exhibited by Gustav Hartmann, of Reichenbach, of a rifled cannon ready to take the field.

Weimar and Darmstadt had some good technical books and periodicals.

Austria also sent little in this class, but the little was of first-rate quality. The *Gewerbschule Jägerzeile*, of Vienna, exhibited a portfolio of satisfactory architectural and rectilinear drawings, and Herr Franz Ritter Van Werthheim, of No. 14, Schwarzenbergplatz, Vienna, exhibited French and

German editions of a work with plates, price 30 thalers (£4 10s.), and entitled *Werkzeugkunde.* This book, of which a counterpart, if not translation, should have its place upon the bookshelf of every industrial school in Europe, is intended, as its name denotes, to convey a popular knowledge of all the tools and implements in daily use, and thought little of on that account, but without which our condition would resemble that of the red Indian, and we should be compelled to live in caves or wigwams, clothe ourselves in skins or bark, and derive our only sustenance from wild fruits, roots, and the proceeds of a chase in which the bow and arrow would play the part of firearms and explosive ammunition.

France, that is to say, the French Minister of Public Instruction, exhibited in Class VI a magnificent and complete collection of books, models, and every appliance suitable to the most advanced state of national technical education, but the favourable impression created by this splendid display of implements for mental culture was somewhat dispelled by a careful study of a series of very beautifully executed maps by M. Manier, entitled *Statistique de Progrès Intellectuel en France et en Europe.* According to these charts of human knowledge, France is still behind many of her neighbours, not only in technical but even in elementary education. Jules Simon has said in a self-satisfied strain that, *Le peuple qui a les meilleures écoles est le premier peuple; s'il ne l'est pas aujourd'hui il le sera demain.* But there would hardly appear to be sufficient statistical evidence to prove that the greatness of France is as yet traceable to the cause given in that liberal formula; for these tables state that, during the period 1858–67, there were, of 380 communes in the Department Maine et Loire, 288 wherein 25·82 per cent. of the population could neither read nor write. It also appeared that in 1866, of a total population of 33,000,000, 28 per cent. of the men, and 48 per cent. of the women could not read ; while 40 per cent. of the men and 60 per cent. of the women could not write, *i.e.*, could not sign their names. In the Department of Dordogne 58·18 per cent. of the men and 76·17 of the women, who were married, were unable to sign the register. This was in 1867 ; in the same Department, 43·82 per cent. of the *conscrits* could neither read nor write ; and evasion of school attendance, which is a good index of the value popularly set on education, as it requires more or less connivance on the part of parents, reached the high figure of 42·50 per cent. on the school-going population. Yet this is a picture, drawn by its own schoolmasters, of the country of which Napoleon III said years ago, *Dans le pays du suffrage universel tout citoyen doit savoir lire et écrire ;* and which spends 1·25 per cent. of its national income on education.

With the exception of the fine official display above referred to, the results exhibited of this expenditure were meagre. *Les frères de la doctrine Chrétienne,* established at Passy, displayed methods of instruction, models, and such like, and some very good specimens of drawing. The architectural and machine drawing exhibited by the *Noviciat préparatoire,* were remarkable for sharpness of outline and regularity of colouring. The *Pensionnat de Passy* exhibited a few good crayon drawings of plants, animals, &c., done by boys and girls under 17 years of age, and some exhibits of the *Ecole de Dessin,* of the Rue d'Apas, Paris, were universally admired ; yet all these exhibits partook rather of the nature of upper middle class, or higher, than of middle, popular, or technical education, and were all flowers culled as it were from Parisian forcing-beds. From the provinces there was nothing but statistics of no very reassuring kind; and taken as a whole the French collection in this class, while showing the importance with which the authorities clothe the subject, also seemed to show that little progress has been made since Mr. Matthew Arnold reported upon French popular education in 1860, as "unpretending" and "of a low level;" and would indicate apparently that the yearnings and heartburnings of our artisans who visited Paris in 1867, for improved technical instruction at home, were misplaced; inasmuch as the results in taste and workmanship, for which they envied their French brethren (of whom a dozen are affirmed to be capable of carving a head in the material they work to one so developed in Great Britain), are due to the innate perception of art and the beautiful which belongs to the former, and which he has opportunities of improving every Sunday and holiday in the galleries of the Louvre and the Luxembourg, rather than to the regular dissemination of technical instruction. "The architecture of Paris is a great school," and the mere fact of walking daily down the Rue de Rivoli on his way to work, can hardly fail to exercise an educating influence on the Paris artisan. Since, however, we lack this medium of conveying instruction, and persist in our refusal to open our museums and galleries on the days and hours when alone the working-man can visit them, it behoves us all the more to endeavour to provide for our artisans such counterbalancing advantages as can be found in an extended system of *Gewerbschulen*, and schools of art and industry, instead of sheltering ourselves behind the only half true and, after all, sad consolation, that our neighbours and our rivals are really but very little better educated than we are ourselves.

Probably one of the best results of extended technical education to a country would be to raise

o

the standard of its manufactures. A larger margin of profit to the manufacturer, and consequent competence to give enhanced wages to the hands, accrues from the sale of articles of luxury than from that of articles of first necessity. Technical education would thus enable the working carpenter to become a cabinetmaker, and the skilful cabinetmaker, in his turn, to mount still higher in the ladder of his profession. Cheap work or cheap labour would be -imported, or would import itself under the law of supply and demand, as might be required to supplement the work turned out by those who either could not or would not better themselves.

Louis XIV and Louis XV with their *Gobelins* and *Sèvres* manufactories would appear, if this line of reasoning be correct, to have possessed intuitive knowledge of political economy as applied to increasing the wealth of nations. It is evident that the country which exports expensive manufactures, and imports its chief necessities, must perpetually be accumulating wealth, and that it will end by getting the command both of the labour and the money market. This, indeed, is the alleged defect in Mr. Cobden's French Treaty. The wear of silks and expensive tissues has become cheapened and popularized in England; and to meet the purchases we thus annually make from France, and which exceed the value of the cottons and cheap textures we supply in return, a regular drain of gold out of England into France is established. This drain has long existed; but while it only amounted in the five years immediately preceding the Treaty to a total of £16,000,000, in the five years subsequent to the Treaty, it reached £20,000,000; and while in the last of the five years preceding the action of the Treaty this drain of gold, or excess of imports from, over exports to, France, was represented by

£5,000,000, on the last of the five years above quoted, subsequent to the Treaty coming into play, it reached the enormous sum of £10,500,000. Though this does not perhaps necessarily imply a large additional percentage of drain of gold, as compared with the increased trade, yet it is more than probable that the increasing poverty in Great Britain, and the popularly believed general increase of prosperity in France, may, to some degree, be attributed to the results of the figures I have ventured upon quoting, and which, like other national figures of money or population, require some years to become felt and apparent to their full extent. The cause of this excess of our imports from, over our exports to, France, and the consequent derangement of the balance of gold between the two countries, is due no doubt to the extraordinary development attained during late years by the French iron and machinery trades, which renders that country so much more independent of our steel and other mineral productions than the most sanguine Frenchman could have anticipated; and this, in its turn, is mainly due to the cut-throat policy of injudicious strikes: some of our most powerful trade unions themselves putting out the fires and closing the gates of our vast puddling and smelting furnaces for long months at a time, on insufficient provocation, and to their own personal detriment, thus driving the trade into other countries, and teaching the world to be independent of Great Britain; or, to use a vulgarism which has the merit of conveying the exact truth and being easy to understand—thus cutting off their nose to spite their face. However this may be, we have now reached a point where it would positively appear to be a question whether increase of our import and our export trade with France, under existing circumstances, will not only entail increased drain of gold, leaving increase of national poverty behind. The answer to this question I shall leave to experts in the science of political economy.

The exhibits from Switzerland in Class VI were neither remarkable for quantity nor quality. They consisted of a system for self-instruction in rectilinear drawing, and in some musical studies for the piano.

Scandinavia was as practical in the class under notice as in all the sections of the Exhibition that have been previously discussed. Denmark exhibited samples of work and methods of instruction given in the Technical Institute of Copenhagen. This establishment, which has 800 scholars, is divided into seven classes, viz. :—

1. Elementary drawing.
2. Ornamental drawing and modelling.
3. Architectural drawing.
4. Trade drawing for carpenters, &c.
5. Handicrafts, such as engraving, lithography, &c.
6. An evening class for surveying, and natural sciences.
7. Repetition class.

Scholars passing certain standard and competitive examinations are admitted gratis to a technical academy. This establishment further exhibited a great variety of good gymnastic appliances, such as are in daily use there; and a method for learning swimming, exhibited in connection with it by Captain P. Schouwburg, of Copenhagen, showed that the Danes do not fail to appreciate at its proper price an art which, apart from its value as a means of saving life, has so large a claim on the favour of mankind as a simple, cheap, and generally accessible means of recreation, promoting both health and cleanliness. It is not too much to say that no school can be

deemed complete in its machinery which does not
possess a swimming class.

Sweden and Norway had interesting collections
of elementary school methods, and some rough school
models and furniture, suitable for peasant life and
home instruction, which assumes such importance in
a country like Norway, where the population is
about one-twentieth of what it is in Holland to the
square mile, and where the sparse cottages are further separated during the winter months by short
days, deep snows, and impassable mountain paths.

Speaking generally, Great Britain was poorly and
inadequately represented in Class VI.

One *diplôme d'honneur* (ranking above gold
medals) was conferred on—

> Messrs. W. and R. Chambers, of 47, Pater-
> noster Row, London, and of 339, High
> Street, Edinburgh, for their excellent edu-
> cational publications, which are too well
> known and too highly appreciated to call
> for any comment in this place.

A silver medal was bestowed on—

> Mr. J. Solomon, of 22, Red Lion Square,
> London, for magic lanterns and slides, ste-
> reoscopes, telescopes, barometers, spectacles,
> and microscopes.

Many of these articles were fairly classable under
means of recreation ; but apart from the question of
their excellence, it can hardly be alleged that their
utility or special adaptation to the objects of the
Exhibition rendered them a fitting collection to represent a country where out-door and indoor recreative
exercises take so high and popular a place in the
national characteristics of the people as they do in
Great Britain.

Bronze medals in this class were obtained by—

Mr. B. S. Cohen, of 9, Magdalen Row, Great
Prescot Street, London, for black (Cumber-
land) lead pencils ; and by,

Mr. Ellis A. Davidson, of 29, Clarendon
Gardens, Maida Hill, London, for books and
models.

These were good exhibits, and strictly suited to
the object in view. The books were divided into
two classes, viz. : books for home study for workmen,
and a primary series of books for workmen's children.
The first of these classes formed the first volumes of
a technical series, and were entitled :—

Vol. 1. Geometry applied to Trade. Linear
Drawing.

Vol. 2. Projection, showing the Development
of Solids.

Vol. 3. Building construction.

The second of these classes, the primary series,
comprised—

1. Right Lines in their Right Places.
2. Our Houses, and what they are Built of.
3. Our Bodies : an Elementary Text-Book of
Human Physiology.

The drawing models exhibited by Mr. Davidson
were equally satisfactory—

1. Small ladder.
2. Step-ladder.
3. Garden-gate.
4. Field-bridge.
5. Bridge.
6. Cottage.
7. Garden-roller.
8. Doorway.
9. Church.

Finally, *mentions extraordinaires* (without the scope of the Exhibition) fell to the three following houses :—

> Messrs. John Brinsmead and Sons, of 18, Wigmore Street, Cavendish Square, London, for two cheap upright pianofortes, ranging from £21.
>
> Messrs. Dean and Son, of 65, Ludgate Hill, London, for books for children, birthday presents, &c. ; and
>
> Messrs. James Perry and Co., of 37, Red Lion Square, for steel pens, and sundry writing appliances.

When one thinks of the multitudes of interesting exhibits England might have had in this class, which would have rendered her contributions of value and importance in the eyes of foreign schoolmasters, philanthropists, and all others taking a practical concern in the ends pursued at Amsterdam, it is impossible not to feel and express a deep regret that we should have no Board or Department in England charged with the general surveillance of Exhibitions. "They somehow manage these things better in France," is an old cry ; but it applies specially to the present instance, where a small table, easily overlooked, held all the jewels we exhibited in this important class, and where the popular eye was taken by, and comments were freely passed on, the more conspicuous pianos, and the velocipede, which were held to represent John Bull's ideas of technical educational development ; while, but a few paces off, the rich collections of the French Minister of Public Instruction were well calculated to convey a widely different impression, and one by no means favourable to our Continental reputation.

TRADE UNIONS, &c.

CLASS VII, the last of the classes into which the Amsterdam Exhibition was divided, somewhat resembled the postscript to a lady's letter, inasmuch as it contained the kernel and the key of the whole undertaking. It was set apart for the Reports, Statutes, Rules and Regulations of Associations, having for their object the promotion of the well-being of the working-classes; and the task which the Jury set themselves was to appraise the extent to which the various institutions represented fulfilled the avowed aims of their originators and supporters. This class was briefly styled " Trade Unions and Co-operative Associations." It contained but 303 exhibits in all; but that its importance was not to be measured by the numerical ratio of those who contributed to fill the shelves devoted to the reception of the class of literature it collected may be gathered from the fact, that of these 303 exhibits no less than 170 came from the second-rate kingdom of Wurtemberg. Though forming a very complete and valuable collection, illustrative of the condition of this great question within the limits of the narrow country whence they came, these 170 exhibits covered in reality less moral ground than the numerically scanty collections from the great industrial centres of the world—the cradles of the movement—the sources of the torrent, which it is the task of modern politicians to keep within its banks. Exhibits from these countries were pearls of price, and carefully selected, with a view to representing the two edges of the sword that hangs suspended over the neck of our industrial prosperity. Consequently they were numbered, not in hundreds, but in tens, in twenties, and in thirties; and, moreover, in order to enable the Jury of this class to arrive at sound and righteous judgments, power was given them to fill up any void or gap they might detect in the co-operative chain of evidence they were appointed to consider, by the insertion as exhibits, competent to receive awards, of any institutions or associations whose tenets and whose practices seemed deserving of international recognition, and who, by some accident, through modesty, ignorance, or *nonchalance*, might have failed to represent themselves.

For the sake of order, and convenience of reference, the whole collection comprising Class VII was divided under the following heads :—

> Benevolent Societies.
> Provident Funds.
> Savings Banks.
> Co-operative Stores.
> Co-operative Labour.
> Sick Funds.
> Pension Funds.
> Trade Unions.

Omitting the first of these, which have to do with public or private charities, and really have no place in a list of institutions organized by working-men themselves for their own purposes; and the last, which will be discussed by themselves, the remaining six may be more conveniently classified under one or other of three denominations, viz. :—

> 1. Societies of Consumption.
> 2. Societies of Production.
> 3. Societies of Credit.

The first of these has hitherto found most favour

in Great Britain, the second in France, while the third is ubiquitous wherever the German tongue is spoken. In Belgium all three are found, but in the sister Kingdom of the Netherlands the first and third alone exist, and that in limited though augmenting numbers. The first is a real benefit to mankind, the second may become so if applied as a remedy to the worst defects of trade unions (as is proposed by the Comte de Paris in his excellent work on this subject), and the third is a harmless accessory to the first and second. To those who seek for information on this theme, "Rochdale" is the password for the first; 1848 is the era which gave an impetus to the second, of which, so far as I know, but one or two isolated and imperfect specimens existed before; and Schultze-Delitsch is the honoured name of the disinterested man who founded, in 1850, the people's banks in Germany, which represent the third. On all these methods for promoting well-being among the working-classes, interesting details, and much that will doubtless prove new to English readers, will be found in a work published in Paris in 1869 entitled, *Du Mouvement Co-opératif International, Etude Théorique et Pratique sur les Différentes Formes de l'Association : par Eugène Pelletier, Fondateur de la Compagnie Française des Chocolats et des Thés;* a little book which, written ostensibly to sell the chocolate of a great Co-operative Association of 1,500 retailers, has a wider interest as tracing from their commencement many of the most remarkable forms this movement has as yet assumed.

Being unwilling to repeat what can thus be found elsewhere, I shall pass with these preliminary remarks on the three great species into which Co-operative Associations (as distinguished from Trade Unions) may be divided, to the manner in which they were represented at Amsterdam, and to the

principles that were followed by the Jury in dealing
with them.

The Jury for Class VII was composed of 13
members, including a President, Vice-President, and
Rapporteur. It did me the honour to name me its
President, and it will always be to me a subject of
the deepest regret that, notwithstanding the fact
that Vice-Admiral Harris, Her Majesty's Minister at
the Hague, was sincerely anxious to give the fullest
effect to the Earl of Clarendon's expressed desire
that every facility should be afforded to enable me
to take my place at Amsterdam, it proved practically
impossible for me to disconnect myself sufficiently
from the daily routine of the chancery work of Her
Majesty's Legation to permit of my taking up my
residence for the time at Amsterdam, and devoting
myself exclusively to the service of the Jury. The
utmost that proved practicable, therefore, was to
watch its proceedings generally, and leave the virtual
Presidency to M. Donnat, the Vice-President, nephew
of M. Rouher, a distinguished Frenchman, well
known for the enlightened interest and careful study
with which he has approached many of the most
important social questions of the day.

The first difficulty which beset the Jury at the
outset of its labours was the impossibility of all its
members, or even of any one of its members, reading,
or much more making himself conversant with, the
rules, statutes, reports, &c., of several hundreds of
societies, written in English, French, German, Dutch,
Danish, Swedish, &c., within the limited time allotted
for the adjudication of awards. To meet this difficulty the Jury ultimately resolved to adopt certain
fixed rules and tests to be of general application ;
and rather than undertake the practical impossibility
of judging associations, of which some, though not
founded on sound social and financial doctrines had

yet worked well on the whole, according to their results, it was resolved to stamp with approval, and hold up to public imitation, those associations only which appeared to the Jury to be firmly based on principles not of a nature, even if pursued with enthusiasm, to convulse society, or foster dreams impossible of realisation without arresting the progress of modern civilization.

This line once drawn between the good and bad, and the chaff winnowed from the wheat, they were to inquire, as closely as possible, into the sum of difficulty vanquished in the founding and maintenance of approved associations; and a strong desire was manifested, and supported, in principle at least, by the majority of the Jury, to reject, as failing in the vital element of independence, all even of approved associations dependent on another class than that which composed them for the finances necessary to their development. Advances of money to workpeople by their employers, even for such laudable purposes as procuring sewing-machines, &c., were regarded with disfavour, as placing the workman too much in the power of his benefactor, and as tantamount to an approval of a mode, highly civilized it is true, of placing the yoke of bondage, serfdom, or of slavery, upon the neck of the working-man. Both sides of this question were fully discussed; but, as has been said, the majority of the Jury decided on upholding the necessity of placing the labourer, above-board at least, independent of his employer; and though it was not desired by any to sever the happy combination of the employer and the benefactor, it was held that the benevolence should come spontaneously—not as the result of a treaty between capital and labour, and thus liable to individual abuse. In the hands of a harsh taskmaster, a recognised blending of the benefactor with the employer might easily be conceived to lead to a renewal in some shape or other of the old demand for bricks without straw; while, on the other hand, such blending of benevolence and power in a weak or unwise man, might easily give rise to the danger of doing too much for the labourer (as is done for example in the Dutch pauper colonies), and of relieving him from the responsibility which rests upon him under the motto, applicable to the whole of human kind, *Aide-toi et Dieu t'aidera.*

The only Dutch association that, in the opinion of the Jury, possessed the required conditions to a sufficient extent to justify them in conferring upon it the highest award, a *Diplôme d'Honneur*, was the Amsterdam Society for Promoting the Interests of the Working-Classes, established in 1854 under the patronage of the Prince of Orange. It has upwards of 650 members, who each pay 5 florins a year, and is divided into the five following distinct sections :—

Amsterdam Society for Promoting the Interests of the Working Classes.

1. Scavengers' Brigade for sweeping and cleaning the streets and gutters on moderate terms, thus procuring employment for many otherwise unable to get work, and improving the sanitary condition of the town.

2. Benevolent Fund for affording temporary relief to members in times of illness or when disabled by accident.

3. Industrial School for sons of workmen. This branch was established in 1861, and receives subsidies from the city of Amsterdam. The King of the Netherlands endowed it with a large and valuable collection of models, implements and tools, in 1866. It has now 125 scholars, from 13 to 16 years of age, and 13 teachers. School hours are from 8 till noon, and from 2 till 8 o'clock. The instruction is purely technical.

4. Lectures for the working-classes, established

in 1866. From fifteen to twenty lectures are given during the winter ; the doors are open to all comers, and they are attended according to the weather and the interest of the topic by from 600 to 1,000 workmen.

5. For procuring employment for needlewomen. In this section great good has been cheaply attained by the giving of instruction gratis in the use of sewing-machines.

This Association contributed towards sending some Dutch artisans to visit the Paris Exhibition of 1867. As has been seen it receives extraneous assistance, and is not entirely self-supporting and co-operative in its character ; its success, however, is none the less complete on that account. More than one of its sections would have been perhaps more properly placed in Class VI ; but its real and most marked character is combination of the working-men of the poorest class to provide themselves with a living ; and from this point of view it is entitled to take rank among co-operative labour societies.

The only gold medals bestowed on Netherlands exhibits in this class fell to the Workmen's Reading Institute of the Hague—an Association conducted on sound principles, but presenting no unusual features calling for particular notice.

Three silver medals were awarded to the Dutch Associations in this class : —

1. The Netherlands Association, for abolishing the use of strong drinks, established at the Hague ; for its facts, and not for its principles.
2. The Zaandam Society of "Help Yourselves," an association essentially co-operative, in the best sense of the term.
3. The Haarlem Society, *Weten und Werken*

("To Know and to Work"). This Association seeks to raise the position and the understanding of the working-man, by means of winter lectures, readings, debating clubs, and other social gatherings. CLASS VII.

The only bronze medals given in this category were:— Bronze medals.

1. The Working Man's Association, established at Middleburg in 1865.
2. The Credit Society, or Savings Bank, of Franeker.
3. The Leyden Society, *Tot Nut en Genoegen* ("For Use and Pleasure"). "Tot nut en Genoegen."

This last may be taken as a fair type of the shape combinations of workmen usually assume in Holland. It dates from 1857, is one of the oldest of its kind, and has undergone no important modifications of its constitution since its establishment. Its members are printers, that is to say, type-setters, pressmen, &c.; but so long as they number under ninety they may, under Article 3 of their Statutes, enrol binders and others into their union. Throughout these statutes no reference occurs to wages, work hours, or strikes; they are strictly confined to regulations respecting the entrance money and the administration of the funds, for objects of necessity or pleasure, for the maintenance of the sick, for providing an out-door excursion and feast on "Kopper Monday" (usually the second Monday in the year), &c. Subscriptions vary according to requirement, cents being levied as frequently as funds are needed for purposes of relief. This Society is in a flourishing condition, and affords real support to its members in times of trouble.

Honourable mentions were conferred in two cases "Mentions honorables."

CLASS VII. on Netherlands associations represented in this important class, viz., on the *Winkel*, or Shop Societies, of Deventer and Gouda. These are co-operative clubs and stores started by workmen engaged in the same trades for the purpose of promoting their physical, social, and intellectual benefit.

It will thus be seen that, so far as Holland was concerned, the timidest of the timid among politicians would have found nothing to make him tremble in the jury work at Amsterdam. The soundest principles were laid down and rigidly maintained. It will next be interesting to inquire into the nature of the Dutch Associations whose claims to an award were not endorsed by the appointed judges.

Of these rejected Societies there were about forty; but they did not offer much variety of purpose or detail.

Blacksmiths' union. One of the most characteristic of them was the Blacksmiths' and Ironworkers' Association of the Hague, established in 1862. This is purely a benefit society, the funds being exclusively applicable to maintaining the sick, burying the dead, and promoting harmony among themselves; this object is generally sought by the regular giving of as many *fêtes* in the course of the year as the funds at their disposal will allow. There is generally at least one ball given to the wives of members of each Society in the course of the winter. The subscription to this Society, which is called after the god of subterranean fire, Vulcan, is 10 cents a week, and for this a member, in case of certificated sickness, receives two florins a week for thirteen weeks in succession. If his illness continues, members have to pay an additional two cents a week; the sick member continuing to receive two florins. If a member returns himself sick, and on examination it is proved he was "shamming," he forfeits all claim to relief during the next

three months. Sickness or injuries brought on by
fighting, drinking, or a member's own fault, have no
claim to relief. Burial expenses are entirely met by
the fund. There is a widows' fund, kept separate
for such of the members as choose to belong to it.

The association of this kind that seems widest Printers' union.
spread throughout the Netherlands is the Typo-
graphical Society. Its head-quarters are at Utrecht,
but it has branches at Alkmaar, Amsterdam, Arnheim,
Breda, Deventer, Dort, and so on all through the
letters of the alphabet, at almost every town or place
where a newspaper is published, or books issue from
the press. These branches take different names,
other than those of the localities, to distinguish
them; such names as "Friends in Faith," and even
longer mottoes as, "Behold how good and joyful a
thing it is to dwell together in unity;" but though
called by different names they form part of a great
whole, and their members subscribe two cents a week,
payable quarterly, to the head-quarters at Utrecht, and
other sums varying from 6 to 10 cents a week to the
local branch to which they belong. In its statutes
the objects of this association are declared to be :—

1. The general promotion of the material prosperity of all its members, who must be, or have been
at some period of their lives, working-men employed
in the printing, binding, or other affiliated trades,
such as lithography, engraving, or even acting as
shop-boy in libraries or stationers' shops.

2. The establishment of a pension fund.

3. To endeavour to procure work for members
out of work through no fault of their own.

4. To enable very promising members to study
their trade abroad, so as to be able to bring home to
Holland the latest improvements and inventions.

5. To promote zeal and good workmanship by
occasional giving of prizes for very meritorious work.

6. The dissemination of knowledge by the publication of a weekly newspaper principally devoted to questions of interest to the trades concerned, so as to keep the members at the height of the latest information that could be of service to them respecting prices, markets, &c. This journal to be conducted by an elective editor, and to abstain from discussing politics or religion.

7. Finally, to promote everything that can contribute to the honour of their several callings, and to the advantage of the work-givers as well as of the workmen.

Such is the character of, I believe, the widest spread working-man's association in the Netherlands. It is singularly unobtrusive in the exercise of its functions, and to this cause, and to their native modesty, which makes Dutchmen look abroad in search of idols, whether in literature or any other branch of civilization, I attribute its failure to secure more prominent notice at Amsterdam than the mere conferring of a medal of the third order on its Leyden branch. At a recent annual gathering of its General Assembly at Utrecht, in reply to some query of questionable propriety, its Chancellor of the Exchequer replied with dignity that the Association and its objects were recognized by Act of Parliament signed by the King, and that application of funds a hair's-breadth beyond the limits prescribed in its well-known statutes would render the administrators of those funds liable to prosecution in a court of law. Now, as the statutes do not make any reference to strikes as a possible contingency which it is necessary to foresee and provide for, it follows that the maintenance of a strike would render them liable to an action for breach of trust.

In the Hague there exists also a powerful association of upholsterers and journeymen of affiliated

trades. Its objects, as stated in Article II of its
statutes, are :—

1. To provide its members in case of illness with 3 florins (5s.) a week for not more than ten weeks in the course of any 12 calendar months.

2. To pay 10 florins towards the burial of any member.

3. To promote harmony among themselves by holding two, three, or more social gatherings, according to the state of the finances within the year.

The subscription is 12½ cents a week, and a man goes round to collect it, thus saving many of the members a long weekly walk.

This association has in its statutes a final Article, which, taken side by side with the fact that the affiliated shipwrights of Amsterdam and Nieuwe Diep are as yet the only collective body of men who have struck work seriously, demanding higher wages or a reduction of hours, is, to say the least, suggestive. This Article reads—"Whenever circumstances occur for which these regulations do not provide, the administration has a right to act according to the course of events, in the interests of the association." How far this Article could be made available in providing funds for the maintenance of a strike has not yet been proved; but it is the most suspicious thing I have come across in the statutes of any Dutch association of which I have been able to obtain perusal. The name of this society is the "Aurora," and it was established in 1864, the year in which the legal restraints upon co-operation of workmen against their employers were removed in France. This may be only another coincidence, but it also looks suspicious.

Numerous societies, of which one or other of those already mentioned may be considered the type, exist in Holland; almost all of them have been established since 1864 ; and while on the one hand they bear evidence to the social, as distinct from the socialist character of the Dutch working man, on the other they afford equal and abundant proof of the existence of the spirit of combination in Holland and of the contented nature of a people whose principal food is potatoes, flavoured with a little mustard sauce, when they can afford it.

"Hand-werksbloei."

The only society I have been able to discover that in its statutes deals openly with wages and hours of labour, is the Arnheim Association, entitled *Hand-werksbloei* ("Bloom of Industry"). Its object is to promote the interest of the workgiver and of the workman, by reducing the hours of labour for efficiency of workmanship, retaining uniformity of wage. Its members are employers of labour in all trades, who are briefly styled the *Baas* or "Boss," a word which the original Dutch settlers of Hoboken (New York) have permanently engrafted on the American vocabulary. In and around the rich and thickly peopled commune of Arnheim, this society has enrolled well-nigh every workshop and factory under its banner, to the great satisfaction of the workmen themselves, who, on attaining a certain standard of proficiency, find their hours of labour curtailed to an extent representing in the aggregate one day in eight, or even two hours in the day, the former wages being retained. The workmen of these masters are furnished with *livrets*, for which they pay 5 cents (1*d.*), and in which their efficiency is noted and their promotion to shorter hours recorded. They are divided into three classes of efficiency. A master is bound to give up the *livret* to a workman quitting his service, and the members of the association also bind themselves not to re-engage a man (without a general enquiry into his case) who has taken

service with a master or " Boss" not belonging to
their association.

Building and singing societies exist in Holland,
though the former only in one or two of the principal towns, such as the Hague, Zwolle, &c. They
cannot as yet be said to have had any important results; but they afford additional evidence of the
extent to which the Dutch workman devotes his
savings to ends consistent with sound principles and
common sense.

Among the most successful of the savings and
other people's banks which exist in Holland are those
founded by the *Nut Van't Algemeen* Society, to
whose educational and charitable triumphs allusion
has been made in Class VI. Some of these banks
rank among the earliest foundations of the society.
One of the first of them was established at Haarlem
in 1793, and has prospered ever since. They number
140 in all, and are scattered broadcast over the face
of the country. The one established at Rotterdam
pays interest on deposits exceeding £160,000. The
deposits of many of the smaller branches, however,
are under £40. Financial operations are strictly
prohibited; Government and other real securities
being the only investments permitted by the laws of
the society.

The *Nut Van't Algemeen* has also led the van
in Holland in the establishment of co-operative
stores, of which it has already founded fifteen, besides
projecting many more. Their peculiarity consists in
their disbursing to their clients during the winter,
at wholesale price, and under the most advantageous
conditions, provisions and firing, for the sums entrusted to them during the summer and good season.
They are beginning to find great favour with the
working-men of the Netherlands.

CLASS VII.

In times of scarcity of work, this society organizes public works, roads, draining of lakes, &c., and it is thus by assuming a variety of characters,—that of the schoolmaster, of the banker, of the salesman, as occasion arises,—that this powerful association, bound together on the simple principle of doing good, without regard to creed or politics, applies itself to the formation, throughout the length and breadth of Holland, of institutions worthy of the name they bear, as being both physically and morally for the public weal. The only blot on its escutcheon was removed in 1864, a great year of reform on the Continent, when the Jews, hitherto excluded from participation in its benefits, were admitted, and assimilated in every respect to the rest of the community.

For its services in this category the *Nut Van't Algemeen* received at Amsterdam a *Grand Diplôme d'Honneur*.

British awards.

The English awards in Class VII were not numerous, but comprised nearly every exhibit, besides one or more persons and institutions supplied by the Jury to complete the character of the selection. If the names of many worthy and successful British co-operative efforts are not to be found upon this limited muster-roll of eleven awards, their failure to obtain honourable recognition at Amsterdam is attributable only to their own neglect to challenge an inquiry into their statutes and conditions on which alone such recognition could be based. Yet short as is the list now under review, it will be found to contain sufficient samples chosen from among the best and most successful of our co-operative associations both of consumption and production, to give the continent a fair idea of the extent the movement has attained in the land of its birth. At the same time no trade union figures on the list to mar the harmony of the picture, by presenting before the imagination spectral figures of half-starved operatives, wending their way at dusk to a neighbouring field to sit in judgment on one of their brethren, whose honest desire to earn his daily bread and send his children back to school again, has finally overcome his allegiance to his union, and given him the courage to incur the certainty of abuse, of picketing, and rattening in all its villainous shape, which represent, in merry England, the consequences of breaking through a strike.

The first place in the rank of approved exhibits in this class was naturally occupied by the honoured name of Rochdale; the cradle in which the giant power of co-operation was rocked through the dangers which beset its childhood, till it attained an age to walk alone, and stride manfully through the civilized world on its errand of humanity.

Three representatives of Rochdale appeared at Amsterdam and were adjudged awards. Two of them received the highest, the *Diplôme d'Honneur*, and the third the medal of bronze. The two former were the Central Co-operative Society, for the successful application of the federative system to the co-operative movement, and the Society of Equitable Pioneers, for its general results; the third was the Co-operative Corn Mills Society. Of all these the history has been too often written to make repetition pardonable. They have occupied the pens of foreign as well as of English writers, and are as well known on the Continent as they are at home. They belong to the highest order of real benefit societies, being self-supporting, and founded on sound doctrine, social and financial.

A *Diplôme d'Honneur* was awarded, though not without partial dissent from Germany, to the Postmaster-General of Great Britain, for his exhibits

CLASS VII. representing the working of our Post-Office Savings Banks; the objection raised to them being the too active participation of the Government, which was deemed socialistic and opposed to the old-fashioned notions of sound economical doctrine. The only other *Diplôme d'Honneur* bestowed on Great Britain

Mr. Twining. in this section fell to Mr. Thomas Twining, of Twickenham, for his powerful and successful efforts to improve the condition of the working classes, and especially for his hand-book of economic literature, and the Guide to his Museum for the working-classes.

Gold medals. Gold medals were adjudged to the Working Men's Club and Institute Union*, the Working Men's College, and the Working Women's College, all in London. Full accounts of the nature and results of these institutions are willingly furnished by their respective principals and secretaries.

Messrs. Briggs. A gold medal was also most justly awarded to Henry Briggs, Son, and Company, of Whitwood, for their successful application of the principle of admitting workmen as shareholders to a partition of profits.† In 1865 this hitherto private firm hit upon this expedient to procure for the future immunity from ruinous strikes, from which they had suffered severely, and registered their collieries as a limited liability company. The success of their scheme has been most unclouded. Workmen have abandoned their trade unions—no strikes have since occurred, while the profits of the collieries have enormously increased. Profits, after deducting 10 per cent. for interest on the capital invested, and after payment of all charges and allowance for depreciation, wear and tear, &c., of plant, are equally divided between the former masters, Messrs. Briggs and Son, and the workmen now partners in the concern. The fullest

---

* See Appendix for objects and results.
† See Appendix for further details.

particulars of this remarkable achievement will be
found in vol. vi of the Reports on the Paris Exhibition of 1867, containing "the returns relative to
the new order of reward," presented to Parliament
in 1868 ; one of the most interesting and valuable
books of this or any other age, and one which has
not yet been studied as it deserves. Class VII.

Three bronze medals complete the unsullied roll
of British awards in Class VII. They were bestowed
upon Mr. J. Brucciani, sculptor, of London, Mr. Gustav
Meinhardt, of Birmingham, and Mr. Joseph Gibbs,
Private Secretary to the late Lord Mayor, Sir James
Lawrence, to whose personal energy and appreciation
of its real character, the Amsterdam Exhibition was
so heavily indebted. Bronze medals.

The first of the above-mentioned gentlemen, Mr. J.
Brucciani, received his award for plaster casts of the
Queen and Prince Consort, and of the Prince and
Princess of Wales, presented for the decoration of
the British Court. The bust of the Prince Consort
had at the very outset of the undertaking been
unanimously demanded by the Dutch Society for the
encouragement of manufactures and industry, the
projectors of the Exhibition, as an object without
which no International Exhibition, more especially
one devoted to the interests of the working-classes,
could be regarded as complete. This tribute to the
memory of a great and enlightened Prince was
entirely spontaneous on the part of the Dutch workmen, members of the Society above-mentioned, and
was the more remarkable from being confined to the
case of the Prince Consort, and not extended to
the bust of any other princely benefactor of the
human race. Prince Consort's bust.

Mr. Meinhardt received his medal for general
valuable services rendered in connection with the
Exhibition at its commencement. He is manager in
the great firm of Messrs. Peyton and Peyton, who M. Mein-hardt.

also enjoy the reputation of having successfully introduced into their large and wealthy business the co-operative principle, and the equal division between master and men of any profits over (I believe) 15 per cent. on the capital they themselves represent.

Belgium.

The Belgian exhibits in Class VII were numerous and remarkable, and showed the complete extent to which the co-operative net is now spread over the whole of that industrious kingdom. The Associations represented comprised many specimens of combinations of workmen for purposes both of consumption and production; and the statutes of all those whose merits were recognized by awards at Amsterdam were free from the stain of clauses for the support of strikes. Such clauses are, however, now beginning to be inserted in the statutes of some Belgian associations, which thus afford the nearest approach to the social monster termed Trade Unionism, as yet existent on the Continent. The date in Belgium of this immunity from the penalties to which they were subject under the old Penal Code of Napoleon is June 11, 1866; but the legislation to which they owe this immunity does not recognize the right of unionists to threaten, intimidate, or ratten non-unionists, or even one another. Such conduct is still punishable by heavy fine and imprisonment, and the extended immunity is strictly confined to removing the former invidious distinctions between combinations of masters and combinations of men; in other words, up to June 11, 1866, employers could legally combine to keep wages down, while it was illegal for artisans to combine for the purpose of keeping them up. This blot is now erased from the statute book of a free State.

"La Vieille Montagne."

In this section of the Amsterdam Exhibition a *diplôme d'honneur* was awarded to the *Société Anonyme de la Vieille Montagne*, established at

Chênée near Liege, which may be said to be the Class VII. centre, or Rochdale, of the Belgian co-operative movement. Zinc is the metal worked by this Society, which, besides employing at its head-quarters 6,500 hands, a figure representing a population of over 20,000 souls, counting wives, &c., has seventeen large branch establishments in Rhenish Prussia, France, and Sweden. The workmen it employs may all be considered as shareholders in the concern, their labour being regarded as so much capital invested in a common undertaking, for which they receive a regular percentage as wages, and further bonuses (on the Messrs. Briggs' principle) according to the profits of the firm; they are thus individually interested in the financial results of the works, and encouraged to personal exertion.

The wages of the hands employed by the *Vieille Montagne* have in this manner increased 45 per cent. in twelve years, without remonstrance or coercion on either side, and they are continually increasing. The hands have, moreover, built up during that time, by the organized investment of 1, 2, 3, or more cents a week, a reserve or benefit fund of 600,000 francs, a separate savings bank, where they get 5 per cent. on their deposits, a building fund, a co-operative store, means of recreation, such as bands of music, archery, and rifle shooting associations, &c., in some of which the miners turn out on *fête* days dressed in national costumes of the middle ages, with bells ringing, banners waving, and other accessories of display.

A second Belgian *Société Anonyme* on which a *diplôme d'honneur* was conferred, is that established "Société Anonyme" of Bleyberg. at Bleyberg near Verviers, also in the Province of Liege. This Company, which works zinc, lead, and silver, and which up to within ten years ago was often in great straits for labour, being geographically so situated near the Dutch and German frontiers

CLASS VII. that it was mostly fed by vagrant hands from foreign countries, who decamped on hearing of a rise in wages or recommencement of work at home,—or, for the matter of that, elsewhere,—owes its present prosperity to the successful endeavours of its managers to attach workmen to the spot by improving their social condition and supplying all their wants. To this end building funds were established, and the workmen were so successfully encouraged to embark a share of their wages in them, that now one-third of this number are proprietors. Churches, libraries, reading-rooms, primary and sewing schools, hospitals, savings banks, co-operative stores, &c., have grown up with the rapidity of magic. Girls are excluded from working in the mines and foundries, and are now being widely sought for service in the neighbourhood owing to their good bringing up. Mothers are not allowed to labour beyond the precincts of their own dwellings and gardens, the men's wages being calculated as sufficient for their support. The Society allows of no *cabarets* in the vicinity of its works, and limits the number of people in each house.

Other "Diplômes d'honneur."   Three more *diplômes d'honneur* demand notice in this section. The first was conferred upon the *Société Co-opérative de Consommation dite l'Equité, à Liège*; the second upon the *Société Anonyme pour la Construction de Maisons Ouvrières à Verviers*; and the third upon Mr. G. Janssen, of Cureghem near Bruxelles, a practical philanthropist and large employer of labour, who occupies in Belgium the same position for successful and persistent endeavours to better the condition of his workpeople by the establishment of building funds, model dwellings, co-operative stores, &c., as is occupied in France by the world-wide honoured name of M. Jean Dolfus, of Mulhouse.

Several gold medals also fell to Belgian exhibits in Class VII. Among them was one conferred upon the *Société Anonyme de Marcinelle et Couillet*, a Company which combines in the treatment of its operatives many of the best characteristics of the Belgian associations above dealt with.

Gold medals were further bestowed on *La Société Anonyme pour la Construction de Maisons Ouvrières à Anvers; La Société Anonyme pour la Construction de Maisons Ouvrières à Liège; La Société pour prévenir les Abus du Travail des Enfants dans les Manufactures à Verviers*, a very valuable association; and upon *La Société Anonyme de l'Espérance à Verviers*.

All these societies are based on sound social and financial foundations, and are equal ornaments to the civilization of the 19th century and to the little kingdom in which they have grown up.

Lastly, a gold medal fell to *Les Etablissements de Sainte Marie d'Oignies, Manufactures de Glaces et Fabrique de Produits Chimiques à Aiseau lez Charleroi*. This Company employs over 1,000 men, and has laboured without intermission since 1828 to improve their moral and physical position by the promotion of schools, savings banks, the building of model dwellings, churches, and the like. When one of the hands has laid by enough money to buy a lot or little piece of land, and enjoys a good character as a workman, from 500 to 800 francs are advanced to him without interest to build a dwelling. The repayment takes place by instalments, and at the will of the borrower. It is a high tribute to human nature in general, when under favourable conditions, and to the Belgian operative in particular, to be able to state, as the company does in its last printed report, that in no single instance where such an advance has been made has the money been over long in being willingly repaid, or have measures had to be taken to obtain repayment. Sixty-three per cent. of such workmen employed by this company as are heads of families are actually proprietors of the dwellings they inhabit.

This company also has its co-operative stores of all kinds, inclusive of butchers' shops and public kitchens, and credit is given under certain fixed and stipulated conditions. The details of these stores and of their management are very interesting and worthy of close study. Unfortunately, neither time nor space permit of their insertion here; but this is of the less importance, as an admirable and complete report on the " Progress and Results of Co-operation," in this instance, published by the director of the establishment, M. Houtart Cossée, is readily obtainable on application. In this report it is stated that drunkards are dismissed, and holiday-making on Monday not permitted; and M. Houtart Cossée modestly states that the happy results they now enjoy of over forty years' labour to improve the position of their men, have not been attained by what may be termed personal government, but by conforming to the wishes of the hands employed, consulting them freely, and enlisting their hearty support. If this system has, in some instances, caused the advance to be slow, some prejudices requiring time to overcome them, the advance has at least been sure and steadily progressive. This affords another confirmation of the maxim that it is better to do too little than too much, and that the great talent, the happy knack, is to hit off the exact point of demarcation between what should be left to the working-man to do for himself, and what should be done for him, so as to stimulate and not slacken his own exertions.

Silver medals.   Silver medals were awarded to two *Caisses de*

Prévoyance des Ouvriers Mineurs, the one at Charleroi, the other at Mons. Among miners, to whom accidents are of so frequent occurrence, even when every proper precaution is taken by the State, the proprietor, and the workmen themselves, it is probably more necessary to have funds available for widows, children, &c., than among any other body of men. Yet the introduction of such *Caisses* into Belgium is due to the life-long energy of one man, M. Auguste Visschers, who unites the rare qualities which render the enthusiast practical. For thirty years he has laboured in the cause of these Associations in Belgium. Great difficulties had to be vanquished before sufficient unity of action could be introduced into a scheme that could succeed only if formed on the most extensive principle of combination. Isolated funds were liable to be crushed by individual calamities, which they were altogether unable to stand up against; but a national fund for that purpose, subscribed to by the State, the proprietors, and the miners themselves, would be invincible in its strength, and would hardly feel beyond a calculable and a harmless point the financial effects of one of those direful pit or mining accidents which from time to time echo through the European press. This is the result that M. Visschers has attained. He has formed an association counting 86,300 subscribers (being 91·37 of the total Belgian mining population), largely subsidized from without, with a revenue reckoned at 2,370,000 francs, an expenditure assessed at 2,080,000, and a balance in hand of 4,400,000 francs. M. Visschers may be regarded as one of the most successful of the practical philanthropists of the age. He has the honour of having embodied in a popular and lasting shape the national motto *L'Union fait la Force*.

If the time and space at my disposal compel me

now to quit Belgium, and trace the combination wave elsewhere, let it not be therefore imagined that I have exhausted the roll of exhibits or awards in this section. Belgium took a high place at Amsterdam, probably the first place in the Exhibition, taken as a whole, and especially as judged from its loftiest points of view. At least a dozen other Belgian Co-operative Stores were represented, and were worthy of receiving awards. There was the *Société la Bonne Foi*, of Pepinster; the *La Ruche*, and *Ateliers Réunis*, of Brussels; the *Le Bond*, of Malines; the *Mouleurs Réunis*, of Liege; the *La Sincérité*, of Ensival; the *Sans Nom non sans Cœur*, of Ghent; the *Aidez-vous les uns les Autres*, of Antwerp; and, lastly, the *Economat*, of Messrs. Duyk, of Brussels. These were one and all represented in a highly satisfactory manner, and one which makes that little Kingdom a worthy rival of Great Britain in the struggle for industrial distinction.

France.   France was the country, as has been said, whose displays of silks and satins implied a non-appreciation of the special aims of the Amsterdam Exhibition. In Class VII, however, she was by no means wanting in interesting objects for study and reflection, and received numerous high and well-deserved awards. Among these were no less than five *diplômes d'honneur*, the first of which was conferred upon the French Minister of Finance, for various institutions established in the interest of the workmen engaged in the administration of the Government tobacco

The "Régie."   monopoly. The establishments of the *Régie* number 17, and employ in all 18,000 workmen. Each branch has its own medical officer appointed by Government, who supplies medicaments and comforts, gratis; takes care that infectious patients are properly isolated; gives certificates of physical inability to work; and publishes an annual report on the sanitary condition of the people he is appointed to look after.

The workmen employed in these manufactories are divided into classes according to efficiency, and derive regular benefits from promotion from class to class. Each class has its *Section des Arts et Métiers*, especially charged with keeping all the plant and machinery in working order, so as to render the establishment independent of extraneous labour and entirely self-supporting. The stokers and others in different employments receive bonuses in a fixed ratio or percentage for fuel or material of any kind economized and preserved from waste: 10,000 francs are annually distributed as presents to the most deserving workmen, and there is a well-organized and largely subsidized *Caisse des Retraites*. The condition of the workmen has steadily improved under all the measures taken to elevate them; and the whole institution, though bearing the unpopular name "monopoly," is a real benefit to the people it employs, while the tobacco it produces is of standard price and quality, liable to no adulteration, and probably as little deleterious to its consumers as is consistent with the habit to which it ministers. Results like these go far to reconcile one to monopolies when well conducted, and suggest the belief that a few such institutions in Great Britain in place of the boasted private enterprise and competition which is so busily engaged in underselling and adulteration, in forcing every class to become its own shopkeeper, and in breaking travellers' bones, would probably be productive, on the whole, of greater good than harm.

The second *Diplôme d'Honneur* fell to the great M. Dupont. Paris printer, M. Paul Dupont, of 45, Rue de Grenelle, St. Honoré. His house does a business of over 5,000,000 francs a year, and 10 per cent. on the

CLASS VII.

net profits are divided among his workmen, according to their individual merit, and not in regular proportion to their different salaries. This house has followed this course for twenty years, and claims the first place in the application of one of the happiest and most successful ideas of modern times. Each new hand, on admission to the *Ateliers,* receives a silver medal worth 5 francs as a badge of office and link between him and his employer. This establishment has its sick and provident funds of all the usual kinds, its loans of honour to its workmen, its *Caisses de Retraite,* its savings banks, its schools, libraries, reading and singing rooms, its co-operative stores, its familisteries, gardens, baths, in short, every invention of modern days for promoting health, wealth, happiness, and religion. To use the words of M. Dupont himself, " *Ce n'est plus un atelier, c'est une famille composée d'un millier de personnes.*" Let every employer of labour in Great Britain who does not yet come up to this high standard cast his eyes across the Straits of Dover, study this establishment in his own interest, and go and do likewise, or better if he can.

MM. Mame.

The third *Diplôme d'Honneur* fell to MM. Mame et Fils, a second monster printing-house, established at Tours, Indre et Loire. The solicitude of this firm for its workmen, women, and children is said if possible to exceed that displayed by M. Dupont. The features with which the latter has made us familiar are here reproduced, with the additional moral and physical advantages that a country town has over a great capital like Paris.

"Société Internationale des Etudes Pratiques d'Economie Sociale."

Fourthly and Fifthly, *Diplômes d'Honneur* fell to the *Société Internationale des Etudes Pratiques d'Economie Sociale,* established in Paris in 1864 (the year of the law repealing the legislation which forbad trade unions in France), and to the *Société pour*

la Protection des Apprentis et des Enfants employés
dans les Manufactures. The first of these seeks to
accomplish its aims by discussion and publicity ; its
aims being the encouragement of all good co-operation among workmen, but the discouragement of
such combination when it assumes the character of
conspiracy, and becomes amenable to the law. Its
members are senators, *députés*, philanthropists, and
other serious men of high social standing. The range
of its inquiries may be defined as embracing everything connected with the realisation of the following
popular formula of the French *Société des Ferblan-
tiers :—*

" 1. *Par les sociétés de production nous récol-
terons nous-mêmes les fruits de notre travail.*

" 2. *Par les sociétés de consommation nous pro-
curerons à nos familles une vie plus saine et meilleure
en dépensant moins.*

" 3. *Par celles de crédit nous nous passerons des
prêteurs à l'usure, et surtout de cet établissement
philanthropique que l'on nomme Mont-de-Piété.*"

The Society for Protection of Apprentices and
Children engaged in manufactures was established in
1867. In the preamble to its first report it states
its object to be to imitate the example set by Great
Britain of framing a special legislation to promote
its ends and enforce its views. That such legislation
was not less required in France than in England may
be gathered from the following extract from an
interesting report by Mr. Coningsby on the condition
and habits of the French working-classes, published
by the Society of Arts. " The age at which children
are considered old enough to be taken into factories
seems to be lower in France than here. I was under
the impression, until I had visited some of the workshops in Lyons and its neighbourhood, that the
French people were more merciful to their little ones

than we are ; but from what I saw in the south, I am convinced that this is not the case. I have been in all the principal manufacturing districts of my own country, and witnessed the sorrowful spectacle of boys and girls, who should have had several more years of play, hurrying to their work on cold, dark mornings, with careworn faces and stooping figures ; but for a sight which is most calculated to move a man of ordinary sensibility to compassion, one must go into the neighbourhood of the French silk factories, and watch the melancholy procession of babies (they can be called nothing else) dragging their little limbs slowly away from the places where their tiny energies have been tortured out of them."

Three French gold medals in Class VII next demand attention. They were—

1. *La Compagnie des Mines de Houille de Blanzy, Saone et Loire,* remarkable for the completeness of its institutions for the workmen employed. This company has constructed and allotted over 100 dwellings, on an annuity system that is well worthy of being studied.

2. *MM. Leclaire Defourneaux et Cie.,* Painters, of Paris. This house ranks early among those who have applied the plan of participation in profits. Its workmen have always distinguished themselves in times of political agitation by their quiet and peaceable conduct.

3. The *Société Co-operative de Production des Ouvriers Lunettiers.* This was regarded at Amsterdam as a faithful type of the best of the numerous associations (over 50) of this kind existing in France. It was established in 1849, and may thus be said to date from a revolutionary period ; but its members have been distinguished by their quiet behaviour and contented spirit in times of political excitement. The members are all working spectacle-makers, and they

elect their administrative officers, foremen, &c., as required. They do a business of upwards of 25,000*l.* a-year, and have hitherto escaped disputes growing out of division of profits, or want of unanimity in action, differences that have caused the disruption of more than one society of this kind in France and elsewhere. In adjudging this gold medal, some members of the International Jury in Class VII placed it on record that they concurred in the proposed recompense, inasmuch as the *Lunettiers* had succeeded well in the application of a dangerous principle.

Three silver medals bestowed upon France in this class next demand special notice. They fell to—

1. MM. Bouillon and Son, of the *Forges de Larivière,* *près Simoges, Haute Vienne.* This house was established by M. Bouillon, *Père,* in 1837, for converting pig-iron into wire-nails, &c. For some reason or other the population of the surrounding country set their faces against the design of M. Bouillon, and combined not to take work in his factories, which thus became dependent upon vagrant labour picked up from Franche Comté, Switzerland, and Burgundy, and was with difficulty kept up to 50 strong. No time was lost by M. Bouillon in endeavouring to overcome the unpopularity of which he was the object, in the hope of ultimately reconciling the native and estranged population, and thus becoming independent of the imported labour, which, shunned by the neighbourhood, never stayed long, and formed a floating and ever-changing element, to the great detriment of the regular work of the factory. In this view M. Bouillon converted his château into comfortable working-men's apartments, and laboured for their comfort with such success that a very short time elapsed before the neighbouring villages sought

his service. If M. Bouillon's efforts had ceased in the attainment of his immediate object—a labour supply for his factory—he would be entitled to little credit in this place, however deserving a member of society at large in other regards ; but the taste thus cultivated, of necessity at the beginning, grew upon him, until the well-being of his hands, originally promoted for his own benefit, was advanced from a secondary to a primary place in his solicitude. His next venture was to employ felons and convicts on the expiry of their terms of imprisonment, and though this met at first with opposition from the steady and respectable families in his employ, his influence with his men carried the day, to such an extent that no unpleasant allusions to their antecedents were made by their fellow-workmen ; and with hardly an exception they have all been reclaimed to society, and have become industrious artisans. Meanwhile M. Bouillon's business prospered ; and his sons, who follow in their father's footsteps in building schools, and promoting by every means in their power the well-being of their people, now employ upwards of 300 hands. Mothers and daughters are not permitted to work in the factories, but stay at home and attend to their domestic duties.

Other silver medals. 2. *La Compagnie des Verreries et Cristalleries, de Baccarat, Meurthe.* This employs 1,800 hands, and produces glass-ware to the value of 5,000,000 francs a-year. It possesses schools, stores, savings banks, sick-funds, and all the machinery of a well-conducted establishment.

3. *M. Menier, Fabrique de Noisiel-Sur-Marne, Seine et Marne,* for its "paternal administration and generous solicitude,"—words which, after what has gone before, sufficiently indicate the principles on which it is conducted.

Concluding remarks on With these three silver medals I shall close this

notice of France in Class VII. A few bronze awards
and honourable mentions fell to other exhibitors;
but no novel features appear among them to call for
special observation. There is no doubt that the co-
operative movement, both of production and consumption, is making giant strides in France, and
French workmen now avail themselves unstintingly
of the permission to combine to influence wages, given
under the law of 1864. Yet while many a French
strike thus legalised occurs, little heed is paid to it
by the outer world. If on a small scale, it is generally adjusted, with mutual concession, by the *Préfet*
or *Sous-Préfet*, on whose impartiality both parties
usually rely, and whose non-official action they prefer
to the intervention of the official *Prud'homme*. If
on a large scale, it finds its level when its funds are
exhausted ; but in neither case are violence, menace,
or fraudulent procedure of any kind permitted for a
single moment. The ends of justice are best served
by prompt measures ; an important fact which France
appreciates to the full, and which we in England
often overlook. In France the arm of the law is
strong, and better still, it is bold, while, if not popular, it is at least respected, which is of infinitely more
importance to the orderly and hard-working elements
of society. Laws should be framed and carried out
to protect such elements, rather than to afford
immunity to malefactors even of a doubtful shade of
culpability.

The great German nation next demands attention.
Assuredly it will not be found behind its brethren in
co-operative development, nor in legislative securities
against the abuse thereof. In the lists of awards
which fell to German individuals and associations in
Class VII, representatives will be found of most of
the features which we have already descried upon the
face of civilization in the limitrophe states which

CLASS VII. bound it on the west so far north as the mouth of the Elbe. Under these circumstances, it will not be necessary to follow up the roll of German successful exhibits so closely as has been done in the case of France, &c., more especially as the principles maintained by the International Jury were the same, and as the people's banks of Germany, the form which People's co-operation has assumed in that country under the banks. guidance of the skilful hand and head of M. Schultze-Delitsch, are already well known in England—thanks to the valuable Reports of Mr. Morier, Secretary of Legation, resident at Darmstadt. These people's banks now number over 1,500, and dispose of £4,500,000 sterling. They exist in every nook and corner of the Fatherland, and are conducted on the soundest of financial principles. Their name is legion, and their action is irreproachable. In addition to these wide-spread credit societies, the co-operation wave has imported into Germany societies of consumption in great numbers and variety, while societies of production are beginning in many places to raise their honest heads. Besides these we find in Germany *Vereins* of workmen of different and of affiliated trades, for promoting education, recreation, and the physical advantages which follow on unadulterated food and the use of fair weights and measures. Of such societies, one of the most perfect Berlin to be found in Germany is the *Société des Ouvriers* Workmen's of Berlin. It was founded in 1859, and is composed Society. of upwards of 60,000 members. It was completely spontaneous and unaided from without in its origin, and by its own power, and its own good sense in the selection of worthy objects for the investment of its funds, it has created a singularly complete system of instruction, primary and technical, besides many means of intellectual and social enjoyment, such as reading rooms, club rooms, and the like. The laws

that control these associations in Northern Germany
were, until last June, more severe than those in
force in France; and strikes, or the appropriation of
funds for their support, were illegal, and punishable
by fine and imprisonment. By a recent law, however, the Prussian legislation on this subject is
practically assimilated to that of France. The
Société des Ouvriers of Berlin received the highest
award the Jury had it in their power to bestow.

While, as is thus seen, the German workman is
by no means backward in associative tendencies,
large employers of labour in the Fatherland are no
less solicitous for the welfare of their hands than in
other Continental States. The 10,000 workmen
who labour in the monster iron and steel works of
M. Krupp, of Essen, in Rhenish Prussia, have
nothing to envy in the condition of their brethren in
France or Belgium. The number of drunkards is
diminished, schools are provided, *caisses de retraite*
and *de prévoyance* are encouraged, dwellings are
constructed on the most improved principles, wives
stay at home and look after their domestic affairs,
workmen may retire on half-wages after twenty
years' active service, and on full pay after a period
of thirty-five years. Bakeries distribute bread 15
per cent. under the trade tariff, and a sound beer is
brewed and supplied at cost price. Finally, presents
are annually bestowed on the most meritorious workmen. In this last item M. Krupp spends some
thousands of pounds a year.

This, moreover, is no isolated instance. The silk
and velvet looms of Baron de Diergardt, at Viersen,
the brick-kilns of M. Boltze, at Saltzmunde, the
cement works of M. Quistorp, at Lebbin, Pomerania,
and the forges of Messrs. Stumm, near Saarbrück,
all testify to the same enlightened policy of solicitude
for the working man. Neither is South Germany in

CLASS VII.   those matters behind the Northern Bund. Bavaria
and Wurtemberg offer many precisely similar cases ;
and the homogeneous character of the Teutonic
race, from the peaks of the Tyrol to the shores of
the Baltic, is strikingly exemplified by the unanimity
of treatment these questions meet with from all
classes, labouring as well as employing, within those
broad territorial limits.

Austria.   Last, though not least, Austria affords no exception to German unity on this score. Vienna, no less
than Berlin, has its *Arbeiter* and its *Credit Vereins;*
while the cotton mills of Madame Staub, of Küchen,
the woollen *fabriques* of M. Liebig, of Reichenberg,
M. Drasche.   and the coal mines and brick works of M. Drasche,
all testify that Southern Germany is not behind the
Northern Bund in civilization and humanity. The
vast establishments of this last-named employer of
labour are indeed so remarkable as to demand a brief
account. They are scattered broadcast over the
Austro-Hungarian Empire, being situated in Upper
and Lower Austria, in Bohemia, in Poland, and in
Hungary. They employ a total of about 10,000 men,
who, with their wives and families, form permanent
colonies, and never quit his service, the development
of the mines, &c., absorbing the natural increase of
population. The whole 10,000 participate in the advantages derivable from a pension fund, originally
endowed by M. Drasche with 500,000 florins. A
second fund of equal magnitude has been similarly
endowed by him as a *caisse de scoours* for the sick and
injured. In addition to this he has built hospitals
for his colonies, and all his workmen receive lodging
and fuel gratis, and without reference to their
regular wages. He has built for their accommodation
upwards of 400 houses. Schools, churches, reading
rooms, clubs, and bursaries, for enabling successful
competitors to proceed to the higher schools and

universities also exist, and are augmented as occasion demands. These efforts of M. Drasche have contributed to the creation of so general a feeling of contentment among his men, that when, in 1848, other employers of labour were having their factories burnt down and pillaged by their own paid hands, the colonists of M. Drasche formed themselves into armed bands to protect their master's property.

It would be a most interesting study, but one very difficult of prosecution, to go carefully over Europe, and discover by statistics whether such noble examples are more frequently met with on the Continent than in Great Britain. I am not prepared to say off-hand whether such would prove the case or not. Vol. VI of the Reports of the Paris Exhibition of 1867, gives a long list of names assuredly second to none in the domain of practical philanthropy. Such names as Akroyd, Bliss, Briggs, Beaumont, Titus Salt of Saltaire, &c., stand out as monuments of what exists, and of what may be done by Christian treatment on our soil ; but these, and others equally deserving, may disabuse themselves of the belief, if indeed they entertain it, that England stands alone on this highway to better things and to a time when such treatment shall be universal and compulsory by law. When this goal is reached trade unionism will have no *raison d'être*, and strikes will be as much a matter of history as the wars between the Picts and Scots, or the Red and White Roses.

The Northern Kingdoms, faithful to their antecedents in other classes of the Exhibition, were second to none in the quality at least of their exhibits in Class VII. Denmark received the highest awards for its *Arbeider foreningen*, and for its *Arbeidernes Byge foreningen*, both of Copenhagen. Sweden received a well-merited gold medal for a similar association of working-men at Gothenburg, styled

Arbitare foreningen. All these are founded on the soundest of sound principles. Many other things that were good, and deserving of close study, came from the north to take their place in Class VII, and in almost every case to carry off well-merited awards. The vast iron works and forestries worked by Mr. Dickson at Gothenburg, and on the Gulf of Bothnia, did not escape the attention of the Jury, whose eyes wandered over Europe in search of good and evil; of which two elements it is strictly true to say that the first predominated. Under the superintendence of Mr. Dickson, in the deep gloom of those northern pine forests, schools and churches are erected, the use of strong drinks is prohibited, savings banks are encouraged, and pension funds are endowed, in the same manner as we have found in France, Belgium, Holland, and the Fatherland, in the remotest gorges of the Black Forest, and in the wide-spreading plains of Hungary.

It is greatly to be regretted that the American Continent was not represented in Class VII, so as to complete the character of the collection therein contained. Although this was unfortunately the case, yet the position of the social questions embraced in the brief title of Class VII within the limits of the Great Republic, did not escape the observation and discussion of the Jury. Tributes were paid to many associations belonging to the New World, to the legislation that controls them, and to the fame of Mr. Peabody, who has united the Old World with the New by perhaps the vastest link of human charity yet forged by the ardent efforts of the nineteenth century.

Finally, the noble works of great Sovereigns, Princes, and Princesses did not pass unnoticed at Amsterdam; for while nothing was too lowly or too distant to attract the attention of the Jury in Class

(margin notes: Class VII. ; America.)

VII, nothing was too high placed or too near at hand to escape their criticism or be overlooked. The result of this section of their inquiry was the conferring of *Diplômes d'Honneur* on three personages who occupy the first and second places in France and Germany respectively ; and the claims on which in each case their title to these laurels rested will be found detailed in the following lists of royal and imperial benefactions, contributed to the alleviation of human suffering, and to the rendering of this life less hard to those who work the hardest.

His Majesty the Emperor of the French.

For institutions, establishments, and foundations in behalf of the working classes, originated or protected by His Majesty, as referred to in the documents collected and exhibited at Amsterdam by M. Paul Bucquet, Inspector-General of Establishments of Beneficence.

Instruction.—Extension of primary instruction ; establishment of 1,904 infant schools, of 10,092 public primary schools. Number of lessons given to adults increased fourteen-fold. Licence to give public lessons. Foundation of 8,400 school libraries.

Technical instruction or teaching of handicrafts. Law on this subject. Bill on the employment of children in factories. Decree, by virtue of which mining engineers are charged with the duties of inspectors of children employed in factories.

Training for handicraft ; Bill on technical instruction.

Subsidies.—Foundation of the Asile Impérial de Vincennes for convalescent working-men (11,000 admissions per annum), 1855. Foundation of the Asile des Convalescents de Lamothe Sanguin for the working men of Loiret (1868). Foundation of the Asile Impérial de Vesinet (1855) for convalescent working women (6,000 admissions per annum).

Institutions for the treatment of the sick at their own homes (1853). Re-organization of medical attendance, free of charge, to agricultural labourers ; (1853) (232,000 persons of this class availed themselves of it in the year 1867).

Foundation of the Hospital Plombières, of hospital beds, of the Refuges "Napoleon" in the Hautes Alpes, of the orphan house at Versailles.

Extension of subsidies made by the State ; foundation of 172 new hospitals, of 3,912 offices of relief ; adoption of 34 lunatic asylums, and foundation of 28 pauper workhouses ; prohibition of begging in 59 departments.

Protection of the Interests and Promotion of the Morality of the Working Classes.—Law on legal assistance ; abolition of arrest.

Law to facilitate marriages among the poorer classes, on the legitimisation of their bastard children, and on resuming the care of those children when placed in charitable institutions (1850). Law on emigration (1850). Law on trade unions (1864). Law on public meetings. The oath of the workman to be received in courts of justice (abolition of Article 1781 of the Code Napoléon : the master's oath to be received, &c.)

Bill for the abolition of the law subjecting factory operatives to have a workman's book ("livret").

Improvement of Material Condition.—Dwellings for working-men and small families, established at the cost of the Emperor, viz., Cité Napoléon in Paris, sixteen houses, Boulevard Mazas ; one house for unmarried workmen ; forty-one houses, avenue Daumesnil ; eight houses on the Champ de Mars ; three houses at Bayonne, Cité Napoléon at Lille ; gifts

of 300,000 francs to the Society of Mülhause; Class VII
Decree assigning 10,000,000 francs for founding
houses for the working classes.

Establishment of public baths and washhouses at
reduced prices, 500,000 francs granted (1853). For
effecting sanitary improvements in populous districts.
Law on unwholesome dwellings (1850). Forming
squares, promenades, parks. Opening, in 1861, of
the people's kitchen, called after the Prince Imperial,
in Paris. Annual subsidy of 100,000 francs given
by the Emperor.

Law for the completion of by-roads.

Inquiry into the state of agriculture.

Collection at the Great Exhibition of 1855, of a
class of articles for the households of the working-
classes.

Collection at the Great Exhibition of 1867, of
the 10th group: articles especially adapted to the
improvement of the physical and moral condition of
the people.

Relief from Taxation.—Reduction of the land-
tax, of the tariff of imports and exports. Exemption
from taxation of dwellings below 200 francs.

Relief from bridge-tolls (11,000,000 francs applied to their redemption).

Extension of gratuitous instruction in schools
(1,767,251 children admitted gratuitously).

*Institutions for promoting the Acquisition of Pro-
perty, and for encouraging Economy and Saving.*—
Increase of wages in consequence of extended public
works.

Establishment of workmen's dwellings at Bayonne,
with qualification on the part of the workman to
become the proprietor, on payment of 300 francs per
annum for 15 years (200 francs for rent, 100 francs
for the ultimate purchase of the house).

Re-organization of savings banks. Between

1851 and 1867 increase in the number of depositors 149,295; increase in the amount of deposits 110,705,618 francs 32 centimes. Increase in the number of savings banks 173.

The balance on hand in the savings banks was, on June 30, 1867, 404,533,708 francs 59 centimes.

Establishment of savings banks for old age (1850). From 1851 to 1867, increase in the number of deposits 291,510; in the amount deposited 7,578,571 francs 94 centimes.

The balance on hand was on June 30, 1869, 3,318,257 francs interest, representing 75,717,437 francs 16 centimes invested.

Assurance brought within the Means of the Working Classes.—Foundation of two public assurance offices: one a life assurance; the other for accidents arising in the course of agricultural or industrial employment (July 11, 1868).

Mutual Support.—Encouragement of societies for mutual support.

Law on the societies for mutual support, July 15, 1850.

Decree devoting 10,000,000 francs to the societies for mutual support.

Subsidy of 500,000 francs to the establishment of pension funds.

From 1851 to 1867. Foundation of 3,592 societies; increase in honorary members, 92,013; increase in ordinary members, 516,310; increase in reserved fund, 36,661,131 francs; balance on hand, June 30, 1869, 169,345,500 francs 72 centimes.

Co-operation. Co-operative Societies.—Foundation by the Emperor of the co-operative society's fund (August 5, 1866).

Discounting securities of the societies of production, of mutual credit, of individual workmen. Of 34,171 securities presented, 9,425 are below 100 francs ; 17 centimes for every 100 francs discounted.

Gift of 500,000 francs to the funds by the Emperor.

Gift of 300,000 francs by the Emperor for the promotion and establishment of the Weavers' Co-operative Society at Lyons.

Gift by the Emperor of forty-one houses to the co-operative associations of real property at Paris.

Burial Clubs.—Foundation by the Emperor of "Aumôniers de dernières prières." (Decree of March 21, 1852), charged with gratuitous funeral rites of the poor.

Her Majesty the Empress of the French.

The Empress Eugénie.

Her Majesty the Empress of the French :—For institutions and foundations established by or under the protection of Her Majesty, as contained in the documents collected by M. Paul Bucquet, Inspector-General of Beneficent Institutions.

Primary and Technical Instruction.—The infant schools, by Decree of March 30, 1854, are placed under the protection of the Empress.

Her Majesty the Empress founds, in 1853, the institution "Eugène Napoléon," by the donation of 600,000 francs presented by the city of Paris to purchase a diamond necklace for Her Majesty (300 orphan girls receive technical instruction in the institution Eugène Napoléon).

Institution of "Pupilles de la Marine" (1862), 415 pupils, orphans, or children of seamen, received from 7 to 13 years of age.

Institution of Popular Lectures ("conferences populaires") in the Imperial Asylum of Vincennes (1856). Political Economy. Law. Moral Philosophy. Sanitary Science.

R

CLASS VII.   *Subsidy or Assistance.*—Her Majesty gives
100,000 francs for new beds in the Hospital for
Incurables (1853).

Her Majesty founds the Hospital Eugène, in the
Faubourg St. Antoine (March 10, 1854): 3,300 sick
children admitted annually. Foundation of the
"Asile des Convalescents Sainte Eugénie," at Lyons
(July 9, 1866).

Protection.—Institutions for neglected and deserted children, foundling hospitals, are placed under
the exalted protection of Her Majesty (1853). Gift
of 100,000 francs to the societies described above.

Her Majesty has under her protection the
" Crèches " (1862), the " Maison Impériale des Quinze
Vingts " (1854), the General Establishment of Beneficence ("Etablissements Généraux de Bienfaisance"),
Imperial Deaf and Dumb Institutions at Paris, Bor-
deaux, Chambery ; the Institution for Blind Children
at Paris ; the Establishment or Institution of Mont
Genevra ; the Imperial Asylums at Vincennes,
Vesinet, Charenton ; the Association for the Protection of Apprentices, and Factory Children (1867) ;
the Association for Assisting and Providing for the
Deaf and Dumb, the Schools for Deaf and Dumb,
and Blind Children at Paris ; the Central Association
for Ship-wrecked persons (1863).

Mutual Assistance.—The Empress founds associations for mutual assistance in behalf of seamen at
Dieppe, Dunkirk, &c. (1859).

Guardianship and Apprenticeship.—Foundation
of the Orphan House of the Prince Imperial (September, 1855). Placing orphan children in the
families of respectable working men, apprenticeship,
protection of the orphan children (600 orphan
children are provided for).

Loan Societies.—Foundation of the association of
the Prince Imperial (1862).

Foundation of the credit fund. Loans to work- CLASS VII.
men for the purchase of tools and materials.
Assistance in exceptional and temporary distress of
families requiring help : 22,109 loans, to the amount
of 6,278,038 francs. Capital invested, March 3,
1869, 2,154,249 francs 48 centimes.

Her Royal Highness Victoria, Crown Princess of Crown Prin-
Prussia, Princess Royal of Great Britain and cess of Prussia.
Ireland.

1. Preliminary steps for establishing the association at Berlin, for enabling women to earn their
living (" Erwerbsfähigkeit ").
2. Promotion of all the institutions of this
association.
3. Much personal trouble in all the undertakings
and operations of this association.
4. Union of separate associations to the one
already existing, in accordance with a scheme
specially contrived, and constant supervision of the
working of the same.

The Association for enabling women to earn
their living (" Für Erwerbsfähigkeit des Weiblichen
Geschlechtes "), has more particularly turned its
thoughts, and directed its operations to women of the
middle and lower classes, especially with a view to
secure to unmarried women a better condition than
has hitherto been possible, as well as to give married
women suitable opportunities of assisting their
husbands. The association would wish to attain
these results :—

(a.) By discovering suitable situations in commerce, and other vocations.

(b.) By indicating where work is to be procured.

(c.) By giving the opportunity to sell their own
work at very moderate prices.

(*d.*) By instruction in such knowledge as is necessary for the commercial classes, so that women may obtain better employment and improve their circumstances.

(*e.*) To attain the object referred to in (*d*) there have been established—

(1.) The Industrial Institution (Gewerbe Institut) for girls at Berlin, under the direction of Professor Clement, and under the especial protection of the Crown Princess ;

(2.) The commercial school for girls, near Lohff, in which only elementary knowledge will be taught ; and,

(3.) A sale room ("Victoria Bazaar"), where women's work is sold.

(*f.*) By founding the "Victoria Stift," where single women are provided with lodging at a low charge. A kitchen is attached.

(*g.*) By the Drawing School of Schulz and Troschel, accompanied by lectures on art and industry.

(*h.*) By founding the "Victoria Lyceum," which has for its object the spread of a higher knowledge of art and science among women.

(*i.*) By regular lectures, to be given by the most talented persons in Berlin, so as to promote the objects of the association.

The Crown Princess accords to the pupils of the above institutions, at all times, free admission to these lectures.

(*k.*) By indicating and presenting productions of industry to serve as models, with a view to improve the taste by copying these productions.

Concluding remarks on Class VII.

Before taking leave of Class VII, I cannot refrain from hazarding the opinion that any trade union or co-operative association which should, failing ascertained means of support, make celibacy up to 30 or 35 years of age, and even then, unless a good future could be foreseen, a condition of membership, would render an important service to society. If it be advanced against such discouragement of matrimony among the young and improvident that a large unmarried population is an element of immorality, I would maintain in reply that the large pauper population, which is the fruit of reckless early marriages among the wage classes, is a yet greater element of immorality, and a fertile source of the worst defects of our civilization. Education is the engine to which we must ultimately look as a cure for improvident marriages; for among the better and the best educated classes of society they diminish with all the regularity of a fixed law; yet pending the diffusion of education, trade unions have it in their power to conduce towards this end. It is fashionable, I know, to point to population as a source of wealth and strength, but it is really not so unless the resources for its support develop with its own increase, and in the same ratio. In Great Britain this has ceased to be the case, and our increase of population now seeks refuge in emigration, goes to swell the Fenian ranks or other buccaneer associations, or raises the poor-rates, if it stays at home, thus only tending to impoverish us in time of peace, and to embarrass us in time of war or complication. This is the case that is alleged to have occurred in Java, where its fruits are beginning to be severely felt. The rice fields being circumscribed in order to promote the growth of Government coffee for export, and the population having greatly increased, the rice fields are necessarily divided among more families. Meanwhile the rice imported by Government is insufficient to make up the difference. Each family thus gets less, or inferior food, and con-

sequently seeks other paths, if not to fortune, at
least to daily bread. Experience is beginning to
teach that these paths are not always, nor indeed
often, those of honesty or loyalty.

I am well aware that the indolent Asiatic cannot
be compared to the industrious Anglo-Saxon, any
more than the limitation of the rice-fields of Java
can be compared with actualities at home. Yet the
broad features are the same. The land cannot be
made to produce more sustenance, the mills and mines
are full of hands and have no room for more ; meanwhile the population increases, and the results in the
one case will resemble the results in the other. In
both cases growth of population means no longer
growth of wealth, but growth of poverty and of the
poor-rates. I venture to submit this view of the
position to trade unions, who, by applying checks to
the improvident growth of the population, would
probably attain their end of keeping up the price of
labour better than by the cut-throat means to which
they now resort.

This heaping up of population in Great Britain,
or in Java, or wherever it occurs, is the source of
nearly all the greatest difficulties the nineteenth
century has to cope with. In our own islands it has
become intensified at the centres of our industrial
wealth,—in London, Manchester, Liverpool, Glasgow,
Paisley, Coventry, and the like ; and until some
means are found to drain off the surplus population
and to distribute it where it is better able to support
itself, the efforts of philanthropists in erecting *cités
ouvrières* and in opening great markets—in other
words, in alleviating the hard lot of the heaped-up
population, but really only rendering it possible for
it to heap itself up still more, however meritorious
and munificent of themselves,—by no means strike
at the root of the evil. Hence it is with great satis-

faction that those who appreciate the evils of this state of things have learnt that the trustees of the latest Peabody gift have awarded preference to building on suburban sites within a ten-mile radius of London, thus laying the first pipes of a drain for carrying off to realms of purer air and less condensed distress the surplus population of the metropolis. It is probable that when this want of vital drainage is better understood, some machinery, Governmental or the reverse, may be invented for effecting what is needed, and that, a decade or so hence, the powers who rule may invent or further some system of inspection and surveillance of the poorest classes of urban society, having for its object the removal of labour from where it is not required, and unable to find fair wages or befitting accommodation, to such points of Great Britain or her dependencies as stand in need of it, or are at least more capable of supporting it.

That such an agency is needed none will deny, though how far it is possible to create it the future must decide ; meanwhile, no one possessed of the ordinary reflective powers with which we are endowed can contemplate the social position of the nineteenth century without arriving at the conclusion that no Government performs its proper functions, and no administrative organization, however perfect otherwise, is possessed of the highest claim to the epithet enlightened, that does not strive to conquer and divert into self-supporting channels the stagnant waters of society, that are daily growing more stagnant and more difficult to deal with.

CONCLUSION.

Appoint-
ment of
Exhibition
Juries.

HAVING now followed the Exhibition through the
seven classes into which it was divided, it is important
to learn on what principles the Jury work was conducted. An Exhibition Jury has hitherto been
appointed on one of two methods : by decree or by
election. If the former, by decree of the Sovereign,
the Minister, or the personage charged with the
Presidency of the Exhibition *ex plenitudine potestatis;*
if the latter, usually by the exhibitors, and sometimes
from among themselves. In the case of Amsterdam,
as has been seen, the International Jury for deciding
awards was appointed by Royal Decree of the King
of the Netherlands, a course in accordance with most
of the more important exhibition precedents. The
Minister of the Home Department was charged with
the execution of the Decree, and under his authority a
code of regulations for the guidance of the Jury was
speedily issued. As this document was the Commission, as it were, which constituted the Central
Jury, or *imperium in imperio,* a Revising Court for
criticising the decisions of the Class Juries, of whose
action several complaints have found their way into
the columns of the daily papers, I here transcribe it
in extenso. It consisted of 18 Articles, viz. :—

Jury regula-
tions.

"Art. 1. Les membres du jury sont repartis en sept
classes, suivant l'ordre de celles où les produits sont
exposés.

"Art. 2. Le Jury de chaque classe nomme son
Président, son Secrétaire, et son Rapporteur.

"Art. 3. Les produits sont jugés exclusivement

au point de vue de leur importance, pour les besoins matériels et moraux des classes ouvrières, sans distinction de nationalité.

" Le Jury aura principalement à tenir compte du bon marché de la production et du bas prix de la vente.

" Art. 4. Les récompenses mises à la disposition du Jury sont les suivantes :—

" 1. Grands Diplômes d'Honneur.

" 2. Médailles de première classe.

" 3. Médailles de seconde classe.

" 4. Médailles de troisième classe.

" 5. Mentions honorables.

" Les produits qui ne rempliront pas les conditions indiquées à l'Article 3 pourront cependant, s'ils le méritent sous quelque rapport, être l'objet d'une mention extraordinaire.

" Art. 5. Des médailles de troisième classe ou des mentions honorables pourront être accordées aux co-opérateurs des exposants, qui auront reçu des diplômes d'honneur ou des médailles de première et deuxième classes, mais seulement sur la proposition de ces derniers.

" Art. 6. Les membres des Jurys de Classes sont autorisés à s'adjoindre des experts pour se faire éclairer individuellement.

" Art. 7. Si, pendant les opérations d'un Jury de Classe, le besoin d'éclaircissements plus précis se fait sentir, le Comité Central de la ' Société pour l'Encouragement du Travail Industriel et Manuel des Pays-Bas' (' Het Hoofdbestuur der Vereeniging ter bevordering van Fabrieks-en-Handwerks nijverheid') nommera un ou plusieurs experts, qui seront tenus à rédiger un rapport. Les noms de ces experts pourront être tenus secrets.

" Art. 8. Chaque Jury de Classe fournira un rapport détaillé et motivé, où seront consignés les avis

émis par la minorité aussi bien que par la majorité
au sujet des decisions prises.

" Ce rapport devra contenir :—

" 1. L'énumération des produits dont on aura
reconnu la falsification ou la mauvaise qualité.

" 2. Les rapports des experts.

" 3. Les propositions des récompenses avec indi-
cation des produits et de l'ordre de la récompense
demandée pour chacun d'eux.

" Ce rapport sera transmis au premier Secrétaire
du Jury avant le 9 Août.

" Art. 9. S'il s'agit de récompenser un exposant
qui vend au détail, le prix de vente des produits
devra figurer dans le rapport du Jury de Classe.

" Art. 10. Les rapports du Jury seront tenus
secrets jusqu'à la publication qui en sera faite par le
Gouvernement.

" Art. 11. Les membres du Jury éliront pour
chaque nation un délégué, afin de former, sous la
direction du Président du Jury, un Jury Central,
auquel sera adjoint un Secrétaire Spécial.

" Art. 12. Le Jury Central, après examen, rati-
fiera sans réserve les récompenses proposées par les
Jurys de Classes, excepté dans les cas suivants :—

" 1. Lorsqu'il aura été constaté que le produit
proposé pour une récompense ne remplit pas le but
de l'Exposition, ou que la récompense aura été pro-
posée avec une moindre sévérité que celle qui a
présidé aux décisions des autres classes. Dans ce
cas la décision sera prise par le Jury Central.

" 2. Lorsque le Jury Central trouvera le juge-
ment des Jurys de Classes insuffisament motivé.
Dans ce cas des éclaircissements plus précis seront
demandés. Si ce dernier moyen n'est pas encore
reconnu suffisant, le Jury tout entier sera convoqué
pour statuer.

" Art. 13. Le Jury Central admettra des réclamations, de quelque part qu'elles viennent, dans le seul cas où il sera prouvé par les intéressés qu'il y a eu erreur pas des causes indépendantes du Jury.

" Art. 14. Aussitôt que les récompenses dans une classe auront été décidées, on composera un tableau donnant les noms et les résidences des lauréats ainsi que la nature des produits qui seront l'objet de la récompense.

" Ce tableau sera expédié au Ministre de l'Intérieur, pour être inséré au Journal Officiel (Staats-Courant).

" Art. 15. La rédaction du Rapport Général sur les travaux du Jury est confiée au Président et au premier Secrétaire.

" Le Rapport Général contiendra comme annexe des notes critiques rédigées par chacun des membres du Jury Central, formant une étude comparative des produits et des procédés industriels reconnus les plus appropriés dans son pays au développement d'une classe spéciale d'ouvriers, ainsi que de ceux qui dans les sections étrangères lui auront paru les plus dignes d'être avantageusement introduits dans son pays.

" Art. 16. Les membres et le Secrétaire du Jury Central, ainsi que le premier Secrétaire, ont le droit d'assister à toutes les réunions des Jurys de Classes.

" Art. 17. Les membres suppléants ont droit d'assister aux visites du Jury. Dans les assemblées des Jurys de Classes ils ont voix consultative seulement.

" Art. 18. Quand il y aura ballotage dans un Jury de Classe, le Président de ce Jury décidera du dernier ressort.

" Quand il y aura ballotage dans le Jury Central, le Jury entier sera appelé à décider.

" En cas de dernier ballotage le sort décidera."

The seven Class Juries into which the International Jury became divided under the above code
of regulations, were composed as follows :—

CLASS I.—*Dwellings.*

Mr. Cohen, President.
Capt. Dashwood, Vice-President.
M. Mondron, Reporter.
M. Berger, Secretary.
M. David.
M. Smidt Van Gelder.
M. Veth.
Le Chevalier de Wertheim.

Supplementary Members.

M. Chapon.
M. Worlizek.

CLASS II.—*Furniture.*

M. Tetterode, President.
M. Aimé Girard, Vice-President.
Dr. Rose, Reporter.
M. O. de Kerchove de Denterghem, Secretary.
M. Hermans.
Mr. Johnson.
Le Chevalier de Liebig.
M. Stobwasser.

Supplementary Members.

M. Ed. Kanitz.
M. Mourceau.
M. Serrurier.

CLASS III.—*Clothing.*

M. Grön, President.
M. Kruseman Aretz, Vice-President.

M. Carcenac, Reporter.
Mr. Alf. Wolff, Secretary.
M. L. d'Andrimont.
M. Eigeman.
Mr. Simmonds.
M. Strakosch.
Le Chevalier de Liebig.

Supplementary Members.
M. Grasveld.
M. Duvelleroy.
M. Worlizek.

CLASS IV.—*Food.*

M. Raeymaeckers, President.
M. Gilka, Vice-President.
Dr. Mouton, Reporter.
Dr. Vrolik, Secretary.
Dr. Gunning.
M. Halphen.
Mr. Simmonds.
M. Strakosch.

Supplementary Member
M. Ed. Kanitz.

CLASS V.—*Implements.*

Le Chevalier de Wertheim, President.
M. Martelet, Vice-President.
Mr. J. Gillon, Reporter.
M. J. Van den Wall Bake, Secretary.
M. Buddingh.
Dr. Grothe.
M. Hartsen.
M. Jensen.

Supplementary Member.
M. Ed. Kanitz.

CLASS VI.—*Instruction and Recreation.*

Baron de Watteville, President.
M. A. von Camp, Vice-President.
Dr. Kroenen, Reporter.
Dr. Van Oven, Secretary.
Mr. Hodgson Pratt.
Dr. Rive.
M. Strackee.
Le Chevalier de Wertheim.

Supplementary Members.

M. Bauernschmidt.
M. Bract V. Ueberfeldt.
M. Armand Desmaresq.

CLASS VII.—*Trade Unions and Co-operative Associations.*

Hon. T. J. Hovell Thurlow, President.
M. Donnat, Vice-President.
M. Clerfeyt, Reporter.
M. Pfaff, Secretary.
M. David.
Baron Mackay.
M. Muller.
Le Chevalier de Wertheim.

Supplementary Members.

M. Morillot.
M. Parcau.
M. Pierson.
Dr. Sax.
M. L. d'Andrimont.

Central Jury.

The Central Jury, with whom rested the responsibility of the final decisions in the adjudging of

awards, was elected *inter se* by the jurymen of each
country, who chose one of their number, a Frenchman, an Englishman, &c., to represent the interests
of his nation ; the choice being as much as possible
so made, as to insure each class, as well as each
country, being effectively represented. The English
jurymen had, in the first instance, chosen me to
represent their interests ; but not having been enabled, as already stated, to take my place upon the
Class Juries, I considered it better to devolve the
responsibility upon Mr. P. L. Simmonds, who had
received from the Lord Mayor permission to style
himself British Commissioner, and who, besides
knowledge of the manner in which the class jury
work had been performed, brought wide previous
exhibition experience to bear upon all doubtful
cases. The gentlemen into whose hands all the
reins were thus gathered, and upon whom responsibility rests for the ultimate adjudication of awards
were :—

> Baron D. J. Mackay, President.
> Mr. Simmonds, England.
> M. Martelet, France.
> M. Grothe, Prussia.
> M. Haupt, Austria.
> M. Van Camp, Belgium.
> M. Van den Wall Bake, Holland.
> M. Pareau, Denmark.

M. F. H. Van Notten was requested to act as
Secretary to this Central Jury, and the manner in
which it performed its arduous task, and the rules
by which it was guided, will be gathered from a
perusal of the following letter of its President com-
municating to the Netherlands Government the
results at which it had arrived, for publication in the
official " Gazette " :—

To M. Fock, Minister of the Interior.

"*Amsterdam, September* 29, 1869.

" Your Excellency,

" The Central Jury of the International Exhibition have the honour to present herewith to your Excellency the report of the distribution of awards to the exhibitors.

" The Central Jury have, as much as possible, maintained the recommendations made by the Class Juries. In any proposal for an award, they have put themselves the question whether the article was directly or indirectly useful to the workman, or if the articles were in all classes judged according to the same standard, and if the nature of the article admitted of a high award.

" All articles that did not answer the object of the Exhibition were placed *hors concours ;* considering, however, that many exhibitors belonging to this category, are especially meritorious, a distinction, for remarkable excellence, is conferred on them, of a '*diplôme d'excellence,*' and, for a relatively lower degree of excellence, of a '*mention extraordinaire.*'

" In several cases exhibitors sent articles which in some respects answered or complied with the requirements of the Exhibition, and in other respects did not ; in these cases the Central Jury asked themselves the question, whether the prize should be awarded for what lay within or without the limitations of the Exhibition, and upon the answer to this question depended the nature of the prize. Thus it does not follow from the fact of a '*diplôme d'excellence*' or of a '*mention extraordinaire*' being conferred, that the recipient of such distinction sent no articles suited and adapted to the direct object of the Exhibition, the domestic economy, of the working-classes.

" A prize of a lower class may be in some cases the highest distinction, because the nature of the article admitted of no higher distinction, although the workmanship left nothing to be desired.

" In some cases the Central Jury have thought it right to abstain from a decision, namely in those where there was a mooted and undecided scientific question.

" They judged that no honour ought to be conferred on exhibitors, however meritorious, by a premature reward. To give an instance, the Central Jury did not think themselves justified in expressing an opinion on theories of agriculture.

" True to this principle of rewarding only what the Central Jury could thoroughly judge of, they have excluded from competition other articles,— cements for instance,—whose excellence cannot be tested during the time an exhibition lasts. Nor have raw materials on which the exhibitors have bestowed but little labour, been taken into account.

" The great difficulty there was in defining the limits of the Exhibition induces the Central Jury to take the liberty of adding the remark, that those who had the management of the Exhibition wisely made the range of admission wide, and left it to the Jury to decide in each case what fulfilled the prescribed conditions. By this means, in the humble judgment of the Central Jury, the object of the Exhibition was better attained than if the Committee of Management themselves, without the possibility of calm and careful consideration and deliberation, had sharply defined the limitations. The Central Jury may then, in conclusion, after a thorough examination of all the subdivisions of the Exhibition, declare, that it has perfectly answered its purpose. The general report will further confirm this opinion. The representatives of the foreign

exhibitors on the Central Jury wish at the same
time to communicate to your Excellency, that,
judging from the sales effected by the exhibitors, it
may safely be concluded, that, in this particular, the
Exhibition will appear to be not without fruit in its
consequences to the Dutch consumer.

"The Central Jury trusts that this Exhibition
will contribute to an increase in the knowledge of
the most suitable ways and means of bettering the
condition of the working-man.

"In the name of the Central Jury.

(Signed)   "D. J. MACKAY, *President*.

"F. H. VAN NOTTEN, *Secretary.*"

Value of
Exhibitions,
and of their
catalogues.

It will not escape notice, that in this letter Baron
Mackay draws attention to the sales made by exhibitors at the Amsterdam Exhibition, as of sufficient
importance, both of themselves as isolated purchases,
and in their character of pioneers of new sources of
food, clothing, and the like, to render them not
unimportant to the Dutch consumer. So far as
England is concerned, this is most strictly true;
though to what exact extent is not possible of calcu-
lation or estimation. On this point, and on the
question of how far those who took part in the
Exhibition were satisfied with the Jury method
followed at Amsterdam, I consulted confidentially
the exhibitors themselves. From the expressions of
opinion thus evoked, it appeared generally to be the
large firms who confessed to considerable orders, and
a belief in future benefits to their business; all concurred in the great value to industry generally of
Exhibition catalogues, which, beginning with 1851,
form a library of works of reference, in which the
progress made in every trade can be clearly traced,
and studied internationally. In fact, it is to the
permanent value attached to the catalogues that

must be attributed the fact that so many exhibitors care more to make a good show in the catalogue, which remains, than in the Exhibition itself, which closes in a few months. Another universally acknowledged advantage of Exhibitions and their catalogues is the opportunity they afford of making inventions widely known. This point is well put in the subjoined extract from a letter addressed to me by Mr. John A. Pols, a successful exhibitor in Class II, who writes under date, October 6, 1869 :—

" The experience of this and many past Exhibitions, proves that they are alike useful to the successful manufacturer and the struggling inventor ; to both of whom international publicity of their names and productions is a matter of the greatest importance ; and as the latter, in his struggles to perfect his inventions, often expends the whole of his available resources, these exhibitions give them the much-needed opportunity of making known the value, economy, and usefulness of their inventions, in case they wish to dispose of their productions, or to sell their processes."

Of the over 150 replies to my inquiries which I received from exhibitors, it is satisfactory to record that 50 per cent. in round numbers expressed themselves fully satisfied with the results of the Exhibition. Now, when it is remembered that about 67 per cent. of the British exhibitors received awards of some kind, it may be presumed that there would remain 33 per cent. of more or less discontented ; and when to these is added the contingent of those who got silver or bronze medals, and were dissatisfied because they were not gold or silver, it will be understood that 50 per cent. of malcontents is no more than might have been expected from a study of the bare statistics. The list of contents and malcontents, however, though bearing a natural general relation to the

Analysis of awards.

lists of awards, yet displayed many exceptions to what might have been expected in this regard ; and by far the major part of the malcontents, recompensed or not, represented small and unimportant houses, whose exhibits, having little to recommend them on the ground of novelty or price, met with little favour from the Jury, or the serious public, who were busily engaged in seeking out new sources of supply, and were not inclined to waste their time or money on exhibition trash or "padding," which nevertheless always carries off, and perhaps justly, a certain share of low awards.

This question of awards is the great stumblingblock of exhibitions. Their percentage on the total exhibits, deemed necessary to insure what is called the success of an exhibition, has steadily increased since exhibitions were invented ; and if their increase should continue, the date, not far distant, may easily be calculated when every exhibit will receive its medal, or its *mention honorable* or the reverse.

For this evil only two possible remedies exist ; either abandon appreciative tokens of every kind, or hedge them round with a machinery not yet invented, and immaculate. It will be evident to all, even to those least versed in exhibitions, that the former of these courses would be the easiest ; and not the least advantage gained would be the absence of intriguing, on the part of those interested, to be represented on the Class or Central Juries.

Hints for future Exhibitions.

In the course of studying the Amsterdam Exhibition from all its points of view, I have, therefore, arrived at the four following conclusions :—

1st. The catalogue should be an official publication, and not given as a concession to any publishing house with leave to make its own terms for advertisements.

2nd. Exhibitors should be required to certify that

the goods they exhibit are of their own manufacture, and to state the wholesale price.

3rd. Wherever there is a Jury at all, there should be a Central Jury of some kind to revise the awards ; but Class Jurymen should be bound under very heavy penalties not to make known their recommendations, more especially previous to the ultimate publication of awards. In the case of France at Amsterdam, the greatest embarrassment was caused by the premature publication of the Class Jury recommendations before they had been considered by the Central Jury. Many of those who were finally adjudged, say gold medals, grumbled because they knew the highest award, a *Dipiôme d'Honneur* had been recommended by the Class Jury; and some who were left out altogether in the last revision, complained bitterly of Amsterdam and of all therewith connected.

4th. Considering the *rôle* Exhibitions play in commerce, and their increasing frequency, it is desirable to establish some efficient Government control over the part taken in them by each country ; and, considering the practical tendency of the age, it is desirable that such control should reside rather with the Board of Trade, than with any other Department, such as the Foreign Office, or the Department of Science and Art.

Of all the Jury suggestions addressed to me, one of the most original, and at the same time most practical, came from the great house of Cliff and Son, of Wortley, Leeds, who wrote :—

"Our idea of awards is this. In an International Exhibition let a circular be sent to each competitor as follows :—

"In the absence of your own goods, whose do you consider entitled to most merit—

" For novelty ?

" For excellence of manufacture ?

" For excellence of material ?

" For cheapness combined with durability ?

" Then let a Jury, as at present formed, take all these statements as their guide, and act as a Grand Jury to throw out the Bill, as it were, if they saw any connivance, or reason to alter the judgment of those who ought to be the best judges."

If this plan were followed, I believe we should hear of fewer complaints.

Character of the official Jury Reports. In Baron Mackay's letter to the Minister of the Home Department, transmitting the final list of awards, it is further mentioned that the General Report, that is to say, the Jury Reports, will substantiate his assertion that the Dutch consumer has profited by the Amsterdam Exhibition. Now these reports of the Class and Central Juries, which will ultimately, though not for some months, see the light, and which, not being yet sent in by the several *rapporteurs* charged with their drafting, I have not had the advantage of consulting as I had anticipated, —will be divided into two categories ; the first confined to supporting the several recommendations for awards, the second, and far more interesting, calculating the results in £ *s. d.* on the daily life of the Dutch peasant,—that is to say, ascertaining what possible improvements have been made manifest in the condition of the man working, say at 1*s.* 6*d.* or 2*s.* a day ; from which country he can obtain, at the cheapest rate, the most durable and satisfactory articles of food, clothing, furniture, and the like. On these preserves I shall not poach, more especially as this Report has already exceeded the customary length, and the extent to which special subjects possess a claim upon general readers ; but I cannot abstain from recommending all who may, at the first blush of the Working-Man's Exhibition of 1869, be disappointed that no miracle has been wrought, that stones have not been converted into bread, nor the barren rock made to run with living water,—to delay their criticism for awhile and await the interesting contributions to social science which will ultimately spring from this as yet pent-up source.

On the subject of the finances and other statistics of the Exhibition, I am also precluded from entering, on account of the delay which has occurred in the publication of the official reports.* So much, however, is known, that the Exhibition was visited by nearly half a million of people during the three months it was open ; and that. with the aid of a small draft on the guarantee fund, and a Government contribution of 15,000 florins, the receipts will cover the expenditure. This not very favourable balance-sheet is due to the bad terms originally made with the Amsterdam Crystal Palace Company, the owners of the building where the Exhibition was held. In addition to a sum of 40,000 florins, the Exhibition authorities agreed to give up to the Company two-thirds of the money taken at the doors ; and the one-third left them proved insufficient to meet the usual miscellaneous items of advertising, printing, &c., to which had to be added, in the case of Amsterdam, the charges on account of building and fitting up suitable accommodation for foreign working-men visiting the Exhibition. The actual numbers of these are not known—the department charged with the manage-ment of that subject and the task of reporting on it, having caught the infection of delay, and not yet published the result of their labours.

As all tales, however dull or interesting, have an end, so had the Amsterdam Exhibition. Opened on

Finances and statistics of the Exhibition.

Close of the Exhibition.

* See Appendix.

July 15th by Prince Henry, it was closed on October 18th by Prince Alexander of the Netherlands, on both occasions in the name of the King ; and even as I was bound to give Baron Mackay's opening address, it is no less my duty to take official notice of the proceedings, of the dinners and the fireworks, which closed, as they had inaugurated, the under- taking, by transcribing the following address with which the President of the Exhibition greeted Prince Alexander on his arrival within the building, to dis- tribute the awards and declare it closed, in the name of the King his father :—

Address to Prince Alex- ander. " Your Royal Highness,

" I take advantage of this opportunity, in the first place, in the name of the Association for the Advancement of Manufactures and Industry, and in the next place in the name of the exhibitors, to tender to your Royal Highness my respectful acknowledgments for your presence here to-day. It affords us another proof that His Majesty regards with approbation the produce of Dutch industry, as well as the efforts made abroad to supply our requirements.

" Industry is grateful to your Royal Highness for your repeated visits to this Exhibition, and trusts that your Royal Highness will continue to devote attention to this important source of national prosperity.

" The distribution of awards to the successful exhibitors, at the close of this Exhibition, suggests many observations which I will not attempt to bring forward during the short space of time I can venture to devote to addressing your Royal Highness.

" One position, however, it appears to me may boldly be maintained : that a prominent and difficult problem of the present day has been propounded in the capital of this Kingdom in a manner that does no dishonour to our Fatherland. The love of truth and the strength of conviction which in all ages have distinguished the Dutch, have not only made it possible for questions of a delicate nature to be discussed without inconvenient results, but also have enabled persons of discordant and even opposite views, by intercommunication and exchange of ideas, to learn to appreciate each other better, and thus pave the way to closer union. The most antagonistic ideas were represented at this Exhibition.

"The difficult, I might almost say thankless, task of the Jury led them, as the list of awards indicates, without sacrificing their own convictions, to recognize all that was really good, produced in different ways in various countries.

"It is not now necessary for me to defend the principle adopted by the Central Jury called in to confirm the decisions which had been arrived at. With the greatest conscientiousness they devoted all their available time to the difficult questions proposed to them, and, in the judgment of well qualified persons, the best possible use was made of the short period which, after all, was longer than that which the Class Juries were able to bestow on their examinations. Besides the already difficult task of regulating the scale of awards, the Central Jury had to answer the question as to what did or did not satisfy the workman in the different parts of Europe. The social condition of every country—where these conditions differ so widely—had to be taken into account. In France, for instance, where the wants and requirements of different classes present scarcely any points of difference; or in England, where the 'skilled artisan' might be denominated an artist rather than a workman, articles wholly different come under the head of domestic economy from those

so classified in the land of the hardy nation which
holds the keys of the Sound. The creation of an
imaginary international workman, of whom a model
could carefully be made according to his supposed
position, would, therefore, have led to no good result.
The Central Jury could never have come to any
decision had they not simply put themselves the
question, Is the article now submitted to us suitable
to the workman in any part of Europe? Where
such suitableness could not be proved, the merit of
the exhibitor was recognized ; but in another way,
and by awards divided into two classes, naturally on
a different scale from the estimate of merit divided
into five classes.

"The Central Jury rigorously defined the limits
of the Exhibition, and kept its object constantly in
view. There appear, consequently, on the list of
diplômes d'excellence and *mentions extraordinaires*,
more articles than one would be tempted to look
upon as within the scope of the Exhibition, than
there will be found among the other successful
exhibits articles to which a scrupulously exact critic
might object.

"Considering that your Royal Highness has
already learnt, in the distribution of awards, what
concerns most nearly the domestic economy of the
workman, I need not enter on a repetition of the
catalogue. I rather crave permission to pause a
moment while we consider the instruction it affords us.

"Nobody can any longer doubt that the movement
we now witness in all the civilised countries of Europe
is the same that was so forcibly expressed long ago
by a French king who deserved a less tragical fate.
The nations of Europe have instituted in this regard
a laudable and formidable competition. They advance
by different roads, but their goal is the same. One

tries to promote the development of the working-man by a sort of parental care and supervision; another, by leaving him as much as possible to his own unassisted and unfettered resources; a third, by uniting the two systems. The conclusion arrived at by this Exhibition on this important point is in so far encouraging that it has adopted no absolute system, but has recognized that the local conditions dominate the question. A general conviction, however, prevails that a great responsibility rests upon those who lead the way to guard their followers against error and misconception, the necessary results of ignorance.

"The dissemination of sound opinions and correct views has, as Michel Chevalier so distinctly pointed out in the preface to the official Report on the French Exhibition, become a vital question. All that was noteworthy in this Exhibition had that tendency to a greater or a less extent. Philanthropy derives lustre from the dedication to it of noble powers; in the object before us they can even less be dispensed with. If the advanced guard is formed by men of science, well armed, the rear-guard should not be left unarmed. There is fortunately no branch of science conceivable which cannot contribute to the solution of this question; every one encounters prejudices which he ought to try to remove by popularizing the knowledge he possesses. Those who help science to make a step in advance ought also to take care that the principles of their science shall not be misunderstood by the public at large.

"Thus shall we be shielded from the dangerous consequences of recklessness; and prudence and skill, the inheritance of examination, shall be applied to the general benefit and advantage. The thirst for extended knowledge shall take the place of the desire to ventilate dangerous and untested notions.

"To the man who has carefully examined this Exhibition, and his opinion alone is weighty and valuable, a hundred questions present themselves which make a new and further examination an act of duty and a source of attraction. The great problems of the subsistence of the people, the sanitary question, the welfare and prosperity of the people, and their educational development were here put forth to view, and painful is the thought how much in these matters has yet to be set in order and corrected.

"Now that science and industry, as at this Exhibition, go hand in hand, the prospect is encouraging, and especially in the Netherlands may we look for a future of prosperity when a Prince of the dynasty we love so well gives us a guarantee that the House of Orange places itself at the head of the movement.

"Besides this discovery the Exhibition has brought about the advantage that foreigners, who often overlook what is passing in the Netherlands, have been able to convince themselves that the great questions our generation has to solve are here examined and investigated from different points of view with no less interest than they are abroad. We have legitimate cause for satisfaction when visitors from foreign countries confess and declare, without affectation or compliment, that their visit to us has made a deep impression on their minds. When an eminent and accomplished statesman, chary of his expressions of satisfaction, told us that the Amsterdam training school for workmen and the industrial school for girls had aroused within him a spirit of emulation, there was implicated in this avowal more than a compliment; we saw in it an encouragement to persevere, a stimulus to advance. We rescued our Fatherland from the billows of the

ocean, we must make it safe against the inroads of
ignorance. Though an exhibition can contribute to
this end, something more—constant exertion—is
required. We did not intend, by this Exhibition, to
set up a thing which would be unproductive when it
was over. No ; your Royal Highness must allow me
boldly to declare that we have a lively conviction
that this Exhibition will elicit new developments.
We wish our Fatherland to be at the head, and
remain at the head, of every grand movement of
our time. From what we have seen here we may
foretell that an exhibition like this, ten years hence,
will be no less remarkable, and that it will bring
forward many new points of view. Our country
must then also occupy a worthy place. But to
attain such a place a very great deal will be required.

"The giant strides of activity, which we notice
everywhere around us, must spur on our countrymen to unabated diligence. Expectations of great
things are entertained, for the estimate formed of us
gives rise to them. In this contest industry and
commerce may lay claim to general and powerful
support. No doubt foreign capital is at our command, but Dutch capital must not keep aloof. The
great undertakings that take advantage of the
favourable physical conditions of our Fatherland, in
which we must no longer content ourselves with
being in name only on a par with the most favoured
parts of the world, ought to have—yea, claim—the
approval of our capitalists.

"Not only at exhibitions do we wish to see the
products of foreign invention displayed ; on the
wharves of Dutch harbours we will give them the
benefit of the prosperity which they will spread
around. Now, if ever, is the time for the development of our trade. We cannot neglect our opportu-

nities with impunity. If we have but roused a
consciousness of this state of affairs, your Royal
Highness may be assured that we shall consider
ourselves richly rewarded for the work we have done.
We shall never forget what an important part foreign
industry, foreign diligence and ingenuity, side by
side with our native products, have played in the
success of this Exhibition. We are deeply grateful
for the marks of confidence thus afforded us.

" In the first place we would express our hearty
thanks to the foreign Commissioners and to the
foreign Jurymen, as well as to our own countrymen,
who afforded us, without exception, all possible
sympathy and co-operation. In what foreigners
have exhibited and in the ideas they have imparted
to us, there is undoubtedly much from which we may
derive profit and advantage. The opportunity of
conferring with their honoured visitors was to the
Dutch Commissioners and Jury as agreeable as it
was instructive.

" Without the foreign and Dutch exhibitors all the
exertions of the Commissioners and Jurymen would
have been in vain ; and although it was impossible
for us to give every one an award, all may feel con-
fident that their names and good intentions will
remain fresh in our recollections. For the regularity
and good order which distinguished the Exhibition,
we are, doubtless in a great measure, indebted to the
precautions so judiciously taken by the various Local
Committees ; all their efforts, however, would have
been fruitless had not the Dutch workmen—and we
were visited by 50,700 of them—proved that they
were well worthy of what was intended for their
benefit and advancement.

" It was especially gratifying to us to observe
that, in almost all parts of the country, people were
found ready and willing to make the visits of work-

ing-men profitable to them, by putting their more extended knowledge at the disposal of our much esteemed visitors of the working-class. We embrace this opportunity publicly to express to them our warmest acknowledgments.

" Dutch workmen showed the value they set on this Exhibition,—may it continue to be for them of permanent utility! The more interest society takes in their condition, the greater is their responsibility. Let them understand our object; let them take counsel with those who know best how to promote their interests; let them shun those who would seduce them to courses in the end injurious to themselves. Without exertion, without persevering assiduity, prosperity is unattainable for them, just as it is for most other members of society, and adversity will sooner or later teach them rightly to appreciate what they once disdained.

" Submission to authority and law is for them, as for all others, the only guarantee of success and of the sympathy which is so willingly extended to them. In their increased prosperity may they never take occasion to frame unreasonable demands, but may they look back, and trace what has been the source of their success. The Exhibition of 1869 belongs to history. As to its shortcomings, as well as its favourable features, we are perhaps not impartial enough, we are too much interested to present either of them fairly. Was the principle, however, to which it conformed practical? This is a question for posterity to answer. Will society, by drawing different classes into closer union, strengthen its foundations, or shall estrangement still further widen the present separation? This is a serious question, and can have but one solution.

" On this we are resolved, that no disheartening prognostications (and when were they ever wanting?)

shall keep us from devoting our best energies to the task before us.

"The great founder of the dynasty of your Royal Highness had no misgivings concerning the future. May this Exhibition afford a proof to foreigners, as well as to our own countrymen, to our contemporaries and to posterity, that the sons of those who were privileged to curb and to repel a foreign tyranny will not hang back whenever they may be exposed to similar dangers.

"May the medal of this Exhibition, wherever it is displayed, be the symbol of this endeavour.

"If an armed peace is the characteristic of the present day, from what arsenal shall we bring out weapons to bid defiance to all time? From the arsenal of industry, art, and science. The nation that knows how most to augment the number of these arsenals will bear the palm of victory. With your Royal Highness, we cherish the hope that the weapons here forged will contribute to assure to our beloved country the blessings that Providence has never withheld, whenever it assumed the manly and independent tone to which our whole history is a stimulus and encouragement.

"The present contest is over, and we now go back to the battle of life.

"May the motto for the battle in which every one of us can assure himself of victory, be now and always henceforth—

"LUCTOR ET EMERGO."

To this address Prince Alexander replied in the following speech, delivered with a power, dignity, and force of conviction far beyond his years :—

Prince Alexander's reply.

"Gentlemen,

"Honoured by the confidence of His Majesty

the King, and called upon by him to close this Exhibition. I am here to rejoice with you at the good results of the undertaking ; and I cannot refrain from testifying my grateful thanks to you for the hearty way in which you have received me.

" I hope and trust that the beautiful example set by the capital of the Netherlands will find imitation elsewhere, and that it will especially contribute to the welfare of the industrious working-class, whose interests are so dear to the hearts of us all.

" My wish is that by such means a friendly intercourse should be brought about and established between the workmen of different countries, and that the Exhibition of 1869 may leave behind a pleasant and enduring remembrance with us all.

" In conclusion, let us express our deep sense of obligation to the Home and Foreign Committees, for their valuable assistance, and our sincere thanks to the honoured exhibitors who made our undertaking so attractive and successful.

" In the name of His Majesty the King I declare the Exhibition closed."

All who have laboured through this somewhat long Report, will naturally ask themselves, when arrived at this last halting-place, and before taking leave of the Amsterdam Exhibition, what have been its practical results ? *Results of the Amsterdam Exhibition.*

To this very proper and most useful question I have no hesitation in replying that, in Holland, where it has literally taught the working man what to eat, drink, and avoid, and wherewithal he may best be clothed, its results have already been considerable, and will become day by day more apparent. To quote but one instance, and one that will react usefully on Great Britain in these days of wide-spread distress and general despair at the decline of trade,

a cry of satisfaction arose at Amsterdam from the
Dutch artisan at the opportunity afforded of comparing side by side the tools of England and their
Belgian imitations, of which some do not even stop
short of counterfeiting the trade-marks of our best-
known Sheffield houses. The result of this comparison is generally admitted to have been in favour
of British cheap hardware over continental articles,
with a disputed superiority on our side in the case
of the very first qualities. More than one Dutch
carpenter informed me triumphantly that his study
of the two would enable him henceforth to distinguish
the real article by its make and general cut from the
crafty imitation.

With many other articles it was the same ; and
this, indeed, is one of the special uses of Exhibitions,
the peculiar value of that at Amsterdam being that
it was principally composed of the very articles which
those attracted to it were best qualified to judge as
experts.

To Holland this Exhibition has further rendered
service by breaking down the barriers of prejudice
and fear which existed in the minds of many, effectually closing the approach to dealing with several
social questions on which legislation has been de-
ferred from time to time since 1855, and which are
now beginning to press for a solution.

A second general result of this Exhibition of
1869, and one of which we have yet to reap the
fruits, is the impulse it has given on the Continent
to the Workmen's Exhibition of 1870, and in their
mutual relation to each other it is probable that
not one of the least of the benefits conferred by the
former on the latter will be the manner in which, by
its very defects, it has buoyed out, as it were, the
road for its successor, pointing out the stumbling-
blocks and pitfalls which beset the fair accomplish-

ment of every *bonâ fide* philanthropic achievement of wide dimensions.

A third result, in which all contributing countries will participate, is the light thrown on the profits of the retail trade. At Amsterdam, it was possible to arrive at a comparison of the wholesale and retail prices of about 65 per cent. of the exhibits, and it need not be said that the opportunity was not neglected by those who appreciated the value and interest of the occasion, and were concerned in the issues of the inquiry.

A fourth result is the moral to be drawn from the action of the Jury in Class VII. This Jury was composed of men chosen on account of their fellow-feeling and sympathy with the co-operative movement as a lever for raising the condition of the working-classes; and this international tribunal confirmed, without a single dissentient voice, the verdict of the civilized world against trade unions in the Sheffield saw-grinders' and Manchester bricklayers' sense of the term.* Let us hope that this judgment, indorsed as it will be by all who love personal liberty and public order, will lend weight to the Legislatures of such countries as have not yet fol-. lowed the wise example of France; and that in legalizing trade unions as such, but not as superior to the penal code, they may not neglect to provide stringent legal enactments to limit and define their power of arbitrary rule, thus rendering impossible future repetitions of the rattening and picketing system, which is more destructive to the liberty of the subject in a country governed as ours is, than even the repeal of the vaunted "Habeas Corpus Act" would be.

Defenders of the odious practices thus branded at Amsterdam attribute the decline of trade to trade

* See Appendix.

unions not being yet international; but, whether
true or false, their theory will be many years before
it is disproved by actual fact, for a very long time
will happily elapse before the despotisms and strong
Liberal Governments firmly established on the Con-
tinents of Europe and America will legalize, or permit of a place being occupied in the statutes or the
acts of a trade union, by picketing, intimidation, and
ratteuing—those singular forms of civilization which
have grown out of an exaggerated respect for the
liberty of association as opposed and superior to
the liberty of the individual—and without whose
assistance international trade unionism would remain
as unproductive as it now is of benefit to British industry, and as powerless to perform the utopian services expected of it.

In conclusion, I beg leave to say that I approached the study of these questions, thinking
manhood suffrage and a "People's Parliament" possible remedies for trade unions, since, if they returned their own representatives to serve in Parliament, they might fairly be expected to trust to the
attainment of their ends by legislation; but I quit
the subject under discussion, firm in the belief that
such extended suffrage would only lead to inter-
necine war between Coventry and Manchester,—
between protection and free trade; and that, therefore, working men are, at least as yet, utterly unable
to legislate in the national interest on trade questions. Time must show whether such moral competence may ultimately develop itself in accordance
with the physical laws which regulate the demand
and the supply. That it may do so I do not deny;
but I do maintain that, judging from the specimens
before us of working-men's legislative tendencies as
displayed in the arbitrary and suicidal statutes of
their own trade unions, it is abundantly well proved

that no ground exists for the belief that the interests of civilization or of national prosperity would be advanced by the sudden promotion of the working-man—the common sailor—to the chief command in the vessel of the State.

The Hague, January 7, 1870.

APPENDICES.

WORKING MEN'S CLUB AND INSTITUTE UNION,

For Promoting the Social, Mental, and Moral Welfare, and Recreation of the Working Classes by the Establishment of Clubs and Libraries.

OFFICE, 150, STRAND, W.C.

This union is formed for the purpose of *helping* Objects. *Working Men to establish and maintain Clubs and Institutes,* where they can meet for conversation, business, and mental improvement, with the means of recreation and refreshment, without being dependent for these purposes upon the public-house ; the Clubs, at the same time, constituting Societies for mutual help of various kinds.

Thousands of young men resort night after night to the tap-room through having no home but a bed-room. Many hang about the street corners and market-places, even in inclement seasons, after a hard day's work, rather than go into the public-house. Great numbers of married men, often with large families, living in one or two rooms, have no means of enjoying that social intercourse with friends so much prized by the middle and upper classes, except by meeting where the accommodation must be paid for by drinking. Hence, among large masses of Working Men habits of improvidence and wasteful selfishness are formed, too often leading to intemperance and poverty, with neglected children and unhappy homes.

The *Club-rooms* in every locality *form the strongest counteraction to these evils;* which arise far more from the desire for company or social enjoyment, a warm fireside and well-lighted room, than in the love of drinking for its own sake.

Home, if we have one, is, *as a general rule,* the best place for any man, in any rank, when his day's work is done. But we must deal with facts as we find them and must *remember the number who have very limited domestic accommodation, or none at all.* Good homes will not often be deserted for the Club. In any case, men make home all the happier on returning to it, for an occasional hour spent in cheerful companionship, or in improving or amusing occupation, when relieved from wasteful or demoralizing temptations.

It is impossible for most Working Men, as at present circumstanced, to enjoy *at home* any of those blessings so prized by the classes above them, which come from the refining and elevating influences of *music,* literature, science, and art generally. They are condemned for the most part to a monotonous routine of mechanical drudgery, with the only variety of a pot of beer and their pipe, or of such amusements as are surrounded by contaminating influences, and are in themselves too often objectionable.

The extent to which Working Men suffer from their dependence, also, upon the public-house *for business purposes* is an immense evil, and one that is still inadequately appreciated. The report of the Registrar of Friendly Societies gives evidence of the incalculable injury resulting therefrom, not merely to those societies, but also to the character and the habits of their members. Gradually, however, the proposed Clubs and Institutes will become the centres of various Working Men's Societies, such as Friendly Societies, Freehold and Building Associations, Co-operative Societies, Circulating Libraries for the district, Temperance Societies, and of any similar agencies calculated to improve the condition of the Working Classes.

The aim of the union in all cases is *to help Working Men to help themselves,* rather than to establish or manage Institutions for them—this being as essential for the moral usefulness as for the permanent success of their endeavours. But it is not one of the least recommendations of this movement, that it is pre-eminently calculated, in every stage of it, to promote that *mutual sympathy and friendly intercourse,* as well as that interchange of benefits between the different classes and sections of society, which is not more stringently required by Christianity than needed for the preservation of social order and national progress.

One main reason of the want of more complete success in the progressive movements of the day is probably to be found in the *incompleteness* of the measures adopted. Vast good, for instance, has been accomplished by the Temperance Reform, but it often fails to retain those whom it has reclaimed from intemperance, in not supplying something to occupy the leisure hours formerly spent at the public-house. Mechanics' Institutions, also, with efforts of a kindred character, have done a great work; but they too generally fail in providing *recreation and amusement.* Their aims have been too high for the great majority of Working Men; hence they have not attracted the masses of the people. As a result we find such Institutions now generally given up to the trading and middle classes. *Recreation must go hand in hand* with Education and

Temperance, if we would have real and permanent improvement.

Yet the Working Men of this country, greatly as they both deserve and need our sympathy and help, are by no means so easily helped as some persons imagine. The failures which occasionally occur in all parts of the country prove this only too painfully. The very anxiety to help them, combined, as it too often is, with ignorance how to do it, frequently forms a formidable hindrance to most praiseworthy efforts. In addition to pecuniary help, which is needed as capital for the first outfit of the Clubs, there is yet greater necessity for gathering in a common centre, experience, information, and personal influence, to be employed throughout the country in that *impartial, unsectarian spirit* which has hitherto characterized the union. Unless this continues to be done, there is manifest danger of the movement becoming stunted or misdirected, sectional in its spirit, spasmodic or feeble in its action, and most discouraging in its results.

Plan of operations.

The Council seek to carry out the objects of the union :—

1.—By making their office a general centre for *meeting and conference* between members of Working Men's Clubs and friends of the movement generally.

2.—By *correspondence* with the officers of existing Associations throughout the kingdom.

3.—By *personal visits*, by their own officers and by honorary deputations from the Council, to places where their presence is desired. At these visits, conferences are held with the gentry, the working men, and with persons in the locality who may be interested in the movement.

4.—By the *dissemination of pamphlets*, or special papers, on subjects lying within the sphere of the

Society's operations, in addition to communications to weekly and monthly periodicals.

5.—By *supplying instructions* for the guidance of persons who may wish to establish and maintain Clubs and Institutes ; together with *rules* to define their objects, and to regulate their proceedings.

6.—By *grants or loans of books* for Club Libraries, and of Apparatus, Diagrams, &c., to societies in membership with the union.

7.—By *small loans of money*, in special cases, to societies in the union.

8.—By the *establishment* ultimately of a *Central Model Club*, which shall provide, among other advantages, a hall or meeting-room for conferences between persons of different classes of society.

9.—By *placing* the *Clubs* in *communication* with *Lecturers* and *Class Teachers;* and by aiding in the promotion of *technical instruction*.

10.—By *holding* at the central office *Conferences* on *public questions*, to which persons of all classes are invited, with the view of encouraging the adoption of such Conferences at the Clubs.

11.—By *correspondence* with the *Co-operative, Trade*, and *Friendly Societies*, with the view of inducing those bodies to establish similar institutions for the use of their members, or to join existing institutions.

Reports have been received of the establishment of forty-two new clubs and institutes during the past year, in the case of thirty-four of which the aid and advice of this Society have been sought. The existence of forty other similar institutions has been reported for the first time. After deducting the number of clubs which are supposed to have been closed during the year, the total number known to the Society is 404, *being an increase of forty-nine as compared with last year*. The total number of

Results attained by this Society.

persons who are members is estimated at upwards of 68,500.

The increasing appreciation of the services rendered by this Society is shown by the fact that sixty-eight clubs have become affiliated, being a greater number than in any preceding year.

The Council of the Society reports the establishment during 1869, of ten new clubs* in the metropolis, bringing the total number to forty-eight. Of these, the Bermondsey Club, in Green Walk, deserves especial mention from the extent of its accommodation, numerous advantages, and great success. The Club was founded and furnished by Mr. Herbert B. Praed, who, while placing the administration virtually in the hands of the members, has been indefatigable in his attention to its interests, helping the Committee with suggestions and arbitration in all cases of difficulty. It is important to mention this, because, if an equally wise and generous course were adopted in all cases, we should not hear of so many failures. The Club consists of 500 members, and twice that number applied for admission a week after it opened. Lectures, Concerts, Classes, Discussions, a Bank, a Library, Clothing and Boot Clubs, a Sick Club, a Brass Band, a Glee Club, and a Chess Club are all at full work, and show in how great a variety of modes a Club may render services to the industrious classes.

* At Clapham, Battersea (for youths), Bermondsey, Rotherhithe, Chelsea, Haggerstone, Muswell Hill, St. Martin's Lane, Nine Elms, Wandsworth Road.

APPENDIX B.

INDUSTRIAL PARTNERSHIPS AND
CO-OPERATIVE SOCIETIES.

Digest of evidence of Mr. Henry Currer Briggs and of Mr. Archibald Briggs before Her Majesty's Commissioners appointed to inquire into the Acts and Practices of Trade Unions in Great Britain.

Mr. H. C. Briggs has had the management of the business of Messrs. Briggs, Son, and Co., since the year 1852. Three collieries — Whitwood, Haigh Moor, and Methley Junction—are now in their occupation.

Describes the disputes as to wages, modes of working, &c., at Messrs. Briggs' and the adjoining collieries in the twelve years (1853-1865) preceding the formation of the limited liability company to which Messrs. Briggs' collieries now belong. The annoyance resulting from these disputes at last came to such a pitch that Messrs. Briggs resolved to adopt the system of co-operation at the collieries. They offered to transfer the collieries to a limited liability company, and to admit their workman and customers as shareholders, they themselves retaining in shares at least two-thirds of the entire capital in their own hands. They also undertook to recommend to the shareholders that whenever the divisible yearly profits accruing from the business, after a fair and usual redemption of capital, and other legitimate allowances, exceeded 10 per cent. upon the capital embarked, all those employed by the Company as managers, agents, or workpeople, should receive one-

half of such excess profit as a bonus, to be distributed among them as a percentage upon their
respective earnings during the year. The wages to
be paid to the workpeople who would work under
this scheme were to be on the same scale as the
ordinary wages of the district. Since the adoption
of the scheme two advances have been made in
wages, concurrently with a general advance in the
district.

Mr. H. C. Briggs was led by several considerations to the view that larger profits could be made
in the collieries if masters and men were to be
working mutually together. The miners seemed to
him, under the ordinary system, utterly reckless as
to the losses inflicted upon employers and workmen
by neglect and stoppage of work for frivolous reasons.
He believed that some of the more intelligent workmen might be led by reasoning and experience to
see the suicidal character of the struggles which had
taken place, and then to influence their fellow-workmen for good ; and he knew that 70 per cent. of the
cost of raising coal is made up by wages for manual
labour, while an additional 15 per cent. is made up
by materials used in the mine, in respect of which
the workmen have ample power of saving by careful
use. He thought that the colliers had a very vague
idea as to the employers' profits, and that Messrs.
Briggs' would lose nothing by publicity. He
thought also that if the workmen were to be shown
that the employers' interests and theirs were iden-
tical, a considerable sum might be gained in working,
and that of this sum it would be only fair to give
the workmen a portion.

The company commenced operations on the 1st
July, 1865. Of the whole number of 10,000 shares,
9,770 have been allotted, and of these 6,450 are held
by the original proprietors, 264 by clerks and men,

114 by non-resident agents, 1,068 by customers, and
1,874 by the public. The shares are £15 each, and
£10 has been paid up. They are now sold in open
market at about £14 5s. to £14 10s., or at £4 5s. to
£4 10s. premium. Of the 785 miners engaged
underground in the several collieries, 83, or one out
of every 9½, are shareholders; of the 214 boys also
employed underground, none are shareholders; of
the 204 workmen employed above ground, 61, or one
out of every 3½, are shareholders. The above-
ground workmen earn smaller wages, and have, it
may be noted, been free from union influence in any
way; whereas the underground men, though not
many of them are now connected with the union,
have all their lives been under its influence.

The directors of the company, who are seven in
number, are elected annually by the shareholders.
The qualification for a director (except in the case
of workmen, none of whom are as yet on the board),
is 50 shares.

The amount of capital which was fixed was based
on the valuation of the pits and plant as it stood in
Messrs. Briggs' books. For two years before the
formation of the Company only 5 per cent. was
realised upon the capital invested. During the first
year's working under the Company 12 per cent. was
paid as dividend to the shareholders, and 2 per cent.
assigned to the bonus fund for labour; and in the
second year 13 per cent. was paid to the shareholders,
and 3 per cent. to the bonus fund. In the first
year £1,800, and in the second year £2,700 was the
amount allotted to bonus. In the first year the
workmen holding shares received 10 per cent. on
their earnings, and the workmen who were not
shareholders 5 per cent.; in the second year the
former received 12 per cent., and the latter 8 per
cent. During the first year only 30 per cent. of the

men qualified themselves to receive bonus, that is, took out books (provided for them at 1*d.* each) in which their wages should be entered, in order that the amount of bonus might be reckoned, but in the second year 80 per cent. qualified themselves. The Articles of Association do not bind the Company to give any bonus whatever. The bonus has been continued for two years, and there is no wish to give it up. The whole of the profit which is realized is not divided. In the last year (ending 30th June, 1867), which was remarkably prosperous, a net profit of £20,417 was made, being equivalent to 207 per cent. upon the capital, and of this, £8,000 was carried to the reserve fund to provide for bonus in another year, if a bad year should come.

Messrs. Briggs retain the entire management of the concern ; that is the same as it was before. The Articles of Association give a vote for every share, and so long, therefore, as Messrs. Briggs retain in their own hands the two-thirds of the shares, which they now have, they will have full control in the management. The working shareholders are content with this arrangement.

A committee of the workmen has been started, and this committee the managers meet occasionally, in order to obtain suggestions as to improvements in working.

The system introduced by Messrs. Briggs, might, perhaps, be better described as a bonus system than as a co-operative system. It is quite clear that collieries worked on the strictly co-operative system, the men at work managing the concern for themselves, would not last a month : the men require to be educated up to such a plan ; and Messrs. Briggs' system may in time give them the education. Moreover, it would be almost impossible in a colliery for the workmen to raise sufficient capital without the aid of capitalists. In a colliery employing 1,000 men, at least £100,000 would, in the West Yorkshire district, be required as capital.

Upon Messrs. Briggs, as the original proprietors of the collieries, the effect of the new plan has been to give them practically more control than they had before, and upon the workmen to contribute to habits of providence and improvement generally, to increase the number of their children sent to school, and to lead them to work infinitely more smoothly with their employers. Since the establishment of the Company there has been a decided improvement in the character of the workmen, an improvement which has been remarked by the rector of the parish. Out of nearly 1,000 men who have received bonus, only two or three spent it badly—that is, they stayed away and were known to be drinking. These men were dismissed, and their dismissal received the strong approval of the other workmen. One effect of the new plan has been to put a stop to the "play days" which used to be frequently taken by the men on very frivolous pretexts, and which cost the employers £120 to £150 a day. Not only is there on a play day loss of trade, but also loss of wages of men who are necessarily kept at work in the mine, and of other expenses.

Customers of the collieries have been induced to take shares, and they exert themselves to keep up the amount of business done. The system has yet to be fully tried, and to do this seven years' experience will be necessary. For the last twenty years the average of the collieries have not, Mr. H. C. Briggs thinks, made more than 10 per cent. upon the capital invested, but he does not think that in the case of his own Company the profits are likely to go below 10 per cent.

Both working shareholders and working non-

U

shareholders receive a bonus, as already stated, but the former receive a larger proportion than the latter, and would object to receive an equal proportion only. The tendency among them is to take the side of the capitalists, and to become capitalists in their notions.

The witnesses do not think that the system of Messrs. Briggs is as applicable to other works as it is to collieries, because in collieries an unusually large proportion of the expenditure (85 per cent. as explained above) is of such a kind as to put it in the workmen's power to prevent waste. The system is probably applicable to those trades in which labour supplies the largest proportion of the cost of production. It is in those trades also that strikes are most frequent and most disastrous.

Union delegates have spoken much against Messrs. Briggs' proceedings, but there has been no further interference by unions in the matter. Union men generally are in favour of the Company. The delegates say that there are two black palls hanging over the district, and one of these is Messrs. Briggs' co-operative system. When the Company was started in 1865, nearly all of the 550 coal hewers then employed were in the union; but now, out of the 785 hewers employed, probably about 40 only pay to the union. These 40 men are all at the Methcley colliery, which is in a hotbed of unionism, and their chief object in remaining on the union books is probably to keep on good terms with their neighbours. Nearly all those who were formerly the leading men in the union of the district are now in the employ of the Company, having taken shares and set to working quietly. They have not been put in any special situations.

There is an accident fund in the collieries, and also a sick fund, which is separate from any union.

In carrying out the scheme no difficulty has as yet been experienced by reason of the present law of partnership.

Similar plans to the plan of Messrs. Briggs have been adopted by Messrs. Fox, Head, and Co., in the iron trade ; by Messrs. Greening and Co., of Manchester ; and by the Tabden Mills Cotton Company, but this Company has not got into full operation. The iron trade has been very bad, and it is said that Messrs. Fox, Head, and Co. have not given any bonus to their workmen, not having made a profit of 10 per cent. Probably the bad state of trade has prevented their scheme having a fair chance. It may be that their refusal to admit any union men has caused the failure.

A GENERAL meeting of the London Committee of the
Netherlands International Exhibition was held at
the House of the Society of Arts, on the 18th March,
S. Redgrave, Esq., in the chair. There were present
—Alderman Sir J. C. Lawrence, Bart., M.P., Sey-
mour Teulon, Gilbert Sanders, G. Coster, P. Le Neve
Foster, Edmund Johnson, and P. L. Simmonds.

The following general statement of accounts was
submitted and approved. It was ordered that the
Central Committee of the Exhibition at Amsterdam
be requested to send to the Society of Arts for distribution the diplomas and certificates awarded to
English exhibitors.

ACCOUNTS.
1869.—RECEIPTS.

Subscriptions :—	£	s.	d.
Vote of Society of Arts	25	0	0
T. Twining	5	0	0
Mr. Sandbach	5	0	0
Brown, Van Santin, and Gereke ..	2	2	0
Enthoven and Son	1	1	0
L. Vankerkaken	2	2	0
Baron Gevers	5	0	0
D. Everwyn....................	5	0	0
F. H. and A. Collier	5	5	0
Hodgson Pratt	2	2	0
J. W. May	5	0	0

* The following is the only statement yet published of the
administration of the funds raised in this country in aid of the
Amsterdam Exhibition.

	£	s.	d.
Wingfield Digby................	10	0	0
The Lord Mayor	10	10	0
Messrs. Baring Brothers	10	10	0
M. Van Thal, jun.	1	1	0
G. Coster......................	25	0	0
S. Morley, M.P.	25	0	0
J. H. Schröder and Company	5	5	0
W. Bunge and Company	5	0	0
Messrs. Hirstmann and Company..	5	0	0
Sir J. Lubbock, Bart., M.P.	5	5	0
A. G. Robinson	5	0	0
The Corporation of the City of London	52	10	0
T. Twining (2nd donation)........	5	0	0
J. M. Johnson and Sons	10	10	0
Seymour Teulon................	2	2	0
R. Hudson	1	0	0
Somerset Beaumont, M.P........	1	0	0
S. Redgrave....................	2	2	0
Rev. W. Rogers................	5	5	0
S. Morley, M.P. (2nd donation)....	5	0	0
	£254	12	0

1869.—EXPENDITURE.

	£	s.	d.
Expended in visiting the provinces, by special order of the Committee	25	0	0
Petty cash disbursements by Secretary, March to December	15	5	0
P. L. Simmonds for services rendered as Secretary and Manager......	146	1	10
J. M. Johnson and Sons, printing circulars, forms for exhibitors, and postages	68	5	2
	£254	12	0

SHEFFIELD INQUIRY REPORT.

*Extract from the Report presented to the Trade
Union Commissioners by the Examiners appointed to inquire into Acts of Intimidation,
Outrage, or Wrong alleged to have been promoted,
encouraged, or connived at by Trade Unions in
the Town of Sheffield.*

THE first subject which engaged our attention was
that of "rattening." Rattening is a mode of enforcing payment of contributions to and compliance
with the rules of the union. The wheel-bands, tools,
and other materials of a workman are taken and held
in pledge until he has satisfied the society by payment of his arrears, or by submitting to the rules
which he has infringed. At first it was denied that
the unions connived at this practice, but we had not
proceeded far with our investigation before it was admitted on all hands that rattening had been for a
long time prevalent in the grinding trades, and in all
trades connected with them.

It is fair to the unions to say, that in the majority
of cases where the demands of the union have been
complied with, and a payment of a small sum for the
expenses of rattening has been made, the property
taken has been restored.

Rattening is always done in the interests of the
union, and very commonly by the direction of the
secretary, who negotiates with the party rattened for
the restitution of his property. In some cases a
member of the union, without express authority,
rattens another member who is known to have

incurred the displeasure of the society, and takes his chance of having his act adopted by the union.

Recourse is seldom had to the police to recover property so taken away, but application is almost always made to the secretary of the union immediately upon the loss of tools, &c., being discovered.

The practice of rattening is well known to be illegal, and persons detected in illegally taking away property have frequently been convicted and punished. The excuse offered by the unions for this system is, that, in the absence of legal powers, rattening affords the most ready means of enforcing payment of contributions and obedience to the rules of the union.

Many articles of Sheffield manufacture require for their completion the labour of various classes of workmen. For example, the manufacture of a saw requires the work of the saw grinders, the saw makers, and the saw-handle makers. All these workmen form separate branches of the saw trade, and are in separate unions. These unions are, however, all amalgamated together for mutual support. In case of default by any member of any of the branches, or in case of a dispute with the masters, as the grinders' tools are the most easily abstracted, and as stopping the grinding stops the whole saw trade, the course commonly adopted is to ratten the grinders, although the dispute may be with the saw makers or saw-handle makers, and on the matter being arranged, the other branches indemnify the grinders for their loss of time and for the expenses incurred. An attempt is often successfully made to saddle the whole cost of the rattening, as well as the cost of supporting the men while out of employment, upon the master, even where he is no party to the dispute, on the ground that he ought to have compelled his workmen to comply with the rules of the union.

The system of rattening has generally proved successful in effecting its object. If, however, the person rattened continues refractory, he commonly receives an anonymous letter, warning him of the consequences of his obstinacy. If this warning is disregarded, recourse has been had to acts of outrage, the nature of which will be understood from a perusal of the cases actually investigated by us.

The following cases, as they affect each union, are taken in the order of time of their occurrence.

THE SAW GRINDERS' UNION.

1853. (30 Vict., c. 8, s. 2.) The earliest case is that of *Elisha Parker*, into which we inquired with the written sanction of Her Majesty's Principal Secretary of State for the Home Department.

Elisha Parker is a saw grinder, living at Dore, about five miles from Sheffield. In the year 1853 Parker was working for Messrs. Newbould, who employed two non-union men, and he was repeatedly required by the union to discontinue working for Messrs. Newbould; this he refused to do.

In July of the same year a horse of Parker's was found hamstrung in a field where it had been grazing, and it had to be killed. Broadhead, the secretary of the Saw Grinders' Union, confessed that he had hired three members of the Saw Grinders' Union (Elijah Smith, John Taylor, and Phineas Dean) to commit this outrage.

1854, March. Some gunpowder was laid in the night time at Parker's door and exploded, but the explosion did but little damage. A few minutes later there was an explosion of gunpowder in the house of another man, one Bishop, a saw maker, who lived at a little distance from Parker, and who had apprenticed a son to the saw-handle makers' trade. The evidence was not satisfactory as to who did these acts, but we have no doubt they arose from trade disputes.

About 11 o'clock at night Parker was roused by the noise of stones being thrown on the roof of his house. He took a double-barrelled gun, which he kept for his protection, and went out. Immediately on getting outside his door a gun was fired at him from a plantation on the opposite side of the road, about 20 yards off. He advanced a little into the road, when a second shot was fired, and Parker was wounded with small shot in the left arm and neck. A third shot was then fired, which hit Parker's right arm and knocked him down. The right arm has been disabled up to the present time. At least two men were engaged in this outrage. One of them, John Hall, was hired to do it by one George Peace, a member of the Saw Grinders' Union, at the instigation of Broadhead, who found the money out of the funds of the union. Peace was a neighbour of Parker's, and had no quarrel with him, and described himself as being at the time a farmer, saw grinder, and colliery master. *1854, Whit-Sunday.*

Hall was sent to America soon after the occurrence, the funds for his voyage being provided by Broadhead.

James Linley, who formerly had been a scissor grinder, had shortly before this period become a saw grinder, and kept a number of apprentices, in defiance of the rules of the Saw Grinders' Union. *1857, November 12th.*

He was shot by Samuel Crookes with an air gun, on November 12th, 1857, at the instigation of Broadhead, in a house in Nursery Street, and was slightly wounded.

James Linley was lodging with his brother-in-law, Samuel Poole, a butcher, whose wife and family were living in the same house. Crookes, at the instigation of Broadhead, threw into Poole's house a can of gunpowder, which exploded and did some damage to the shop, but hurt no one.

1859, January 11th.
1859, August 1st.
Crookes and Hallam tracked Linley from house to house nearly every day for five or six weeks, intending to shoot him. On the 1st August they found him sitting in a public-house in Scotland Street, in a room full of people, the windows of which opened in a back yard, and from that yard Crookes shot Linley with an air gun. The shot struck him on the side of the head, and he died from the effects of the injury in the following February. Crookes and Hallam were hired by Broadhead to shoot Linley.

1859, May 24th.
Samuel Baxter, of Loxley, was a saw grinder, but " kept aloof from the trade." Crookes and Needham, at the instigation of Broadhead, put down the chimney of his house a can of gunpowder, which they exploded ; no one was hurt by the explosion.

1859, October 18th.
Joseph Helliwell was not a member of the union, and had not been brought up to the trade of a saw grinder. On the 18th October, 1859, he was working at saw grinding for Joseph Wilson (who refused to employ union men), and he was blown up by the explosion of gunpowder, which was ignited by the sparks from his glazier when he began to work. Broadhead gave three cans of gunpowder to Dennis Clark to blow up Helliwell, and Clark and Shaw placed half a can of powder in Helliwell's trough. Helliwell was blind for nearly a fortnight, and it was a month before he was able to resume work.

1859, November 24th.
Joseph Wilson, master of the above-named Joseph Helliwell, had " set the trade at defiance," and had determined not to employ anyone connected with the union.

On the night of the 24th November, 1859, Wilson's house, in which his wife and family were asleep, was blown up by the explosion of a can (containing a quart of gunpowder) in the cellar, under the children's room; no one was hurt, but great injury was done to the house and furniture. Broadhead employed Crookes to commit this outrage.

Shortly after this time, but the exact date was not proved, an unsuccessful attempt was made by Crookes, at the instigation of Broadhead, to blow down a chimney of Messrs. Firths. Messrs. Firths had at the time two non-union men in their employment named John Helliwell and Samuel Baxter.

John Helliwell had left the union and took discounts, *i.e.*, worked for less than the scale of prices regulated by the union, and had more apprentices than were allowed by their rules. _1850, December._

Crookes and Hallam, at the instigation of Broadhead, watched for Helliwell on several occasions, on the Midland Railway, in order to shoot him while at his work at Messrs. Firths. They were, however, misinformed as to the place where he worked and failed to find him. Before they had succeeded in their object they were requested by Broadhead to let Halliwell alone for the present, as there was "a job to be done" at Messrs. Wheatman's and Smith's, which was of a more pressing character.

Messrs. Wheatman and Smith had introduced machinery for grinding saws, to the detriment, as Broadhead conceived, of hand labour. Broadhead gave Crookes £2 to purchase gunpowder, in order to blow down Messrs. Wheatman and Smith's chimney. Crookes and Hallam bought 24 pounds of powder, placed it in a can strengthened by a lash line wound tightly round it, and attached a fuse to it. They at first intended to place it in the chimney, and went on several nights to find an opportunity, but owing sometimes to the workmen being about, and at other times to the chimney being too hot, they were unable to do so. Ultimately they placed the powder in a drain in the neighbourhood of the chimney, and _1860, January 17th._

exploded it, and the explosion caused considerable damage.

Harry Holdsworth did not acknowledge the union, and refused to discharge one Jonathan Crapper, a saw grinder, who had a dispute with the union, and employed some jobbing grinders who did not contribute to the union. In October and November 1861 he received several threatening letters. On the night of December 1st, 1861, a can of gunpowder was exploded in the cellar under his warehouse, which did damage to the building to the amount of £100.

In the year 1861 the Jobbing Grinders' Union was associated with the other three branches of the saw trade, and Joseph Hoyle was their secretary. Broadhead applied to him to compel the non-union jobbing grinders to join the union, and Hoyle consented to their being rattened, and agreed to bear his share of the expense, which he stated he believed would be about 10s. The men were not rattened, but Holdsworth's warehouse was blown up, and after the committal of this outrage Broadhead applied to Hoyle for £6 as his share of the expense. Hoyle obtained the £6 from the committee of the union, but denied that he had authorized the blowing up, and he stated that in consequence of this circumstance his own union had withdrawn from the amalgamation on the first convenient opportunity. Their secession from the amalgamation, however, did not occur till three years afterwards, and we report that this outrage was promoted and encouraged by the Saw Grinders' and Jobbing Grinders' Union.

Messrs. Reaney were the owners of a wheel in the Park, and Thomas Fearnehough, who was obnoxious to the trade, was working there ; Crookes, at the instigation of Broadhead, attempted to blow up this wheel and failed.

Thomas Fearnehough, a saw grinder, had long been obnoxious to the union. Having been a member of the union, he left it eight years ago, and shortly after joined again from fear of bodily harm. In 1865 he left the union a second time, and never rejoined it. He had been in the habit of working on his own tools instead of his master's (which was against the rules of the union), and at the time of this outrage he was working for Messrs. Slack, Sellars, and Co., who had a dispute with the saw-handle makers. The saw grinders had in consequence been withdrawn, but Fearnehough had, notwithstanding the withdrawal of the grinders, persisted in working for the firm. Messrs. Slack, Sellars, and Co., aware of the danger which Fearnehough incurred by working for them, took power for him at Messrs. Butchers' wheel, to which there was no access except through a covered gateway which was carefully guarded. Fearnehough was therefore safe from being rattened.

1866, October 8th.

Two or three months before October, 1866, Henry Skidmore, secretary of the Saw Makers' Society, and Joseph Barker, secretary of the Saw-handle Makers' Society, called on Broadhead, and represented to him that Fearnehough was working for Slack, Sellars, and Co., and thereby injuring the trade, and asked him " if something could not be done at him to stop his working." They were aware that he could not be rattened at Butchers' wheel, but no plan was laid down by them by which Fearnehough was to be coerced, although they agreed to bear their share of the expense of compelling him to submit to the union. On the 8th October, 1866, a can of gunpowder was exploded in the cellar under Fearnehough's house in New Hereford Street, in which he was then living with his family, consisting of two sons and a daughter. No one was hurt, but great damage was done to the house. Samuel Crookes was hired by

Broadhead to commit this outrage, and was assisted
by Joseph Copley, a member of the Saw Grinders'
Union. A day or two after this occurrence, Barker
and Skidmore, with the knowledge of Thomas Smith,
Secretary of the Saw Makers' Union, paid Broadhead
£7 10s., the share of each union for the expense of
committing the outrage. Joseph Barker found the
money (the Saw Handle Makers' Union being then
£18 in debt to the Saw Makers' Union), and Smith
credited Barker with the amount in the books of the
Saw Makers' Union. The entry of this amount was
passed over by the auditors without inquiry in the
December following; this could not have been done
if the audit had been carefully and honestly conducted.

A reward of £1,100 offered for the detection of
the perpetrators failed to elicit any information.

The fact of these outrages having been done in
the interest of the trade was well known to the union,
and although in one or two instances individual
members had protested against them, yet nothing
like an investigation had been demanded, nor had
there been any general vote of condemnation of these
acts until the case of Fearnehough occurred, when
public indignation was aroused, and then the outrage
was denounced, and a reward was offered by the
union for the detection of the offenders. The whole
of the above offences were directed by Broadhead,
and sums amounting to nearly £200 had been taken
by him out of the funds of the union to pay the
parties who committed them. Although these acts
were not proved to have been directly authorized by
the union, there must have been a knowledge, or at
all events a well-grounded belief, amongst its members
that they were done, not only in the interests of
their society, but through the agency of some one or
more of their governing body, and we report that all

the above outrages were promoted, encouraged, and connived at by the Saw Grinders' Union ; and that the "Hereford Street outrage" was promoted and encouraged by the Saw Grinders', Saw Makers', and Saw-handle Makers' Unions.

The following members of the Saw Grinders' Union have been engaged in the concerting or perpetration of outrages :—

Broadhead, William.

Clark, Dennis.

Copley, Joseph.

Crookes, Samuel.

Dean, Phineas (dead).

Hallam, James.

Peace, George.

Shaw, George.

Smith, Elijah (dead).

Taylor, John (dead).

The File Grinders' Union.

George Gillott, a file grinder, had ceased to pay to the union, and had more apprentices than were allowed by the trade. He was working at the Tower wheel, where it was almost imposible that he could be rattened. On the night of April 25th, 1857, while he and his wife, two children, and two apprentices were in bed, a can of gunpowder was thrown into the cellar of the house, and exploded. No one was hurt, but one wall of the house was blown down, and great damage was done to the building and to the furniture. There was entire absence of any private cause for this act, and though the perpetrators are undiscovered, and we have no evidence directly implicating the union, we do not hesitate to report that this was a trade outrage. *[1857, April 25th.]*

William Torr, a file manufacturer, had a dispute with the union on account of his paying his men less than the union scale of prices. The union men in his employment were drawn out by the union ; his factory was picketed, his warehouse broken into, a cistern containing a preparation for hardening files *[1864, November.]*

was tapped three times, his bellows were cut, and the books of his trade were taken away and never restored. The offenders are undiscovered, but the circumstances of the case, and the admission made by Cutts and Holland, joint secretaries of the File Smiths' Union, that these acts had certainly the appearance of being society matters, draw us to the conclusion that these outrages were encouraged and connived at by the File Grinders' Union.

THE SICKLE GRINDERS' UNION.

1860, July 26th.

Christopher Rotherham had been a sickle manufacturer for nearly 50 years, at Dronfield, five miles from Sheffield. Shortly before 1860 his men refused to pay to the union, and he thereupon received several threatening letters to the effect that his premises would be blown up if he did not compel them.

About the year 1860 his boiler was blown up, and shortly after a can of gunpowder was thrown, at night, into a house belonging to him at Troway (inhabited by two of his nephews, who worked for him, and were not members of the union), and exploded. No one was hurt, but great damage was done to the house. He has had at different times nine pairs of bellows cut, twelve bands cut to pieces, and his anvils thrown into his dam.

1865.

In 1865 a two-gallon bottle, filled with gunpowder, with a lighted fuze attached, was placed in the night time in his warehouse. The fire of the fuze from some cause became extinguished before it reached the powder. Adjoining the warehouse were sleeping rooms, which, at the time the bottle was placed in the warehouse, were occupied by a mother, three sons, and a daughter. This he said "beat him," and he forced his men to join the union, adding

that since that time " they had been as quiet as
bees."

George Castles, the secretary of the Sickle and
Reaping Hook Grinders' Association, told us that in
the September of last year he saw a cash book of the
union, containing entries of payments made at the
time some of these outrages occurred, burnt in the
committee room, and also that leaves had been torn
out of other books of the union which might have
implicated the union.

We have to report that these outrages were promoted and encouraged by the Sickle Grinders'
Union.

THE FORK GRINDERS' UNION.

In this year a resolution had been passed by the
union that no fork grinder should work except for
one of ten specified masters who were sanctioned by
the union.

William Mason, Thomas Roebuck, and *Samuel
Gunson* were non-union men, and were working for
masters not sanctioned by the trade. One night
Mason was assaulted by about 30 union men, five of
whom were summoned before the magistrates, and of
these two were fined. Three weeks after this assualt,
namely, on 17th February, 1859, gunpowder was
placed in the troughs of Mason, Roebuck, and
Gunson.

In Mason's case the powder exploded immediately Mason began working, and burnt his arm, face,
and neck ; he was wearing spectacles, and these
saved his sight. Roebuck fortunately perceived the
powder before he began work, and he found about
1 lb. of gunpowder in his trough.

Gunson being in America, we have not been able
to ascertain the particulars of his case.

The books of the union applicable to this period

*1859, Febru-
ary 17th.*

x

were not produced before us. They were said to
have been destroyed, for the purpose, as stated by
the secretary, of hiding their contents. The secretary of the union said that he believed these outrages were trade affairs; and we report that they
were encouraged and promoted by the Fork Grinders'
Union.

THE BRICKMAKERS' UNION.

1857.
James Robinson, a master brickmaker had had
disputes with the union before 1857, and in this
year he had in his employment four non-union men
who had been seven years in his service. At the
latter end of the year 1857 four men came to Robinson, saying that they were sent by the committee of
the union to take the place of the four non-union
men. Robinson refused to turn off his old hands.
The union ordered the union men to leave, which
they refused to do. In the following summer 17,000
bricks were trampled upon and destroyed. This was
done by four or five men at the least.

1859.
One of Robinson's cows was found stabbed while
grazing in a field adjoining his brick-yard, and had to
be killed.

1859,
October.
On the   day of October, 1859, at 3 A.M., an
attempt was made to blow up the house in which
Robinson, his wife, his son, and four daughters were
living. Three gingerbeer bottles, filled with gunpowder and nails, with lighted fuzes attached, were
thrown at a chamber window of Robinson's house.
Two struck below the window sill and fell outside
the house. One was thrown through the window
and was broken against the wall of the room, by
which means the powder escaped and exploded
harmlessly.

1863,
November.
An unsuccessful attempt was made to burn a
haystack worth £150, situated 10 yards from his

house, and close to a stable in which were his cows and horses. A length of calico saturated with naphtha and turpentine had been pegged round the stack ; the ends of the calico were carried down so as to touch 11 boxes of lucifer matches, and a roll of paper, to act as a fuze, which extended along the ground. The paper had been lighted and had burnt about a yard, but owing to the dampness of the atmosphere, or some other cause, the light had gone out.

One of his horses was found dead in his field. During the night it had been stabbed in the side by a pointed instrument. 1861.

The perpetrators of these outrages have never been discovered, although active steps were taken by the police at the time. The secretary stated to us that he believed these outrages were done by the union.

Henry Bridges, formerly a master brickmaker, was not in 1861, a member of the union. 1861, April 21st.

On the Saturday before the 21st April, 1861, one of his men, named Thomas Poole, had a quarrel with John Baxter, a member of the committee, in reference to the payment of what is called "outworking money."

On the night of 21st of April between 40,000 and 50,000 bricks, five or six barrows, and a pressing machine, the property of Bridges, of the value of £40, were destroyed. This must have been the work of five or six men.

Bridges applied to Baxter as to the cause of his bricks being spoiled, and Baxter said it was because he (Baxter) had been insulted by one of Bridges' men.

The books of the Brickmakers' Society, containing their transactions for the whole of the year 1861, were destroyed, and William Hy. Owen, a former secretary, admitted that if they had been produced, they would have shown that money was paid by the union for the commission of these outrages.

We report that these outrages were promoted and encouraged by the Brickmakers' Union.

THE FENDER GRINDERS' UNION.

1861, November 5th.   *John Sibray* was foreman to Mr. H. E. Hoole, stove, grate, and fender manufacturer, in the spring of 1861. At that time Mr. Hoole's "heavy" grinders having absented themselves from work for more than a week, Mr. Hoole desired Sibray to endeavour to procure other men. Sibray engaged Charles Taylor, a non-union man. When the union men returned and found Charles Taylor at work they quitted the works in a body, taking the "light" grinders with them. Their places were filled by Rd. White, George White, W. Hulse, George Wastnidge, and others. On the next day Mr. Hoole received a threatening letter; this was followed by several others, and deputations from the union saw Mr. Hoole on the subject of his employing non-union men.

On the 5th November Sibray was assaulted in the street by two men, and about the same time Richard White, George White, and William Hulse, three of the non-union men, were assaulted and beaten, and one of the Whites was left for dead.

1861, November 23rd.   *George Wastnidge,* one of the above-named non-union men, lived in Acorn Street, with his wife, child, and a lodger named Bridget O'Rourke. Wastnidge, his wife, and child slept in the garret, and Mrs. O'Rourke in the chamber below fronting the street. About 1 o'clock in the morning of the 23rd November, a can of gunpowder was thrown through the chamber window. Mrs. Wastnidge hearing a noise, ran down into Mrs. O'Rourke's room and found her holding in her hand a parcel emitting sparks. She seized it in order to throw it through the window, and it exploded in her hands, setting fire to her night dress and seriously injuring her. She ran upstairs, her husband stripped off her burning clothes, and in her fear she threw herself through the garret window into the street. Wastnidge dropped his little boy to persons who were below in the street, and by means of a ladder which was brought escaped from the house. Mrs. O'Rourke was found in the cellar shockingly burnt.

Mrs. Wastnidge was taken to the infirmary in a state of insensibility, where she remained five or six weeks. She has not recovered from the injuries she received. Mrs. O'Rourke was also taken to the infirmary, where she died a fortnight after. A person of the name of Thompson was tried at York, at the spring assizes, 1862, for the murder of Mrs. O'Rourke, and was acquitted.

Robert Renshaw confessed before us that he threw the can of gunpowder into Wastnidge's house, and that he was hired to do so on the promise of £6 by William Bayles and Samuel Cutler, both members of the Fender Grinders' Union, and he stated that it was done because Wastnidge was not right with the trade.

James Robertson, now secretary, and at that time acting secretary of the Fender Grinders' Union, stated that he paid to William Bayles £6 which he had received from Kenworthy, the then secretary of the union, and that he had falsified the books of the union in order that that payment should not be discovered.

We report that all the above outrages were promoted and encouraged by the Fender Grinders' Union.

The Pen and Pocket Blade Grinders' Union.

1861. *Samuel Sutcliffe* was a surgical instrument maker. There was a strike in this trade in 1861, and Sutcliffe had "gone in when the others were out." Broomhead (now dead), secretary of the union, and one Braithwaite, in the same trade, hired Hallam "to make him so that he could not work for a week or two." Hallam and Crookes waylaid him at his own door and beat him on the head with life preservers, and hurt him so severely that he was confined to his bed for a week. Broomhead paid Hallam £5 for the job, remarking at the time that £5 was as much as the committee would allow him to pay him. The books of the union for this period have been destroyed.

We report that this outrage was encouraged and promoted by the Pen and Pocket Blade Grinders' Union.

The Scissor Forgers' Union.

1865, February 22nd. *George Gill*, scissor manufacturer, had in his employment a man named Joseph Hague, who was not in the union. Joseph Hague had frequently been solicited by Joseph Thompson, the secretary, to join the union, and a deputation from the union called upon him and told him, that if he did not join they would do something for him. Three weeks after this a pair of bellows on which Hague was working, but which belonged to Mr. Gill, were cut.

1865, August. *Robert Winter*, scissor forger, refused to join the union, and had in his employment some men who had also refused. The bellows of the men who had refused to join the union were cut, whilst those of the union men were not injured. William Fearnley, a member of the union, confessed to having committed these outrages in consequence of the men not paying to the union, but he denied that he cut the bellows by the authority of the union.

In the early part of this year *Messrs. Darwin*, scissor manufacturers had employed non-union men at a scale of prices less than that sanctioned by the union. Joseph Thompson, secretary of the Scissor Forgers' Union, admitted that he employed John 1866. Clarke to take away their tools and hide them. Clarke, however, was examined by us, and stated that he was employed by Thompson to take their tools and cut their bellows, and we believe his statement. Clarke was tried for this offence at Leeds, and convicted and sentenced to nine months' imprisonment. Thompson paid Mrs. Clarke 6s. a week during the time her husband was in prison, and although Thompson said that he had embezzled the funds and falsified the accounts of the union in order to conceal this payment, and although he had in consequence tendered his resignation, the society passed a resolution to the effect that the money had been taken and paid for services rendered to the union. The books of this union, as we have already stated, were mutilated and falsely kept by the secretary, and they were never subjected to any careful audit.

We report that all these outrages were encouraged and promoted by the Scissor Forgers' Union.

The Scissor Grinders' Union.

Edwin Sykes, a scissor manufacturer, had, when 1866, December. a master grinder, refused to pay to the trade; for this he was threatened by Holmshaw, president of this union, and subsequently he was rattened. In December, 1866, he had in his employment a man, named Pryor, who was not a member of the union, and who had never been apprenticed to the trade.

Holmshaw had told him that Pryor must not work for him, and on his refusal to dismiss Pryor had threatened to "serve him out." On the 26th of the same month his wheel was broken into and damage done to the amount of £24; a large quantity of tools were damaged, and the remainder thrown into the dam.

We report that this outrage was encouraged and connived at by the Scissor Grinders' Union.

THE EDGE-TOOL FORGERS' UNION.

1864.

Mr. David Ward, of the firm of Ward and Payne, edge-tool manufacturers, had frequently been requested by their customers to obtain a first-rate carving tool forger. They brought to Sheffield *James Addis*, a London workman, who had received prize medals for carving tools at the Exhibitions both of 1851 and 1862. At this time tools of the kind made by Addis were not manufactured in Sheffield. Addis offered to pay to the Union an entrance fee of £15, in addition to the usual contributions, and undertook not to claim any benefit from the union for two years. The committee, however, refused to accept him, and Addis returned to London. Some time afterwards Mr. Ward sent for Addis again, and set him to work. Deputations from the union called upon Mr. Ward, withdrew the union men from work, and would consent to no terms except the dismissal of Addis, and a payment by Mr. Ward of £30 to the union to cover the expenses of the men whom the union had withdrawn from his employment.

Mr. Ward paid the £30 and dismissed Addis. In order to secure the carving tools made by Addis, Mr. Ward was obliged to advance money requisite to set Addis up as a small manufacturer on his own account. He thereby ceased to be a workman, and now, instead of forging only, he is obliged to grind and finish his tools, so as to bring them in a complete state to Mr. Ward's warehouse. This is both expensive and inconvenient.

Addis, with the assistance of an apprentice, could earn £7 a week, and has earned as much as £10 a week. Whilst Addis was at work for Mr. Ward, and before the payment of the £30, he was standing one day at the bar of a public-house, when four men, members of the union, fastened the door, and asked him, " How many trade union meetings have we had through you ?" and then kicked him, and inflicted two serious wounds on his head. The parties were summoned before the magistrates and three were fined £5, each, and one £3 10s. Although this outrage was done by members of the Edge-tool Forgers' Union, we have no evidence to show that it was an outrage promoted or encouraged by that union.

The Edge-Tool Grinders' Union.

John Hague, sheep-shear and edge-tool grinder, was never apprenticed, but as a boy worked for his father, who belonged to the trade. He had offered to pay £20 to be allowed to join the union. Whilst working for a person called Greaves, thirteen axle-trees and glaziers, six wheelbands, and twelve pulleys, belonging to Hague, were taken away from the wheel, and were found to be so much burnt as to be rendered useless, a shank stone was broken, and his horsing chopped into firewood. Whenever he appeared amongst union men he was called a "knob-stick." Although the circumstances of the outrage would indicate that it was done in the interests of the trade, yet there was no evidence before us to show that this was an outrage promoted or encouraged by the Edge-tool Grinders' Union.

There is no ground to doubt the correctness of Hague's statement. We think it right, however, to observe that Hague was a very disreputable witness, having been several times convicted, and once transported for seven years.

THE SCYTHE GRINDERS' UNION.

1858.

Messrs. Tyzack and Sons, scythe, saw, file, and steel manufacturers, employ 250 men, and are brought into communication with several unions. They have had continual disputes with the unions, in the course of which they have received several threatening letters, and have had considerable damage done to their property.

1858.

Three pairs of bellows were destroyed at their works at Abbey Dale, in consequence, as was stated, of the scythe finishers in their employment not paying their contributions.

1859, July]

Thirteen scythe grinders' bands were taken because they had engaged a man without the consent of the union.

1863 and 1865.

Several shops were broken open and tools taken away in consequence of some of the men being in arrear with their contributions.

1862, November.

A man called Needham, who had been convicted of a trade outrage, had when in prison made a statement to Mr. Joshua Tyzack, affecting Michael Thompson, the Secretary of the Scythe Grinders' Union. On Needham's coming out of prison, and shortly before November 1862, Mr. Joshua Tyzack made frequent inquiries for him in order to get his evidence against Thompson.

In the month of November, 1862, Mr. Joshua Tyzack was returning in his gig from Sheffield, according to his usual habit, at about 8.30 p.m. ; he had proceeded three-quarters of a mile from Sheffield, when passing a plantation he heard a shot fired, and then a second one in quick succession; he looked round and saw the flash of a third shot about 15 or 20 yards off, and at the same instant a bullet passed through his hair and the brim of his hat. He became unconscious for a moment and sank down in the gig, and in so doing stopped his horse. He almost instantly recovered himself, and as he rose to whip the horse two more shots were fired at him from the same place. Mr. Tyzack stated that in his opinion this attempt to shoot him was made in consequence of the inquiries which he had set on foot respecting Needham, but we are unable to satisfy ourselves from the evidence before us that this was an outrage promoted or encouraged by any trade union.

The Nail Makers' Union.

This union has its head-quarters at Belper, in Derbyshire, but the persons on whose property the following outrages were committed lived and worked at Thorpe Hesley, within the district to which the present inquiry is limited. In this union there is no regular weekly contribution, but when a strike occurs a levy is made to support the men who are out.

In December, 1861, the nailmakers in the employment of Mr. Favell, of Rotherham, were on strike, but *John Hattersley* and *Charles Butcher*, who carried on their trade at their own shops at Thorpe Hesley, persisted in working for Mr. Favell. Hattersley was subjected to many acts of annoyance, and Butcher on going to his work discovered one morning, in the chimney above his hearth, a can full of gunpowder suspended by a rope from the top, which would have exploded immediately the fire was lighted.

On the 21st December, 1861, the shops of these

1861, December.

1861, December 21st.

men were blown up by a can of powder suspended by a rope in the chimney of each shop, and exploded by a fuse. Isaac Emanuel Watson, Joseph Tomlinson, and Samuel Proctor committed these outrages, and were paid for doing them out of the funds of the union (by order of the Committee) by Charles Webster, a member of the Committee, the money being handed to him by James Beighton, the Chairman, for that purpose.

Watson, Tomlinson, and a brother of Watson, were tried for these outrages at the York Spring Assizes, 1862, and found guilty, and sentenced to 14 years' transportation. Upon strong representations being made of their innocence they were pardoned and released. The men were defended by the union, and their defence cost the union £40 or £50.

We report that these outrages were promoted and encouraged by the Nail Makers' Union.

THE IRONWORKERS' UNION.

1867, February and March.

In consequence of the reduction of wages in the early part of this year, a large number of the workmen of *Messrs. J. Brown and Co. (Limited)*, steel manufacturers, went out on strike. The firm made great exertions to get new hands. This was strenuously opposed by the union. For three weeks the works were watched by policemen specially appointed, and the new men were lodged and fed within the walls of the establishment. James Dunhill and Edmund Higgins, two non-union men working for Brown and Co., were found in a public-house by seven or eight union men and assaulted, and on leaving the public-house they were followed into the street and again assaulted. Dunhill and Higgins summoned the men before the magistrates, and they were bound over to keep the peace.

We have not sufficient evidence before us to
justify our reporting that these outrages were promoted or encouraged by the Ironworkers' Union.

We have now given an outline of all the cases of
importance which were submitted to us for investigation.   Mr. Thomas Thorpe, managing clerk to
Mr. Albert Smith, clerk to the magistrates acting for
the Petty Sessional Division and borough of Sheffield,
prepared for us a list of cases supposed to be connected with trade unions, and which had been
brought before the justices within the last 10 years ;
it comprised, in addition to the outrages mentioned
in this report, 166 cases of rattening and 21 cases of
sending threatening letters. A very small proportion,
however, of the persons rattened gave information
either to the police or to the justices.

Most of the outrages we have investigated were
brought before the justices, and although in several
cases large rewards have been offered for the detection of the perpetrators, the offenders have with two
or three exceptions remained unknown up to the
period of this inquiry.

We believe that there are about 60 trade unions
in Sheffield, of which 12 have promoted or encouraged
outrages within the meaning of the Trade Union
Commission Act, 1867.

We have to report that there has not occurred
within the last 10 years any act of intimidation,
outrage, or wrong promoted, encouraged, or connived
at by any association of employers.

We point to the year 1859 as the one in which
outrage was most rife, and we notice with pleasure
that it has diminished since that time.

During the course of our investigation, matters
connected with trade unions (such as the number of
apprentices allowed to each workman, and the class

from which they may be taken, the remuneration of labour, the restraints exercised upon voluntary action, and the rules and general policy of trade unions) have frequently been brought before our notice. These, however, are questions for the consideration of the Royal Commission sitting in London, and we purposely avoid making any observations upon them.

At the commencement of our inquiry, and frequently during the course of it, we explained the provisions of the Trade Union Commission Act, 1867, with regard to the powers conferred on us of granting certificates of indemnity to witnesses who should by their evidence inculpate themselves. We are convinced that the most material disclosures made to us were so made in reliance on our promise of indemnity made in conformity with the Act of Parliament. Had no such indemnity been offered, we are satisfied that we should never have obtained any clear and conclusive evidence touching the most important subjects of our inquiry, and that the system of crime which has now been disclosed, as well as the perpetrators, would have remained undiscovered; we have therefore granted certificates to all witnesses whom we believe to have made a full and true disclosure of all offences in which they have been implicated.

WILLIAM OVEREND.
THOMAS I. BARSTOW.
GEORGE CHANCE.

Dated this 2nd of August, 1867.

MANCHESTER INQUIRY REPORT.

*Extract from the Report presented to the Trade
Unions Commissioners by the Examiners ap-
pointed to inquire into Acts of Intimidation,
Outrage, or Wrong alleged to have been pro-
moted, encouraged, or connived at by Trade
Unions in Manchester and its neighbourhood.*

WE found that the members of several of the
unions of the brickmakers and bricklayers throughout the district had, in expectation of the inquiry,
destroyed their books containing the accounts of
their expenditure and the minutes of their proceedings.

In the case of the Manchester Union of Brickmakers, Samuel Wood, the landlord of the Crown
and Cushion Inn, at Manchester, where that union
held its meetings, having been served with a *subpœna
duces tecum*, delivered to us five chests, one of iron
and four of wood. Wood had the custody of these
chests at his inn, and at first refused to deliver them
up, stating that if he did so without the permission
of the members of the union, they would kill him.
But after a consultation with six or seven members of
the union, he gave the chests up to the police officers
who had been sent to fetch them. They were, however, all locked, and it was proved that those who
had had the custody of the keys had thrown them
away; and, though notice for that purpose was
publicly given, no one came forward to produce
them. We accordingly had all the five chests broken
open, when it appeared that all books containing the

accounts of the expenditure of that union and the minutes of proceedings, and other books and papers relating to the union, which might have been relevant to our inquiry, had been removed. It was proved that those chests were the usual place of custody for such books, minutes, and papers of the union.

We will now proceed to give an account of the cases which were brought under our notice.

THE STOCKPORT OPERATIVE BRICKMAKERS' UNION.

1864.

In the summer of 1864 Messrs. Thomas and William Meadows were carrying on business as brickmakers at Reddish, two miles from Stockport. In June of that year they made an improvement in the manufacture of bricks, by which they effected a saving in the cost of making of 10*d.* per thousand. The union men in their employment claimed for themselves the whole of the sum they saved. Messrs. Meadows offered 6*d.* This the men refused, and left their employment. A week after they had left, three of them, *Thomas Wilde*, Humphrey Child, and William Fallowes, returned to work on the terms offered by the Messrs. Meadows. On the night of the 2nd of August Wilde, who is a brick-burner, was at his work when he was assaulted by six men, and beaten with "cart legs." His head, and face under the eye, were cut open, his leg much injured, and his right arm broken in several places. He was left on the ground, and as the party went away some of them said "he should burn bricks no more." He was in the Stockport Infirmary five or six weeks; and at the time he appeared before us he was evidently still suffering from the injuries he had then received.

Two men, named Holland Cheetham and William Slater, then respectively president and treasurer of

the Stockport Brickmakers' Union, were tried at
Manchester at the following winter assizes for this
offence, and were convicted and sentenced to 20
years' penal servitude. The union paid the costs of
their defence. After their conviction the members
of the union made great efforts to procure their
pardon or a remission of their sentence. They repeatedly urged Wilde to sign papers to the effect
that the convicts were not the men who had assaulted
him ; but though they made him offers of money for
that purpose, and were also willing to admit him as
a member of the union, he constantly refused to sign
any paper which could be construed into an admission
that he had mistaken the men. On the 28th of
March 1865, upon receiving from three men, calling
themselves representatives of the Stockport Brickmakers' Society, a written guarantee that, on condition that he would sign a certain paper, they would
" re-instate him to all the benefits" of the union,
and give him five pounds. Wilde, having consulted
an attorney, signed in his presence the above-named
paper, of which the following is a copy :—

" I, Thomas Wilde, of Small's Buildings, Regent
Road, Salford, brickmaker, the prosecutor in the late
prosecution against Holland Cheetham and William
Slater, tried and convicted at the winter assizes for
Manchester, 1864, and sentenced by Mr. Justice
Blackburn to 20 years' penal servitude, do hereby
testify that I believe the said Holland Cheetham and
William Slater never have had any malice or desire to
injure me personally or otherwise. And I further
say that from Holland Cheetham I experienced at
times great kindness, and when out of employment
he exerted himself for me to obtain a situation. That
William Slater I know but little, except as a workman in the same trade : that I never had any falling
out or quarrel with him which would lead to a motive

Y

for his committing the offence for which he is now
suffering ; and I cannot ascribe to either Cheetham
or Slater a motive for doing me an injury. Under
these circumstances, and taking into consideration
the uncertainty of the testimony I have given, for I
may have been mistaken as to their identity (although
I cannot say that I have), I trust that Her Majesty
will be pleased to give the prisoners the benefit of
any doubt upon the case, and if not liberating them,
at least commute the punishment to a short period
of imprisonment.

    Dated this 28th day of March 1865.

              (The mark of Thomas Wilde.)
(Witness to signature.)

    The two convicts received a free pardon, and
were released after having been in prison two years
four months and seven days. Immediately upon
their release Slater was elected to the office of president of the Stockport Brickmakers' Union, and was
so at the time of our inquiry.

    Wilde has ever since been the subject of persecu-
tion. He was afraid to reside at Reddish, Manchester, or Oldham. The union men refused to work
with him, and he has now left that part of the
country ; and, having changed his name, and being
undiscovered, he has succeeded in obtaining work.

    The account given by Slater and Cheetham is
that it had been settled at a full committee meeting,
over which Cheetham presided as president of the
union, that Wilde should be beaten. No details were
then arranged ; but afterwards, at a meeting of
about eight members of the committee, summoned
suddenly in a brickcroft, on the 1st of August, 1864,
it was resolved that Wilde and Child were to be
beaten that night. £14 was voted for the purpose,
and the execution of the business was entrusted to

Slater. In pursuance of the above resolution, Slater went the same afternoon to Manchester to one James Kay, the "walking delegate" of the Manchester Brickmakers' Union, and Kay agreed for £14 to bring down a gang of men to beat Wilde and Child, which he accordingly did. But Slater and Cheetham both denied that they were either of them present at the time Wilde was beaten. The money, as agreed, was paid to Kay by Joseph Brown, the secretary of the Stockport Union. The minute book of the Stockport Brickmakers' Society, which, no doubt, contained entries relating to this and the following outrages, was burnt the day before our inquiry was commenced.

Mr. John Simpson is a brickmaker, and for four years has carried on business at Stockport Moor, and before that time at Heaton Moor. As long ago as 1860 he had difficulties and disputes with the Stockport Union, which resulted in his having to leave Heaton. In 1863 he was employing a non-union man, named Dunkley, as a brick-burner. On the 8th of May 25,000 bricks were destroyed by men trampling on them; his barrows, tressels, tables, and other tools were cut to pieces. Eight men were concerned in this outrage; their footsteps were traced to a place called Hillgate, where many members of the Stockport Union then lived. Immediate information was given to the police, but no one was apprehended. 1863, May 8th.

After the destruction of the property in 1863, Mr. Simpson had the brickyard watched at night by one and sometimes by two or three men. Peter Platt was watching on the night of the 17th of June, when he was alarmed by the barking of his dog. As he opened the door of his cabin a man struck at him; he backed into his cabin, and immediately a gun was thrust through the window and discharged; he returned the fire with a revolver, and then went out; he saw two men knocking down the "green walls;" 1863, June 17th.

Y 2

he fired at them, and they ran away. As he turned round he saw three other men setting fire to the shed ; he called out to his lad to bring his gun, and the three men ran off. Seven men altogether were engaged in this outrage, but little damage was done, as they were so soon disturbed. This outrage on Mr. Simpson's property was resolved on at a special council meeting of the Stockport Brickmakers' Society, at which 12 or 13 members were present ; £15 was voted for the job, and the execution of it was entrusted to William Slater.

1864, July.   In July, 1864, *Mr. Thornley* was a master brick-maker at Heaton Norris ; he would not employ union men. The same committee as in the last case re-solved to destroy his property. Holland Cheetham, president of the Stockport Brickmakers' Union, William Slater, the treasurer, and the above-named James Kay, and two others, members of the com-mittee, trampled on 40,000 or 50,000 bricks, and burnt Thornley's sheds, boards, and other implements. The party went provided with chips and matches, and Kay set the shed on fire. The party were paid £10 or £12 by either the treasurer or the secretary of the society.

The Manchester Brickmakers' Society claim an extent of four miles round Manchester in every direction, an area of 120 square miles, as their peculiar district, within the limits of which they permit no bricks to be made except by Manchester union men, nor any bricks to be used except those made within the district. They accomplish the latter object by means of an alliance with the Manchester Bricklayers' Union, the members of which will not set any bricks not made within the above-named district. Levenshulme is claimed by both the Man-chester and the Stockport Unions, and is a kind of debateable ground between them.

In the summer of 1867, *Mr. Thomas Aitken* was building the print-works at Levenshulme, and making the bricks for building upon his own ground. In 1866 and the early part of the following year both the brickmaking and bricklaying were being done by Manchester union men. In consequence of the foreman putting on two Stockport bricklayers, all the Manchester men, both brickmakers and bricklayers left their work. Mr. Aitken then contracted with one Joseph Rigby, a non-union man, to make bricks. On the night of the 15th June 4,500 bricks were trampled on and destroyed by five or six men. 1867, June 15th.

On or about the 28th of August, 1867, at the same place, 19,920 bricks were trampled on by five or six men, who were traced from the brickyard in the direction of Manchester. 1867, Aug. 28th.

Messrs. Edward Barrett and *Peter Bailey* are brickmakers within the so-called Stockport district, at Didsbury, and Heaton Norris respectively; they employ Stockport Union men, and are on good terms with the union. On the night of the 15th of June, 1867, 40,000 bricks belonging to Mr. Barrett and 47,000 belonging to Mr. Bailey were destroyed. About 20 men were employed in each of these outrages. About a fortnight after this Mr. Barrett had some boards burnt. They attribute this destruction of their property to the Manchester Brickmakers' Society. They each offered a reward of £200 to any one who would give such information as would lead to the conviction of the offenders, but in both cases ineffectually. They were compensated for the loss they had sustained by the Stockport Brickmakers' Society, as they had suffered in consequence of the dispute between the two unions. 1867, June 15th.

We had no doubt from the evidence that the above outrages were done by members of the Manchester Brickmakers' Society.

The Ashton-under-Lyne Operative Brick-makers' Union.

The outrages committed in the district of this union arose almost entirely from the employment by the master brickmakers of non-union men.

About the year 1859 the union brickmakers struck for an advance of wages. The masters refused to give the advance demanded, and the men thereupon refused to work. The masters were compelled to seek hands elsewhere, and supplied the places of the union men with non-unionists. The employment of non-union men was against the rules of the society, and deputations from the Ashton Union waited upon the masters to remonstrate with them, and to require that they should employ union men only. The masters in general refused compliance with the demands of the union; whereupon they were subjected to a series of outrages, of which the following were proved before us.

1859, Nov 4th.

James Taylor, master brickmaker, had formerly a brickyard at Cockbrook, Ashton-under-Lyne. In the year 1859 he had in his employ several men who had entered or were on the point of entering the Ashton Union, which had been broken up, and was then being re-formed. In the summer of that year, Mr. Taylor, being dissatisfied with the manner in which his men did their work, paid them off as soon as they had finished the job for which they had been engaged, and took on a fresh set of men who were not members of the union. In October, Thomas Harrison, secretary to the Ashton Union, and another man whose name is not known, called upon Taylor, and asked him to take his former men back again. This he refused to do; upon which one of the two men said, "he (Taylor) must take what followed." Taylor resided within a short distance of his brickyard; and

on the morning of the 4th November, between one
and two o'clock, he was called up by an old man who
was employed by him to burn bricks at night. He
went down immediately to his yard, and found his
sheds on fire. One of those sheds was in process of
erection, and all the boards and spars had been laid
ready to put on the following morning. These had
all been removed into the old shed, and having been
piled up in a heap, together with some barrows and
screens, naphtha had been poured over them, and the
whole set on fire. This shed with its contents was
destroyed, and a considerable portion also of the new
shed burnt down ; but the fire having been discovered,
further damage was stayed. A number of bricks
were also destroyed at the same time. Five or six
men, all members of the Ashton Union, were engaged in committing this outrage; and Charles
Barlow confessed before us to having been one of the
number.

Taylor continued to employ non-union men until
the end of 1861 ; and then, from fear of further
damage being done to him, he discharged them,
and employed members of the union instead ; from
which time, until he gave over brickmaking in 1864,
to use his own expression " he went on comfortably."

Messrs. Clifford were master brickmakers at
Stalybridge, in the Ashton District. In the year
1860 they were employing non-union men. From
time to time applications were made to their men to
join the union, but they refused. Not long after, 1860.
15,000 to 16,000 bricks were destroyed, by being
trampled upon. This damage was proved to have
been done by members of the Ashton Union. Five
men were engaged in the act, one of whom was John
Ensor, at that time President of the union. Thomas
Barlow admitted that he also took part in it.

In October of the same year, after a resolution 1860, Oct.

passed at a meeting of the union that "something must be done to Cliffords," some members of the union paid a second visit to the brickyard. Messrs. Clifford were erecting a new shed, and there was a considerable quantity of materials and implements upon the premises. The men collected all the planks, tables, tressels, mouldings, boards, barrows, tubs, riddles, shovels, and everything they could find, added some dried grass or stuff which was on the ground, poured naphtha over the heap, and set it on fire. A man named Joseph Frith, who had been President of the Ashton Union, confessed to his having been concerned in this outrage.

1861.

In the following summer 16,000 bricks belonging to Messrs. Clifford were trampled upon.

1862, June 28th.

Notwithstanding these outrages Messrs. Clifford continued to employ non-union men. On the night of the 28th of June, 1862, John Ward, John Ensor, Robert Ryan, John Toole, Thomas Barlow, Frederick Hipwell, —— Gregory, and Michael Burke met at a shop behind Ward's house, to arrange another attack upon Cliffords' premises. They then separated, and met again about 12 o'clock at a fence near the brickfield; Ensor, Ward, and Burke had each a pistol, the others carried bludgeons. Thence they proceeded to the brickfield. At the kiln, which was burning, there were a policeman and two or three other men, who were laughing and talking. The fire of the kiln prevented the union party from being seen, and they succeeded in trampling upon some 20,000 bricks without being discovered. They then left, returning the same way they had come. On arriving at Small Shaw, a place about three miles from Cliffords' brickfield, they were met by George Harrop, inspector of police, and police constable *William Jump*, who happened to be on duty there that night. When first seen by Harrop, the men were walking in a body on the footpath, but when they came within about 50 yards of the police constables they all left the footpath and walked in single file on the grass in the field. After they had all passed, with the exception of two, Harrop stopped before the last but one, and said, " My man, what is the meaning of all this ?" He attempted to pass without speaking, whereupon Harrop said, " Nay, you have done nothing wrong, you need not fear," and put up his hand to the man's breast. The latter then seized Harrop by the arm and shoulder, and said, " Now men, now men, now," two or three times, quickly. Harrop then seized tight hold of him with his left hand by the coat collar. He attempted to break Harrop's hold by going under his arm with his head stooping down. By this time the other men had collected together, and stood about six or eight yards from the spot where Harrop and the one man were struggling. Burke discharged a pistol at Harrop, the ball from which knocked the stick out of his hand, and struck him over the right eye ; two other shots were fired in quick succession, the balls in each case passing close to Harrop's head. Then Ward and another man attacked him with bludgeons, and a desperate struggle ensued. Harrop having possessed himself of the bludgeon of the man whom he had first laid hold of, struck Ward on the head, who dropped and went on his hands and knees towards the left, where at this time constable Jump was engaged in a scuffle with three others of the party. He then struck the other man with whom he was struggling, and forced him to retire. At the distance of 15 or 20 yards stood a man, who threw large stones at Harrop, one of which struck him on the arm. Harrop went after that man, and while pursuing him he heard two reports of fire-arms in the direction in which he had seen Jump engaged. He returned, and found Jump crouched down against the stump of a tree. He had been shot in the breast, and died almost immediately.

Ward, Burke, Hipwell, Thomas Barlow, Ryan, and Toole were apprehended on suspicion of being concerned in this outrage. John Ward and Michael Burke were tried at the summer assizes at Liverpool, 1862, for the murder of Jump, and were convicted. Ward was hanged, and Burke sentenced to penal servitude for life. Gregory, Hipwell, Ryan, and Toole were discharged in consequence of the evidence not being sufficiently strong against them. Additional evidence was subsequently obtained, but Gregory and Ensor had then left the neighbourhood, and Ryan and Toole could not be found. Thomas Barlow and Hipwell confessed to having been of the party, and Hipwell admitted that he was the man who threw the stones at Harrop.

The Ashton Union undertook the defence of the men charged with Jump's murder, and applied to the Amalgamated Brickmakers' Union for subscriptions towards defraying the expenses. This Amalgamated Union, comprising the Unions of Ashton, Manchester, Oldham, Stockport, Wigan, Liverpool, Sheffield, St. Helens, and Birkenhead, had been formed some time before, for mutual help and protection. Each union subscribed to the funds of the Amalgamated Society, and these subscriptions were usually paid at the quarterly meetings held at Manchester. Thomas Harrison, at that time president of the Ashton Union, attended the quarterly meeting of the Amalgamated Union, as delegate, for the purpose of obtaining contributions towards the expense of defending Ward and the other men. He explained to the meeting the object for which he sought their assistance, and the application was taken into consideration. Ultimately all the unions subscribed to the defence fund, but the amount raised proving insufficient, a second appeal was made by delegates from the Ashton Union, and further sums were obtained. The money subscribed amounted to £400, of which £200 was paid to Mr. Roberts, the attorney for the prisoners, and the remainder spent in making Ensor and Gregory "secure," by getting them out of the way. The money was entrusted to John Barlow, the then secretary, and Thomas Harrison, the then president of the Ashton Union, for these purposes, but no entry was made in any of the books of the unions relating thereto.

We have no doubt that the Amalgamated Union subscribed towards the defence of the men charged with the murder of Jump with a full knowledge that the murder was committed by the men returning from Clifford's brickyard, and that the outrage committed by them on Clifford's property was done in the interest and with the concurrence of the Ashton Union.

William Tetlow was a brickmaker, and worked 1861, May. for his father, a master brickmaker, at Hurst Brook, Ashton-under-Lyne. The latter had offended the Ashton Union by employing non-union men. He had originally employed members of the union, but in consequence of their refusing to work for him unless he gave them the advance of wages demanded, he was obliged to put up with such men as he could find, and took on non-union men. In May, 1861, needles were put into his clay. Upon this, Tetlow, who was not in a large way of business, ceased to employ strangers, and the work was done by members of his own family. An additional reason for not employing union men was, that he had no work for them in the winter, and if employed in the summer, they would look for their work in the winter, when Tetlow and his family could do all the work themselves.

In November, 1861, an attempt was made to blow up and burn Tetlow's house, by throwing bottles containing gunpowder and naphtha into it. Three bottles containing naphtha, with lighted fuzes attached, were thrown into a room downstairs, and exploded, setting the furniture on fire, and doing considerable damage. Two bottles filled with powder and nails were thrown at the window of the bedroom where Tetlow and his wife were sleeping, but, striking against the window frame, they exploded outside, shattering the framework. This outrage was proved to have been committed by seven members of the Ashton Union. Thomas Barlow and Hipwell confessed to having been of the party; Charles Barlow could not remember whether he was there or not, but he stated that "he had been concerned in so many of these affairs, that it had slipped his mind if he was there."

On other occasions, subsequent to this, Tetlow's bricks have been destroyed, and he has often been threatened by the union men, and shamefully ill-used.

John Rogers was a master brickmaker in the Oldham Road, in the Ashton district. In 1861 he was employing union men; they demanded an advance of wages. Mr. Rogers was willing to give them half the sum demanded, but this they refused and struck work. Their places were supplied with non-union men. Rogers' conduct was brought before a meeting of the union. Ensor and another member were sent to him as a deputation to endeavour to arrange matters with him, but without success. The matter was again brought before a meeting of the union, when it was suggested that something should be done to make him have union men. Rogers put a watchman, named Samuel Newton, on his premises, to protect them. On the morning of the 15th

November, 1861, Newton met a man as he was coming to his work, who said to him, "You are going to your work I see; you had better stop at home, something might happen to you." On the following night, about 12 o'clock, a party of six or seven men, members of the Ashton Union, went to Rogers' brickyard, for the purpose of destroying his bricks. Two of the men were armed with pistols, and the party went determined to resist, in the event of being apprehended or disturbed. Newton was inside the shed when they arrived at the brickfield. Hearing a noise outside, as if an attempt was being made to loosen the board from the bottom of the shed, he went out. On going up to the end of the shed he came in contact with a man, and, putting his lamp in his face, he asked him what he was doing there, adding, "There was no road, and he might get into the brickpits." The man made no reply, but fired at him; the shot went close by the left side of his head. Newton said, "This is nice work, shooting at a man, and not speaking to him;" and then, stepping back, he drew a pistol out of his pocket, with the intention of firing it. Another man, at that instant, sprang up from the back of the shed, and shot Newton in the head as he was in the act of discharging his pistol. They all then ran away. A few days after a ball and slug were extracted from Newton's head, and it was eleven weeks before he was fit for work. Thomas Barlow and Charles Barlow confessed to having been concerned in this outrage also.

Joseph Barlow was a master brickmaker at Droylsden, in the Ashton District. He is brother to the above-named Charles Barlow, and uncle to Thomas and John. Joseph Barlow was in disfavour with the union, from not employing union men. A deputation was sent from the union to warn him; and one night, between 12 and 1 o'clock, two stone bottles filled with gunpowder, were thrown at his bedroom window, but, striking against the woodwork, they exploded outside. He, with his wife and child, was in bed at the time. The following morning the fragments of the two bottles were found underneath the window, together with a third bottle, which had not exploded. On another occasion a quantity of clay, sufficient to make 400,000 bricks, was "needled."

1861.

Mr. Barlow was compelled to place a watchman on his premises. One *John King Butterfield*, was employed in this capacity, and it was also his duty to put coals on the fires at night. Some time in 1861, Butterfield was told by union men that something would be done to him if he watched or did the firing for Mr. Barlow. He continued his duties as before ; and some time after the threat, about 12 o'clock at night, his horse was hamstrung in the stable, and otherwise so injured that it had to be shot.

In consequence of these repeated outrages Mr. Barlow was compelled to turn away non-union men, and to employ union men instead.

John Barlow and Thomas Harrison, at that time respectively secretary and president of the Ashton Union, admitted that these outrages were committed at the instance of the union, and had been paid for out of the union funds.

1861, Feb.

Thomas Shepley superintended the business of his father, who was a master brickmaker, at Hyde, in the Ashton district. A branch of the Ashton Union had been established at Hyde for the convenience of the members living there, but this branch was subject to the rules of the parent society. In 1860 Shepley employed union men, but, on their striking for an advance of wages, non-union men were taken on in their place. Upon this, the usual request was made to Mr. Shepley by the union, to discharge the non-union workmen, but he refused to comply. In February, 1861, a hut or cabin in his brickyard was broken into, and his men's tools and wheelbarrows destroyed. A paper was found pinned on the door of the hut, containing a notice threatening the men's lives if they continued to work for Mr. Shepley.

The May following a considerable quantity of clay was damaged by needles and short nails being put into it.

Mr. Shepley had in his stable two valuable horses. One night in the following August, between 11 and 12 o'clock, four men, who were members of the union, proceeded to the stable; two of them watched outside, while the other two entered the stable. One of these, with a razor which he had taken for the purpose, severed the hind-leg sinews of both horses, which afterwards had to be destroyed. *1861, May.* *1861, Aug.*

Amongst the non-union men who worked for Mr. Shepley was one named *Joseph Wyatt.* In the year 1860 Wyatt had been a member of the Ashton Union, but having been fined 30s. for expressing his determination to work at Shepley's yard independently of of union men, he left the society. In 1861 he was made manager of the yard. Wyatt lived about two miles from the yard, and was constantly watched and threatened by union men as he was going to and returning from his work. On several occasions he found lying in his path apples and oranges which had the appearance of having been poisoned. Wyatt gave information of the circumstance at the time of its occurrence, to the police authorities, but no examination of the fruit was made. He could, however, in no way account for these oranges and apples being so frequently and in such numbers placed in his way, except on the supposition that they were poisoned, and intended to injure him. *1861.*

1861.

 William Hibbert carried on the brickmaking business near Hyde. He employed non-union men, and a bad feeling arose, in consequence, between him and the union. In 1861 a large quantity of needles were thrown into his tempered clay. In consequence of this, and from apprehension of further damage to his property he discontinued the trade.

1858 to 1863.

 John Hartley was a master brickmaker at Dukinfield, in the Ashton district, who had always employed non-union men. During the years 1858 to 1863 damage was done to his bricks upon five or six different occasions, but the actual loss sustained was not great. On one of these occasions, namely, in the year 1862, the outrage was committed by two members of the Ashton Union, Richard Brown and John Middleton Walker. These men were discovered in the act, were apprehended, committed, and sentenced to six months' imprisonment for the offence.

1861.

 Thomas Hague had been a master brickmaker at Hyde for 16 years. He had generally employed union men, but in the year 1861, in consequence of repeated turn-outs, he resolved not to employ them again, and supplied their places with non-unionists. Soon after this, about 7,000 of his bricks were spoiled, and both he and his men were frequently threatened. The non-union men employed by him were continually going away, and when asked why they left, they said "they dare not work."

1861.

 On one occasion, in 1861, a man came to Mr. Hague as a delegate from the union. He said that "he (Hague) was much respected, but they had "come to the determination to shoot him." Under the influence of this threat, and in fear of his life, Hague turned away the non-union men in his employ, and took on union men. With these he.finished the "bit of clay" he had in hand, told them they must make bricks for themselves in future, and gave up the business.

John Warden was a master bricklayer at Newton Wood, in the Ashton district, and was carrying on his business there in 1860. He employed non-union men. In the spring of this year he was solicited to join the Brickmakers' Union, but refused. In July, eight members of the union, three of whom upon their own confession were Frederick Hipwell and Thomas and Charles Barlow, went to his brickyard. They collected together the various tools, implements, and other things they found there, consisting of barrows, trestles, boards, and other materials, piled them together in a heap, poured naphtha over them, and then set them on fire. The then Secretary and President of the Ashton Union admitted having paid £15 out of the union funds to the perpetrators of the outrage. 1860, July.

William Henry Wylde was a master brickmaker in Turner Lane, in the Ashton Union. The union men in his employ struck for an advance of wages, and he then took on non-union hands. On the night of the 19th February, 1861, six or seven Ashton Union men went to Wylde's brickyard, and put a quantity of needles and broken glass into his clay. 1861, February 19th.

At that time Wylde had a man in his employ, named *Moorhouse*. The men, having destroyed the clay, proceeded to the shed to see if there was a watchman there. One of them knocked at the door; and Moorhouse, who happened to be inside, went to the door, and said, "Who's that; is it you, Ned?" meaning the watchman. Some one answered "Yes." He opened the door, and immediately one of the men attempted to fire a pistol at him, but it missed fire, and then the man struck him on the head with it. Moorhouse struggled and freed himself, and as he was running away he was fired at, but not 1861.

hit. Charles Barrow confessed to having been one of the party

Five or six months after this Wylde took the union men again into his employ, the non-union men either having left of their own accord, or having been enticed away by the union men. After the union men had returned Wylde had no further trouble with the union. He gave up business, however, about four years ago, in consequence of trade outrages. "They had reached," he said, "such a pitch that nothing could be done with it."

John Kirk was a master brickmaker at Ashton. In 1861 he was employing non-union men, and in January of that year an attempt was made to set his house on fire. About one o'clock in the morning three bottles were thrown into the window of his bed-room, in which his father-in-law, an old man of 82 years of age, and a sister-in-law, were sleeping. He and his wife occupied an adjoining room at the back. Two of these bottles, which were of glass, contained naphtha; and the bottles being broken by the concussion, the naphtha was spilled on the floor, and fragments of the bottles flew about the room. The third bottle, which was of stone, and contained gunpowder, did not explode, as the fuse attached to it either had not been lighted, or, if lighted, had gone out. There was also a fourth bottle containing powder, which struck against the window-frame and exploded outside, filling the room with smoke. Six members of the Ashton Union were engaged in this attack upon Kirk's house. One of them was armed with a pistol, and kept guard with another man, while the others threw the bottles into the house. Two of them, Charles Barlow and Frith, confessed their participation in the outrage; the latter, as has been before mentioned, having filled the office of president of the union.

In the following April Mr. Kirk had a quantity 1861, April. of clay damaged by needles being put into it.

Messrs. Martin and Smethurst were master brick- 1862, April. makers at Guide Bridge, in the Ashton district. In 1861 they were employing non-union men. In the month of April, 1862, from 5,000 to 10,000 of their bricks were destroyed by being trampled upon. This damage was done by members of the Ashton Union. Hipwell and Thomas Barlow confessed to having been of the party.

To prevent further damage being done to their 1862, June 27th. property, Messrs. Martin and Smethurst engaged Richard Dunning to act as watchman during the night time. On the night of June 27th, in the same year, the night before police constable Jump was shot, two of their men were burning at the kiln in the brickyard. Dunning, armed with a gun, was watching ; he saw two men come together into the brickyard ; they separated ; one went near to the kiln where the two men were burning, the other came on to the railway bridge, nearer to the spot where Dunning was standing. Dunning saw the former shoot at the kiln-burners, and immediately fired his gun at man on the bridge. The two men then ran away. One of the kiln-burners was hit in the back with shot.

At the time of these outrages Messrs. Martin and Smethurst were not making bricks for sale, but for their own use in building a cotton mill. They had supposed it would matter little to the trade whether they employed union or non-union men. We believe this outrage to have been committed by union men.

Thomas Blocksage was a master brickmaker at Dukinfield in the Ashton district. In 1860 he was employing union men. Some of the work not having been done to his satisfaction, he stopped a small sum out of their wages. In consequence of this they turned out, called a district meeting, and the union fined him £5 for the loss of a day's labour to the men, who refused to return to work until the fine was paid. Mr. Blocksage at first refused to pay the fine, but subsequently gave way. Being annoyed, however, at the treatment he had received from the union, he threw up the contracts he had then on hand, ceased work for two years, and did not resume brickmaking until 1862.

1862.

On recommencing business he employed non-union men only; and in the summer of 1862, 50,000 to 60,000 of his bricks were trampled upon, and some of his walls of bricks pushed down. Seven men, members of the Ashton Union, were engaged in this work of destruction. Hipwell and Thomas Barlow admitted being of the party. The arrangement of this outrange had been entrusted by Thomas Harrison, the then president of the union, to James Kay, the delegate of the Manchester Brickmakers' Union, who received from Harrison out of the Ashton Union funds £25 in payment for this and another outrage. In consequence of this outrage Blocksage's premises were placed under the protection of the police. On a subsequent occasion in the same year, late at night, a number of men were seen by a policeman concealed under a hedge in the immediate neighbourhood of the brickyard, but before any of them could be apprehended they made off.

1864.

In 1863 and 1864 deputations came to Mr. Blocksage from the union, to request that he would ask his men to join the society. His reply was, that if his men wanted to go into the union they might do so, and that he should not object to it. His men declined. Soon after a visit from one of these deputations in 1864, an attempt was made to set his shed on fire, and in the latter end of the same year one of his horses was stabbed in the stable. His men were often threatened by members of the union.

Notwithstanding the attacks made upon his property, Mr. Blocksage expressed his opinion that the union men " had dealt very leniently with him, as he " had other property at stake by which they might " have punished him severely."

John Clifford, at present a labourer, was in 1864 a brickmaster, carrying on business at Ridgy Lane, Stalybridge, in the Ashton district. In May, 1864, several members of the Ashton Union called upon him, and complained of his employing non-union men, and of the wages he was then paying, which were a little less than the club price. They wished him to turn away the non-union men, and to take a gang of their men instead, adding that it would be better for him if he did take their men. Clifford refused to comply with their request. A few days after, on Whitsun Friday night, 11,000 of his bricks were trampled on.

1864, Whitsun Friday.

In the beginning of the following November a shed was set on fire, and two-thirds of it destroyed. Some hurdles had been collected together, placed in the shed, and then fired. On the same night a valuable dog which was in the shed belonging to Clifford was killed, and upwards of 2,000 bricks destroyed. Clifford's house was situated about 200 yards from the brickyard. At the latter end of November, about 12 o'clock at night, a bottle filled with combustibles was thrown into the window of his bedroom, where he, his wife, and four children, were then sleeping. It caught the back of a chair, and then rebounded into the street, where it exploded. The bottle had been wrapped in a bit of rag steeped in gas tar. The next morning there was found, buried in a heap of ashes, about a quarter of a mile from the house, another bottle containing powder with a fuse at-

1864, November.

tached, which probably there had not been time to throw, as Clifford immediately upon the explosion whistled for the police, six of whom came directly to the spot.

After this last outrage Clifford employed a watchman to guard his premises. He provided him with a revolver and two large dogs, the watchman refusing to undertake the duty unless he had them for his protection.

Clifford was abused and threatened by the union men, and dared not go to Ashton after dark. Believing his life to be in danger he gave up the brick-making business in August of the following year, as, to use his own words, he "thought it better to give it up than to lose his life."

1866.

James Harrison and his brother were in business as brickmakers at Ashton in the year 1866. There was upon their property a considerable quantity of clay, which, when ground, was available for making bricks, but which, if not ground was useless. There was clay sufficient to produce 100,000 bricks a year. In order to make this clay practicable Messrs. Harrison proceeded by way experiment to grind it by machinery; but their men objected to its being ground, because they considered it was infringing upon their labour, although they had their own tables and stools to work it when ground. No sooner had Messrs. Harrison commenced grinding than they were waited on by a delegate from the Ashton Union, with two of their own men, who declared they would not work for them if they, Messrs. Harrison, "did like that." Messrs. Harrison said they should try it, and the men went away. As they were going one of the men said, "Come, we have plenty of money in the box, and thou wilt not always be master." This conversation took place in the middle of the week. Messrs. Harrison told their

men to keep a sharp look out, as they thought they
would be on them pretty quick ; and on the Sunday
following, about 12 o'clock at night, while the watchman was getting his supper, the shed was fired. The
shed was fitted up with shelves, on which coals, chips,
and other stuff had been crammed and set on fire.
There was a considerable quantity of timber in the
shed, and if the fire had not been discovered immediately it must have been burnt down.

In the summer of the present year, 1867, *James* 1867.
Turner, a neighbour of Messrs. Harrison, was going
along the footpath by their brickyard, about 10
o'clock at night, when a man dressed in white clothes
came up to him, struck him two very violent blows
on the face and forehead with a stone, cutting his
lip and breaking his nose, and then ran away, leaving
him insensible. Turner and the watchman of Messrs.
Harrison were about the same size, and the outrage
could only be accounted for on the supposition that
he was mistaken for the latter.

The greater number of the foregoing outrages
committed in the Ashton district, already mentioned,
were confessed to be parties—members of the Ashton Union—who were personally concerned in them ;
and it was also admitted by John Barlow and Thomas
Harrison, who were respectively secretary and president of the society during the greater portion of the
years 1860, 1861, and 1862, the period when these
outrages were most frequent, that they had all been
promoted by the officers of the union, with the concurrence of a large majority of its members, and had
been paid for out of the union funds. Neither Barlow nor Harrison was able to speak with accuracy
as to payments made on each particular occasion.
"There were so many jobs," they said, "that they
"could not remember whether they paid for them or
"not ;" but they stated that "they had no doubt

" the outrages were all paid for either by themselves
" or by the then acting officers of the union."

THE MANCHESTER OPERATIVE BRICKMAKERS' AND BRICKLAYERS' UNIONS.

In 1862 *Joseph Frith*, who at that time was a
master brickmaker, and a member of the Ashton
Union, sent some bricks from his premises, which were
in the district of the Ashton Union, to Belle Vue Gaol,
which is in the Manchester Union district. The
two carters who went with the bricks were both
beaten, and by the direction of members of the Manchester Union.

If a person in the Manchester district were to
obtain bricks from another district no brickmaker
in the Manchester district would supply him with any
unless he sent back what he had thus obtained in
violation of the rules of the Manchester Union. This
was represented to us as a common occurrence.

In the year 1864 there was a company called the
Ardwick Brickmaking Company, which was in the
Manchester district, and which made bricks by
machinery. For some time they had been in the
habit of having timber from Messrs. Bennett and Co.,
timber merchants, whose premises were in Hyde
Road, Manchester. The members of the Manchester
Union are all hand brickmakers, and it is against
the rules of the union that bricks should be made by
machinery. It seems that in consequence of their
carters, who went with the timber to the Ardwick
Brickmaking Company, being threatened, and also
of one of their horses having had its throat cut, the
Messrs. Bennett had refused to supply the company
with any more timber. At the beginning of January,
1864, the timber which was in the yard of the
Ardwick Brickmaking Company, and which had

come from Bolton, was covered with pitch and tar,
and then set on fire, and, though not destroyed, was
rendered useless for the purpose for which it had
been intended. This was done at night by four men,
and there was no reason for the outrage, but that the
company made bricks by machinery.

The same company had also a gray mare, which 1864, May.
was burnt to death in May of the same year, 1864.
The brickmakers who perpetrated this outrage broke
open the stable door between 2 a.m. and 3 a.m., tied
the mare fast by the head to the iron hay-rack, put
shavings under her and all over the stable where she
was, and then set fire to them. The fire was discovered by a neighbour in time to save the stable
from being burnt ; otherwise five other horses, which
were in it, would have shared the same fate. The
reason why the gray mare was selected for destruction apparently was that this mare was usually employed in carrying timber to the machine brickmakers.

The same Company had a boy of about 12 years 1864, August.
old in their service, whose name was *Thomas Cole*. In
August, 1864, this boy was sent about 7 p m. with some
letters to the post office, which was about a quarter
of a mile from the Company's premises, and the way
to which lay through a comparatively unfrequented
district. As he went, he was seized by some brickmakers, who, one of them taking him by the shoulders
and the other by the legs, threw him into a pit of
water. The pit was 40 or 50 yards in length, by 30
yards in breadth, and at that time was about 10 or
12 feet deep in water ; the sides of it were steep,
the banks being about 12 or 14 feet above the surface
of the water. The men, after committing this outrage, ran away ; and had it not been that a mechanic,
who accidentally came up, and seeing what had
happened, went into the pit, and got the boy out,

the boy, being unable to swim, would have been drowned.

1864, November.

In November, 1864, the same Company had their joiners' shop set on fire at night by some brickmakers; and in the following month, December, a bottle of some combustibles was thrown into the cellar of the house of the manager of the Company. The bottle contained gunpowder and a sort of flannel, which had been saturated with spirits, and before the bottle had been thrown into the cellar, two lots of hay and straw had been pushed through the cellar window. There was attached to the bottle a fuze which had been lighted, but had apparently gone out. There was in the cellar a quantity of firewood, very near to which the bottle had been thrown, and if that had caught fire, the house must have been burnt down.

The machinery which this Company used for brickmaking was constantly breaking down, the cause of which was unknown; but the nature and frequency of the injuries were such, that the injuries could only have been done by some persons employed on the premises, and no reason could be given for them, or for any of the above-mentioned outrages committed against persons in the service of this Company, except that they made bricks by machinery. It was in consequence of the persecution to which they were subject, and which was attended with such serious loss to them, that the Company gave up their business.

1862, February.

William Alfred Atkins was a machine brickmaker in Cheetwood Lane, in Manchester; and after he had been repeatedly threatened because he made bricks by machinery, the roof of the engine house on his premises was blown off by gunpowder in February, 1862. There was frequently something put into his machine, or the wheels of it, so that it often broke down ; and sometimes the water had been let out of the boiler, so that it might blow up. His bricks had frequently been damaged. The men he employed were non-union men, some of whom had been severely beaten with sticks ; and no cart could come to his yard but it was watched, and the carters threatened. Atkins himself had received a letter containing a sketch of a coffin, and telling him to prepare for death.

A burner, named *Wood*, in the employ of Messrs. 1863. Atkins, and who was a married man with a family, had a bottle full of gunpowder and slugs, with a fuze attached to it, thrown into his bedroom window, about 11 p.m., some time in 1863. He was then living in Cheetwood Lane, in Manchester. Fortunately, though in the room, he was not in bed at the time ; but he heard the crash, and, seizing the bottle, he threw it out of the window, when it exploded outside the house. The slugs were found all round the place where the bottle had exploded.

In 1863 a carter, named *Wogden*, in the employ 1863. of Messrs. Atkins, had his hay-stack set on fire. This same carter had on two separate occasions been fined £5 by the Manchester Brickmakers' Union, and had been obliged to pay the money, for having wheeled machine-made bricks. If these fines had not been paid, he would not have been allowed to work anywhere in the district.

This system of terrorism and outrage went on for two or three years, till at last Messrs. Atkins and Co. were obliged to give up their business.

In 1863 *Messrs. Elliotson and Dickson* had six 1863. houses, which they were building near Regent Road, in Salford, pushed down, because they were using machine-made bricks. The houses had been built up to the first story, when 50 brickmakers went one night, and levelled them to the ground. We have no doubt that this was done by members of the Manchester Brickmakers' Union. The machine-made bricks which Messrs. Elliotson and Dickson had been using had been made by Messrs. Atkins and Co.

1863.

The union district of Manchester and that of Ashton-under-Lyne are, as alleged by the members of the Manchester Union, divided by the canal at Droylsden. The members of the Manchester Union will not allow any bricks to be brought out of Ashton into their district. *Messrs. Bates and Co.*, who were builders and brickmakers, had one yard on the Ashton side of the canal, in the Ashton district, and two yards on the Manchester side, in the Manchester district, about a mile from the canal; but the Ashton Union disputed the boundary between the two districts, and asserted that the two yards of Messrs. Bates and Co. were within their district. However, because Messrs. Bates and Co. had carted some bricks made by themselves in their yard on the Ashton side of the canal into their own yards in the alleged district of the Manchester Union on the other side of the canal, a large quantity of their bricks were in 1863 trampled upon and spoilt.

1863, April.

In April, 1863, *John Lomas* was building some houses in the Manchester district, with bricks made by machinery. James Kay, the delegate of the Manchester Brickmakers' Union, came to him, and told him the union would "forgive him" if he carted the machine-made bricks back, and used only hand-made bricks in future. On Lomas refusing to comply with this demand, Kay replied, " If you do not send them back again, you may mark the consequences; I will shift your head:" by which expression Lomas understood him to mean he would blow his (Lomas's) head off. Shortly afterwards the buildings on Lomas's premises were blown up, and set on fire by means of canisters full of gunpowder, which had been placed there for that purpose.

In 1863, *Robert Ellerton*, a bricklayer, was building some houses in Crowther Street, Salford, with machine-made bricks, and had got them nearly a floor high, when at night the greater part of them were pushed down. 1863.

In the spring of 1864 he was building some houses in Radnor Street, Manchester, and for that purpose was using bricks made by machinery as well as those made by hand. He was informed by James Kay, the delegate of the Manchester Brickmakers' Union, that measures would be taken to prevent him from carrying on his work, because he used bricks made by machinery ; and the consequence was that Ellerton had to give up a contract he had entered into for building twelve houses in that street. It was proved that it was better for a bricklayer to use machine-made bricks, as they were cheaper, and there was not so much waste in them 1864.

Mr. Bramall was the contractor for the Assize Courts at Manchester, and employed men belonging to the Manchester Union. In April, 1864, a strike took place among the bricklayers' labourers ; and then the bricklayers themselves, and afterwards the joiners also struck. The places of the men who had thus struck were filled up by non-union men, members from the unions of the joiners, the bricklayers, and the labourers (all of which unions were at Manchester) picketed the men at work with Mr. Bramall ; and on the 22nd May, 1864, three of the bricklayers, *Wilfred, Ratcliffe*, and *Upton* (who were union men, but who had stayed on when the others had left, and were at work at the Assize Courts), were waylaid as they went home, and very much injured. Two of the men, John Nolan and Thomas Daly, who had committed the assault, were taken up for it, and sent to 1864, May 22nd.

be tried at the sessions. However, before the trial came on, the main witness, viz., Wilfred, who had been very badly used, was got out of the way, and taken up to London by some members of the Bricklayers' Union. The father of another witness, George Henry Carr, was paid ten guineas by some members of the same union to induce his son to refuse at the trial to swear to the identity of Nolan; and Nolan was consequently acquitted. Ratcliffe and Upton, the other two men who were assaulted, were also taken up to London by members of the same union, and got out of the way by the time the trial came on.

Daniel Callaghan, a bricklayers' labourer, had belonged to the union; but because he could not pay the levy, which was 2s. 3d. every Saturday night, he he was turned out of it. He was, by order of the committee of the Bricklayers' Union, stopped at his work; and on one occasion John Nolan, the delegate of the Bricklayers' Union, threatened to throw him into some boiling lime, and endeavoured to put his threat into execution, but was prevented doing so. Callaghan was afterwards violently assaulted, his eye much injured, and his teeth knocked out. From the injuries he received, from which he never quite recovered, he was for some time unable to do any kind of work, and he could not even walk in the streets without fear of being assaulted by the union men. Before some of the men who had committed the assault could be apprehended, the union paid the passage of one of them to America, and another left Manchester.

1864, May.   *Benjamin Armitage* was in 1864 building a new mill in Pendleton with machine-made bricks. He employed a watchman, named *George Goodie*, on his premises. About 12.30 p.m., in May, 1864, Goodie was attacked by 20 or 30 brickmakers. They pulled the newly-built walls of the mill down, and severely beat and injured Goodie, saying at the same time that they meant to kill him. Goodie was so injured that he was unable to work at all for 16 weeks, and has never recovered from the injuries he then received.

George Taunton, a master brickmaker, whose works were in the Manchester district, in June, 1864, had some bricks spoilt, for which he could not in any way account, except that he had strongly advocated bricks being made by machinery. 1864, June.

John Ashworth, a master bricklayer, who carried on his business at Salford, in the Manchester Union district, had in June, 1864, a large quantity of bricks destroyed. There was no doubt that this outrage was committed by the members of the Manchester Brickmakers' Union ; and the only reason why it was committed was because one of his sons, who was working for him, was not a member of the union, though all the other men who were working for him, including another son, were so. In addition to this destruction of his property, all the union men (excepting his son) left his service. A man named Patrick Cullens, was taken up on suspicion of having been concerned in the destruction of Ashworth's property ; and for that reason two members of the union, named George Mannering and James Kershaw, came to Ashworth and told him that he must pay £50 to the union before he should be allowed to make any more bricks. Ashworth refused this demand, and from not being able to get any union men to work for him he employed non-unionists, and began to make bricks by machinery. The brickmakers and bricklayers then combined against him, and he could find no market for his bricks. This combination extended over the whole of the Manchester district, but not beyond it. This state of things continued till August, 1865, when Mr. Ashworth received the following letter :— 1864, June.

" To Mr. Ashworth,

" Friday Morning, August 15, 1865.

" Dear Sir,

" I think it my duty to inform you that at a
meeting of the Operative Brickmakers, held in their
own hall yesterday, there was a committee appointed
to consider the best means of shooting you, or otherwise putting an end to your existence. In writing
this I put myself in quite as much danger as yourself,
if it should come to the knowledge of this society of
ruffians, and so beg that you will not let my trouble
be thrown away, but put yourself upon your guard
at once. Now, considering that I have done my duty,
I beg to subscribe myself,

" A WELL-WISHER.

" P.S.—If you should value this communication
any, please advertise the receipt of it in to-morrow's
' Guardian,' in the following words :—' Received,
Well-Wisher's Letter.—J.A.' "

1865, August
13th.

There was a man of the name of *John Parkes*,
who, in height, size, and dress, very much resembled
one of Mr. Ashworth's sons. About ten days after
Mr. Ashworth had received the above letter, viz., on
the 13th August, 1865, about 11 p.m., Parkes was
walking on the road, about 70 yards from Mr. Ashworth's house, when he was attacked by three men,
and violently beaten on the head and elsewhere, so
as to be rendered insensible for nine days. All the
front of his head, and the whole of his left side, from
the head to the foot, were injured. His eye, from the
injury which he has not recovered from, was cut open.
These injuries seem to have been done with a bottle,
which was found near the spot, broken into many
pieces. Another bottle was also found, full of blast-
ing gunpowder, with a fuze attached to it.

In consequence of what had happened, and his

continued inability to sell his bricks, Mr. Ashworth gave up his business.

The township of Whitefield is out of the Man- 1866. chester district, but is the next township to it, and there is a bricklayer's union in that township. *Edward Hindley*, a builder, had in 1866 a contract for the bricklayer's work in constructing the Prestwich Reservoir. The work to be done was in the Manchester district, and he was using Manchester bricks. His workmen belonged to the Whitefield Union, and he had a boy, of the age of 17, who worked for him. The members of the Whitefield Union at first complained that the boy had not been bound as an apprentice; and said that unless he became one, all the men should leave their work. Upon this Hindley had the boy bound to him. The Whitefield Union men then said that the boy was too old, and that no one should be bound as a bricklayer's apprentice who had passed the age of 15. The men accordingly stopped work, and the Whitefield Union men persuaded the Manchester Union men, both brickmakers and bricklayers, to prevent Hindley having any more bricks in the Manchester district.

A man named *James Dalton*, who was a married 1867, man, with a family of children, and had ceased to be February. a member of the union, had been severely beaten by members of the Manchester Union, and threatened to be thrown into a limepit, for having carried bricks made by machinery. From the threats which were constantly made against his life, he had been compelled to leave Manchester for a twelvemonth. He returned, however, to Manchester, in February, 1867, when he was again beaten severely by members of the Manchester Union. On one occasion, when some members of the Manchester Union had come to his house for the purpose of beating him, and had not been able to find him, one of them struck his daughter, a little girl between 11 and 12 years of age, on the face with his fist, and knocked her down. In consequence of the persecutions to which he had been subjected by the members of the Manchester Union, he had been unable to get work in Manchester.

Dalton obtained a warrant against Fyland, the man who had threatened to throw him into a limepit, but Fyland absconded. Thomas Riley, who had severely beaten Dalton, was apprehended and sentenced to one month's imprisonment ; and John Riley, Murray, Deffly, and McLaughlin, who also on another occasion had assaulted Dalton, were bound over to keep the peace. Fyland and all the men who had committed these assaults were members of the Manchester Bricklayers' Labourers' Union.

1867, July 6th.

Messrs. Nasmyth and Co., engineers at Patriscroft, whose works are in the Manchester district, were unable to procure bricks suitable for their purpose in that district, and accordingly sent to procure some from another. They were informed by members of the Manchester Union that no bricklayer would be allowed to set bricks which had been brought into the Manchester district from any other. Messrs. Nasmyth and Co. then determined to make bricks for themselves with clay on their own property, and for that purpose employed a man named Twigg, who was not a member of the union. They were told that they should only employ members of the union, and that if they did not do so, they must take the consequences. Twigg was offered £5 to leave their service, which he refused to do. On the 6th July, 1867, Messrs. Nasmyth and Co. had some bricks destroyed by being trampled upon.

We have no doubt that these outrages were all promoted and encouraged by the Manchester Brickmakers' and Bricklayers' Unions.

Colliers' Unions.

Mr. John Knowles was the managing partner of 7th March. a firm who were colliery proprietors at Pendlebury, which is about four miles from Manchester. There is a trade union among the colliers at Little Lever, near Bolton, and the firm of *Messrs. Knowles* had not for the last 20 years employed union men. They had collieries also at Pendleton, Edge Croft, Clifton Hall, Clifton Moss, Stone Clough, Little Lever, Ratcliffe, and the Cleggs, near Rochdale. The hands in their employ were about 3,000 altogether. In November, 1866, about 1,400 men left their service, and joined the union. At that time the colliery trade was in a depressed state, and the firm sent to other parts of the country for hands. They obtained about 300 men from Staffordshire, and 200 from Cornwall. The union men who had left the service of the firm had been tenants of cottages belonging to the firm ; and as their tenancies could not be immediately determined, Messrs. Knowles prepared beds, and the necessary accommodation for the new hands, in their works and store rooms at Pendlebury. In March, 1867, one of the store rooms there was set on fire ; and, had not the fire been immediately discovered, the loss of hundreds of lives must have been the consequence. The store room, in which the fire took place, was full of oil, tallow, and hemp ; and in the room adjoining, some of the new-comers were residing. Close to the spot where the fire had taken place was a gasometer, with a large pressure of gas on it ; and not very far from that was a powder magazine, containing about a ton of gunpowder, and also a room in which gun cotton was kept. We have no doubt, from the evidence, that this was the work of an incendiary, and that it took place in consequence of the dispute with

2 A 2

the union. As it was, the damage done was about £800.

William Holford was one of the new hands employed by Messrs. Knowles. Between 11 and 12 o'clock at night a bottle, full of combustible materials, was thrown into the bedroom, where he and his wife were sleeping. The bottle exploded, but fortunately did no injury. Holford had previously been frequently called "knobstick," and had been told by the union men that he should rue having come to Pendlebury.

Other non-union men in the employ of Messrs. Knowles were much insulted by the union men, and some of them were seriously injured. 'One man, *Henry Jones*, was knocked down and rendered senseless, and cut under the eye ; and another, *Matthew Bodling*, was knocked down, and left for dead on the ground. His ear was split open, his skull knocked in, and his cheek bone broken ; he was also severely kicked on his side. From the effect of these injuries he is never likely to recover.

The strike of the men in the employ of Messrs. Knowles cost the union about £16,000. Many of the union men were allowed by Messrs. Knowles to return to their employment, but only on condition that they would give up all connexion with the union ; and at the time of our enquiry about 80 of those who had gone out on strike were still out of work, and receiving pay from the union.

MANCHESTER WARPERS' UNION.

1857,
November.

Charles Mason was a warper, living at Newcastle Street, Hulme, in Manchester ; and there is a trade union of warpers, at Manchester. Mason taught his wife and two of his sisters to warp. The members of the Warpers' Union remonstrated with him for this, and said they would not permit it, as it was against their rules to allow women to warp, for, if women were introduced into their market, the wages of the men would be reduced. In November, 1857, about 11 p.m., Mason was persuaded to go into a public-house in Manchester, where he found several members of the Warpers' Union. They offered him some ale, but on observing that the colour of it was unusual, and also that there was some sediment in it, his suspicions were aroused, and he refused to drink it. He then left the public-house, when the men followed him, one of them, named Doherty, forcing himself into conversation with him as he walked along the street. When he got near his own house, and was still in the street, a rush was made at him, and a man named Hall threw vitriol into his eyes. He suffered great pain, and for 12 months was unable to do any work at all. Hall and Doherty, both members of the union, were tried at the Liverpool Assizes for the offence; and, on being found guilty, Hall was sentenced to six years' penal servitude, and Doherty to four years. In April, 1861, Doherty was released, having completed his term of servitude; and a few days afterwards, without any application from Doherty, it was resolved by the union that a sum of £20 should be given to him. In accordance with this resolution, the president of the union, at a meeting, when not less than 100 members were present, gave to Doherty the £20.

The Oldham Operative Brickmakers' Union.

James Wrigley, a brickmaker at Oldham, was 1858. employing a burner who was not a member of the union. In consequence of this, all his other men, who were members of the union, left his service, and shortly afterwards, in 1858, his shed was set on fire, and some of his barrows and planks were burnt. He had also needles put into his clay, and his bricks spoilt. The consequence was, that he turned away the non-union men in his service, who had done him no damage, and took into his employ union men, to whom he attributed the injuries he had received. He has never been disturbed in any way since.

1859.

John Holt, who carried on business as a master brickmaker, at Royton, near Oldham, in 1859, had bricks destroyed, and needles put into his clay, for having employed non-union men. Those who did this outrage also collected all the tools, barrows, &c., they could find on Holt's premises, put them together into a shed, and then set fire to the shed. Some of Holt's workmen were seriously injured by trying to work the clay after the needles had been put into it.

We have no doubt, from the evidence, that these outrages were done by members of the Oldham Union.

1859 and 1860.

John Smethurst, who was a master brickmaker in the Oldham district, had bricks destroyed in 1859 and 1860, for having employed non-union men. From the annoyances and injuries which were done to him from time to time, and from being kept continually in dread of something happening to himself or his property, he gave up his business in 1862, and has ceased to continue in the trade.

Isaiah Greaves, a master brickmaker in the Oldham district, took into his employ a man named Davenport, who had left the Oldham Union in consequence of having been fined. The members of that union came to him several times, and demanded of him that Davenport should be discharged from his service, but he refused to yield to their demand. In

1858.

consequence of this refusal by him, Greaves in 1858 had his bricks destroyed, and needles put into his clay; and in October, 1859, a grenade was thrown

at him just as he was going into his house. It took
a part of his trowsers, stocking, and a portion of his
skin away, but, fortunately, did not do him more
damage. The grenade was found to have contained
knife blades and horse-nails, and various sharp instruments. In 1863, when he was still employing
Davenport, Greaves had his engine-house blown up.
Those who did this outrage had taken off the cylinder
top, and had put down a can of powder inside the
cylinder, with a fuse attached to it, and had then
screwed the cylinder down again.

1859.
1863.

In consequence of the demand that had been made
upon Greaves to discharge Davenport, and of what
had happened to him, a meeting of the master brickmakers took place, when they determined no longer
to employ union men, and accordingly discharged all
the union men in their service.

John Brooks was one of the master brickmakers
who had been party to this resolution, and had acted
on it by discharging the union men in his service on
the 17th September, 1859. Afterwards, and in that
same month, he had two stacks of hay set on fire,
about 12 o'clock at night ; but fortunately the fire
was seen, and on an alarm being given, was put out.
In several places near the stacks were found lucifer
matches, and chips put together ; and in the same
field where the stacks were, a card with the name of
John Barker on it, a member of the Oldham union,
was discovered.

1859,
September.

In October or November of the same year some
cows belonging to John Brooks were poisoned. One
of the cows was opened and examined, and was
proved to have died from poison ; and in the field
where the cows were, were found a number of cakes,
which, upon being analysed, proved to be made of
meal or bran and water, mixed with arsenic.

1859.

In the following May, Brooks also had a quantity
of bricks spoilt, and needles put into his clay.

We have no doubt that all these outrages were
committed by members of the Oldham Union.

The Bolton Joiners', Masons', and Bricklayers' Unions.

1866, May.   *Jonah Thompson* carried on business as a builder
at Bolton. In 1866 he had employed a man named
Caton as a mason. Caton came to Thompson on the
15th May, 1866, and demanded his wages before,
according to the usual course of business, they were
due. He came with another man, named Williams,
also a mason, who had never been in the employ of
Thompson, but who, nevertheless, demanded money
of Thompson. The reason they gave for this demand was, that they wanted money to go on a
"spree." Upon Thompson's refusing their demand,
they collected a crowd of 300 or 400 persons in the
street opposite his premises, and caused a great dis-
turbance. Caton and Williams were taken up before
the magistrates, and bound over to keep the peace.
It appeared that Caton and Williams were members
of the Masons' Union, and in consequence of the
proceedings against them there was a strike of the
masons in Thompson's employ.

1866.   In 1866 Thompson had also employed a man,
named Clarkson, a member of the Builders' Union,
who, about the 13th June, 1866, on being discharged
from Thompson's service in the middle of the week,
demanded the immediate payment of his wages.
Thompson refused to pay him before the usual pay
day at the end of the week. Thereupon Clarkson
assaulted Thompson's wife and knocked her down.
For this assault Clarkson was sentenced to a month's

imprisonment. In consequence of the prosecution of
Clarkson, and of the previous proceedings against
Caton and Williams, delegates from the joiners',
Masons', and Bricklayers' Unions drew off from their
work about 44 of Thompson's men, and his premises
were picketed. Thompson then supplied the places
of the men who had left him by non-union men, who
were exposed to much insult and injury. One of
these men, *Charles Harris*, had his head cut open
with a brick. The man who committed this assault,
and also Charles Harris, were got out of the way by
the bricklayers, so that no one was prosecuted for
it. Thompson also stated, that at the time of the
inquiry both himself and his men were annoyed and
threatened, wherever they went, by members of the
Joiners', Masons', and Bricklayers' Unions.

There is a general union of joiners, called the
"Operative Carpenters' Union," which extends all
over the country, and consists of about 10,000
members. There are lodges belonging to the
general union, in the different towns in England,
where there are joiners. In Bolton there are two
lodges, as there are a great many joiners there. The
committee of the general union, consisting only of a
dozen members, meet in Manchester. The members
of the committee are elected within a radius of six
or seven miles of Manchester. At certain meetings,
which are called delegate meetings, delegates are
sent from the different lodges to represent them.
The men who are members of the lodges or of the
general union are not allowed to work with any men
who are not at all events members of some union. The
Joiners' Union, *i.e.*, the general union, paid the men
who picketed Thompson's premises. It was attempted
to refer the dispute between the several unions and
Thompson to a mediator between the parties, but
the attempt failed; the unions demanding that all

the expenses arising from the strikes, which appear to have amounted nearly to £1,000, should be paid by Thompson, and also that he should make an open acknowledgment that he was wrong.

THE BOLTON SELF-ACTING MINDERS' UNION.

The men who mind the self-acting mules in the spinning yarn trades are called self-acting minders. There is a trades union of them at Bolton. This union at Bolton is connected with other unions of the same sort, of which the central place is Manchester. There is a meeting at Manchester, every three months, of delegates from the several unions of minders. The delegates come from numerous places throughout the country where the unions exist. Cheshire, Yorkshire, and Derbyshire, besides Lancashire, were mentioned as the principal counties from which delegates are sent. These unions are all amalgamated. They will not allow a man to work below a given rate of wages, nor any of their members to work with a non-union man. If a master employs non-union men, he is put down as a "black," and then, it was added, "no respectable" man would go near his shop.

Messrs. John Thomason and Sons had a cotton mill at Bolton; and on the 15th of December, 1866, the self-acting minders in their employ, who were members of the union, turned out of work, upon some complaint that the cotton was not good, and that they could not make good work of it. The number of men who thus left was 21, and Messrs. Thomason got in their places 21 hands who were non-union men. The consequence was that the premises of Messrs. Thomason were picketed, and every attempt was made by intimidation to prevent the non-union men from working. One of the non-union men, named *Winward*, was used very badly, ^{1866.} being beaten by the unionists, and much hurt. Another, named *Mason*, was insulted and threatened with violence; and some stones, of about two or three pounds weight, were thrown between 2 a.m. and 4 a.m., through his bedroom window, but fortunately no damage was done to him or his wife, as, from their apprehension of danger, they were then sleeping in another room.

The Bolton Ironfounders' Union.

There is at Bolton a society which is called the Little Bolton Branch of the Ironfounders' Society of Great Britain and Ireland. There are general meetings of this society, both quarterly and special, and they are governed by an executive committee of the whole society in London. This committee is elected by seven branches of the society near London. The governing branch elect two members; Greenwich, one; East London, two; North London, one; and Chelsea, one. There are altogether about 107 branches, which exist throughout the country, in England, Wales, and Ireland. The rules of the society are, however, made at a meeting of delegates, which takes place about every five years, sometimes in London and sometimes in Manchester. There was a special general meeting of the society at Bolton, on the 1st of August 1866, at which it was resolved that there should be a demand for a rise in wages.

Jonathan Edge was an ironfounder in Bolton, and employed about 70 hands in 1866. In August of that year, in consequence of that resolution, a demand was made by the men in his employ for a rise in their wages. Mr. Edge refused to give it; and consequently the men in his employ, who were unionists, left his service. Their places were supplied by non-unionists, who were insulted and intimidated by the unionists upon every occasion. The premises of Mr. Edge were picketed, so that it was difficult for the non-unionists to get to their work; and for that purpose they had to be escorted by the police. Some of the non-unionists were assaulted, and one of them, named *Atkinson*, was very severely beaten and ill-used by a member of the union.

At the latter end of 1866, Mr. Marsden, of the Britannia Foundry at Bolton, gave his men notice that he should reduce their wages 2*s.* a week. The case was brought before the society at Bolton, who sent it up to the executive committee of the Iron-founders' Society in London. The committee there investigated it, and ordered the men to leave Mr. Marsden's service, which they did. Mr. Marsden at first withdrew his notice of reduction of wages; but afterwards, in consequence, it was stated, of some resolution of the masters, gave notice again for a reduction of wages, and the union men left his service.

There is a General Masters' Iron Association, the Lancashire Branch of which is in Liverpool. Mr. Marsden, on his men (about 32 in number) leaving his service on account of the reduction of wages, sent the names of these men to the secretary of the Lancashire Branch at Liverpool. The consequence of thus publishing their names was, that many of them were unable to get employment, and there were said to be 14 of these men who were at the time of this Inquiry out of work, and receiving pay from the union.

The Bolton Tailors' Unions.

There are two societies of tailors at Bolton (No. 1 and No. 2) which are branches of a General Amal-. gamation Society. The General Amalgamation Society holds its meetings at Manchester. In about 80 towns there are branches of the General Society, to which they subscribe. London has a separate Amalgamation Society of its own, and forms no part of the one which meets at Manchester. The subscription to the General Amalgamation Society at Manchester is 3*d.* a member per quarter; the contribution to the Branch Society at Bolton is 4*d.* a week. The funds of the branch are entirely at their own disposal. If a master wishes to reduce his wages, the matter may be brought before the branch, and they may direct a strike ; but the proper course is to obtain the sanction of the Amalgamation Society. If a resolution is passed that a certain shop is to be "in block," as it is called, all the union men are drawn off, and no one is allowed to work for the offending master. In one of the books of the society were found the following entries:—"April, 1867.— That the men "be called from Mr. Roscoe's and "Brook's shops until the machines* be dispensed "with." "That 300 bills be printed and circulated "of the names of those who would not comply with "the wish of the society." These bills were said to have contained the names of four men, and were published and sent round to the various towns within 12 miles of Bolton, with the object of preventing any members of the union from working with those men. It was stated that the reason why the union men were drawn off from Mr. Roscoe's was that the other men, who were working there, would

---

* The machines alluded to were sewing-machines.

not tell the union what wages they were getting. The union also regulates the hours at which their men should work. There was another entry in the following words:—"Moved, that the hours of work be from 7 a.m. to 7 p.m., and on Saturdays from 7 a.m. to 2 p.m." That resolution was passed because some men were working 20 hours a day, while others could not work 10 hours a day. Another entry, on 27th March, 1867, was "that the society do not recognize machines," which was carried; and another that "masters dispense with machines on 6th April." It was, however, stated that in the following July the opinion of the union was altered on the subject of machinery, and that the union men were allowed to work with masters who used machinery, provided they got what the union considered to be proper wages, and worked in proper hours.

1866.

Mr. Horrocks is a tailor carrying on business at Bolton. A strike took place among his men in November, 1866, the reason of which was as follows: There are, as has been mentioned above, two branch societies of tailors in Bolton, No. 1 and No. 2. Mr. Horrocks employed men belonging to both these societies. No. 1 society struck because Mr. Horrocks employed men belonging to No. 2; then the two societies met, and settled which should be a No. 1 shop and which a No. 2, throughout the town. It was settled that Mr. Horrocks should employ No. 1, though No. 2 wished to work for him. Under these circumstances Mr. Horrocks employed non-union men. A strike therefore took place, and Mr. Horrocks' shop was picketed by men from both No. 1 and No. 2. The non-unionists were insulted and assaulted; and one man, John Campbell, was sent to prison for a month for throwing stones and hitting one of the non-unionists. The violence and systematic intimidation were such that the police had to be employed to protect the workmen ; and this state of things continued for about eight or ten weeks.

We have now given a statement of the principal cases which came under our notice.

We report that there has not occurred during the last ten years, within the district over which our inquiry extended, any act of intimidation, outrage, or wrong, promoted, encouraged, or connived at by any association of employers.

The outrages which we have related, and which rendered life and property insecure, were in our opinion, all of them instigated and sanctioned by the several unions in the districts in which they were respectively committed. They were all deliberately planned and executed in furtherance of a system, which had for its object the subjection of both masters and men to the rules of the union, and the destruction of the freedom of labour.

When the conduct of any master as to the mode in which he carried on his business, or as to the men he employed, was opposed to the regulations of the union, it was brought before a general or a special meeting. Sometimes a resolution was passed that the outrage should be committed. But, whether there was a distinct resolution to that effect, or the opinion of the meeting was unmistakeably ascertained, the measures to be adopted for carrying out the known purposes of the union in this respect were usually left to the officers of the society, who had the union funds at their disposal for this object. There was no difficulty in finding persons ready to carry out such a purpose, whatever crime it might involve. The officers of the union usually selected one " trusty" individual, with whom the contract for the special service was made, and who found the men to perpetrate the outrage, and paid them for it.

The largest sum we found to have been paid for

such a purpose was £20, and the share which fell to
the lot of each man engaged in the transaction was
generally about £1, though the amount varied, and
was often more. James Kay, the member of the
Manchester Union, whose name has been already
mentioned, was said to have been constantly employed for this purpose ; indeed, one witness said
that Kay did nothing else, and lived only by such
employment. This man, James Kay, absconded on
the first morning the Commission met at Manchester ;
and, though every means have been used for his apprehension, he has never since been heard of. In
several unions of the brickmakers, as we have already
mentioned, the books relating to the accounts and
the proceedings of the unions were destroyed, in
order to prevent an examination of them at the time
of our inquiry, and, of course, we are unable to say
what entries those books contained. But, in the
books which were produced before us, we found that
the money paid for these outrages was frequently
entered in the cash book as for " certain expenses ;"
in other cases a sum total was put down in the money
column without any explanation for what the money
had been spent ; and these modes of making up the
accounts seem to have been so well understood that
the auditors never objected to them, but passed the
accounts. The account books, as well as the minute
books, were always on the table at the regular meetings of the union when business was conducted, and
open to the inspection of the members ; and, though
few may have taken the trouble to inspect them, we
have no doubt that the expenditure of the money,
and the object for which it had been made, were well
known to every member of the union. It is but too
evident that the members of the different unions
which came under our notice considered that the
outrages we have mentioned had been perpetrated,

and the union money had been spent, in the promotion of a system which they sanctioned and upheld.

Dated this 10th of February, 1868.

PERCIVAL A. PICKERING.
THOMAS I. BARSTOW.
GEORGE CHANCE.

THE MORAL OF THE STORY.

Legislation
urgently
called for. ALL comment on the above clear statement of facts
elicited by the gentlemen whose names are appended
to the foregoing reports is obviously unnecessary.
These reports are dated as far back as 1867; so that
three more years, not unaccompanied by similar
deeds of violence, and open defiance of all law,
human and divine, have now to be added to the
decade of crime whose history is here written for
our learning, and written as it appears, in vain. The
difficulties to legislation in this matter no doubt are
great, but not greater than those that beset the
treatment of every serious social question; yet Parliament and Her Majesty's Government have hitherto
contented themselves with makeshift and imperfect
measures, and manifest every symptom of remaining
satisfied therewith.

The callousness of the country generally to the
great question of the use and abuse of Trade Unions
is most difficult to account for and most deplorable
to witness. Is there not one of our public men competent and prepared to devote himself to the service
of this great cause, while so many less vital issues of
our daily lives and of our national prosperity find
apostles by the score, and engross the attention of
our legislators? Is there no means of awakening
the rich men of this country to a sense of the height

and steepness of the precipice at the edge of which they contentedly slumber, permitting the laws of the land to be trampled under foot by societies of men, who contrive to cover their personal liability with the cloak of their corporate capacity? Is there in the 19th century, and in Great Britain, no means by which independence and free trade in labour may be secured to the industrious millions to whom labour is the only staple commodity they have to dispose of? Finally, is there not one member in our vaunted House of Commons bold enough and wise enough to frame and bring in a Bill of two simple and sufficing clauses; the first confirming Trade Unions, in their corporate capacity, in all the rights of citizenship; and the second making each officer, if not indeed each member of such union, personally liable, under a kind of unlimited liability Act, for every deed of the union. In a word, to reduce the social monster, Trade Unionism, to the level of a civilised institution, enjoying all the liberties of the subject, but subjected in its turn to the laws of the land; which laws, inasmuch as they might prove more difficult to apply to a combination of individuals than to an isolated human being, should be interpreted and executed with the utmost severity, so as to protect the one against the many, and secure to each man, to the fullest extent, the right of making his own terms with his employer for the free barter and exchange of his disposable market commodity, labour, against its corresponding equivalent, wages.

The existing state of things in Great Britain is a public scandal, and justly holds us up to the pity and contempt of foreign nations. It is not yet too late to apply the fitting remedial measures, but it may any day become so with a sudden growth of communist dogmas; and then our awakening from our present state of lethargic torpor will only be comparable to the late awakening of France to hei position on the humbling of her mighty armaments, with this difference, that she, like a phœnix, must and will arise, proud and defiant as ever, from her ashes; but that from the goal to which we, in our sordid, selfish, money-making way, are rapidly approaching, regardless of our duties to the poor and needy, there will be no turning back, when once a certain, and not now distant, point is reached, short of a climax of moral, mental, physical, and national degradation greater than the world has witnessed since 1789.

DUNPHAIL, *Forres*, *N.B.*

THE END.

INDEX.

2 C

www.ingramcontent.com/pod-product-compliance
Lightning Source LLC
Chambersburg PA
CBHW021352210326
41599CB00011B/839